The
RAT
Real-world Aptitude Test

The RAT
Real-world Aptitude Test

PREPARING YOURSELF
FOR LEAVING HOME

Homer E. Moyer, Jr.

CAPITAL
BOOKS, INC.

Capital Books, Inc.
P.O. Box 605
Herndon, Virginia 20172-0605

ISBN 1-892123-42-8 (alk.paper)

Library of Congress Cataloging-in-Publication Data

Moyer, Homer E., 1942-
    The RAT (Real World Aptitude Test): preparing yourself for leaving home
 / by Homer E. Moyer, Jr.
     p. cm.
   ISBN 1-892123-42-8
    1. Life skills--Handbooks, manuals, etc. I. Title.

   HQ2037 .M69 2001
   646.7--dc21

                                               2001017416

Printed in the United States of America on acid-free paper that meets the American National Standards Institute Z39-48 Standard.

First Edition

10 9 8 7 6 5 4 3 2

CONTENTS

III.   **The Answer Section**

To our four children —

Bronwen,
whose anticipated departure for college inspired The RAT;
Max and Eli,
who left home before publication,
but who will have no peace until they have mastered The RAT;
and Kaia Joye,
who will have no choice but to conquer
The RAT before being let out into the real world

To Beret — the true super parent of the family

And to all those fellow parents
who look for ways to give their kids
a boost in navigating
in the real world.

ACKNOWLEDGMENTS

Through a longer-than-would-have-been-preferred incubation period, *The RAT* and its part-time author were sustained by the encouragement and delight of many friends and supporters. Most steadfast in their optimistic support were Cathy Hagle, Mark Ellis, and Dick Foth, each of whom can take credit for helping keep the tortoise on course.

Bronwen, for whom *The RAT* was originally conceived, provided invaluable assistance in researching web sites and tracking down the occasional elusive source or detail. In *The RAT*'s early days, Joy Johansen did valuable research, as did Peter Butter later on. Max supplied an occasional illustration; Beret, Ben, Eli, Adam, and Dave cheerfully provided other assistance in a crunch.

For her instant enthusiasm and continuing support, I am grateful to Kathleen Hughes, the president of Capital Books, and to her assistant editor, Noemi Taylor. And special thanks go to Nancy Prendergast, without whom I likely would have found neither Kathleen nor Capital Books.

Finally, I was repeatedly encouraged by the spontaneous excitement of friends and acquaintances who heard about *The RAT,* even briefly. Among those who provided these invaluable moments of encouragement were Jon McBride, Don and Jane Furtado, Cathy and Scott McCulloch, Jackson Brown, Betsy Huffman, Eric Edelson, Jim Falkner, and Bill Dillelio. Similar thanks go to Togo, Patsy and Sandy, Maggie, Jane and Chaz, and at least two Sandras, each of whom provided timely "atta boy's"; to the group of high school juniors and seniors and their fathers who reacted so positively to the first public discussion of *The RAT* at the annual "Dad's Brunch"; and to the knowledgeable group of friends who dedicated an evening to looking through drafts and making comments, suggestions, and critiques. Finally, my assistant, Terry Prosise, encouraged this endeavor with the same calm bemusement that allows her to manage the barrage of her everyday challenges so effectively.

For those who provided encouragement or an insight into specific real-world issues, I am most grateful. For any errors that may appear—and surely there must be some—the responsibility is mine. We will fix them in *The Return of The RAT.*

Homer Moyer

The RAT

(Real-world Aptitude Test)

Introduction and Instructions

The RAT is a test to be taken and passed before leaving home to enter the real world—the real world of work, further education, adventure, or some combination of the three. It is designed to test skills and knowledge you might not learn in school but that could be quite useful in life.

In superficial respects, *The RAT* bears some resemblance to the SAT, the infamous Scholastic Aptitude Test, with which most students are all too familiar. If you are an alert reader, you will already have noticed, for example, that there is some similarity between the two names. Both can be administered at about the same stage of life (or later, when you might assume that your score would be higher). Those who take *The RAT* can score from 200 to 800, as is the case with both sections of the SAT. And, as with the SAT, a perfect score of 800 on *The RAT* is hard to come by.

From the perspective of the test taker, however, *The RAT* is vastly superior and far friendlier. *The RAT* may be taken in the comfort of your own home; you may take as long as you like to finish; and, if you like, you can take it a second or third time without the answers having changed. Most important, the answers are in the back. And whatever your score, it will not be mailed in an official-looking envelope to employers or colleges with whom you may soon be interviewing—or colleagues who may have laughed at you in the past because you didn't know how to change a tire.

The Origins of *The RAT*

The idea of a test of practical skills and know-how began in our house as a playful notion. It was prompted by the sudden realization that our oldest child was to leave home soon for college. Is she, we wondered, really prepared for what she might encounter in the real world? Have 13 years of schooling and 17 years of loving,

1

but undoubtedly imperfect, parenting prepared her? Have we given her the skills, knowledge, know-how, and savvy with which she should be equipped for a somewhat intimidating real world?

We were not, we recognize, the first parents to be seized with these concerns. Literature is sprinkled with advice from parents to departing children. The advice of Polonius to his departing son, Laertes (*Hamlet*, Act I, Scene 3), which shows up in the answer section on "Managing Your Money," is one of the most famous. A more recent classic that reflects the same instinct, *Life's Little Instruction Book*, grew out of Jackson Brown's handwritten notes of advice that he accumulated and presented to his son when he left for college. These parental instincts may thus be eternal.

As *The RAT* began to grow and to take shape, it was not just 16- to 25-year-olds who found it educational and entertaining. Those who were responsible for those about to enter the real world also found that a high score was elusive, or decided that it might be appropriate to exclude one or more entire sections of *The RAT* for some improvised, unpersuasive reason. As a result, a number of friends are impatient for *The RAT* so that they may give it to someone else to take.

Anatomy of *The RAT*

Although the dividing line is sometimes blurry, *The RAT* focuses on real-word subjects, rather than the usual academic subjects that have been covered on countless pop quizzes and traumatic final exams in school. Instead, *The RAT* addresses 30 real-life subjects. As a result, *The RAT*'s anatomy is a bit more varied than that of its ever-present namesake, the SAT.

Questions.   *The RAT*'s questions are not standardized, and many are quite friendly. There are the familiar multiple-choice questions, for which you know the right answer is there somewhere. And—immediately increasing your chances of a right answer to 50-50—there are true-false questions.

In addition, there are fill-in-the-blank questions. Some ask for multiple answers, some ask you to identify an incorrect answer, and some have multiple correct answers. Some give you the choice of which question to answer. A few ask you to describe or demonstrate how to do something. And, finally, as a small gift to those who take on *The RAT*, there are questions that simply ask the reader to think carefully about something.

Answers.   Unlike other, less friendly, precollege tests, *The RAT* comes with answers in the back. In fact, the Answer Section comprises most of the book. And, if that is not user friendly enough, the questions and answers are cross-referenced to one another.

The Answer Section contains at least one correct answer for every question. And, as further evidence of its superiority over other tests, *The RAT* also includes many questions for which there is more than one correct answer.

When a correct answer requires the reader to demonstrate or perform a task, subjective judgment from parents, friends, or an understanding passerby may be necessary. When the correct answers are unique to the individual taking the test, the reader is to operate on the honor system. And for those few questions (potentially easy points) to which any thoughtful answer will be, by definition, correct, the Answer Section simply suggests a few possible choices but leaves the final answer to the reader.

Finally, a word about the answers in the Answer Section. Any answer found in the Answer Section may be counted as correct. There are some questions, however, for which there may be additional correct answers. Critical readers may even choose to quarrel with one or two of the answers, an indignity with which even the SAT probably has to contend.

In any event, even the most careful answers are not performance guarantees. The author accordingly prefers not to hear from readers who think that *The RAT*'s instructions for the fox-trot are inadequate or who wish to quarrel with its guidance on the proper use of silverware. We particularly don't want to hear complaints about our answers on carpentry or, worse yet, finances. Before rewiring your house or investing your savings check with a professional.

Nonessential Information. Rather like Crackerjack boxes with sticky prizes in the bottom, *The RAT* contains extra information that is valuable but not essential to determining a correct answer. For the benefit of those students who have dedicated their academic lives to the principle that one's mind should not be cluttered with information that will *not* be on the test, this information is identified by various signposts. Thus, test takers whose only objective is a high score on this particular test may simply skip over these bonus entries, which are interspersed randomly among the answers. Nonessential information is identified in three ways:

Merely Informative

This label is an important signpost. Information that is labeled "MERELY INFORMATIVE" and enclosed in a box like this one is not required reading. It is true that what appears in these boxes may be interesting or instructive or helpful to success in real life, but in test terms, they can be skipped.

continued on next page

On the other hand, since *The RAT* has no time limits, the random browser or curious reader is free to dip into the nuggets of information that may be found in the Merely Informative boxes. Doing so, however, risks getting a touch of something that teachers call "intellectual curiosity," a condition that doesn't always flourish during the teenage years. So if you just want to get to the heart of the matter, you can skip these boxes until later.

More Where This Came From . . .

This signpost, which appears in shaded sections of *The RAT,* signifies references to other books or sources that have even more information about the topic being discussed. These references are academically honorable shortcuts that allow you to take advantage of someone else's digging through libraries or bookstores. In books that are less fun than *The RAT,* these sections are called secondary sources or bibliographies. In *The RAT,* they are tips for further information and sources on which some of the information included here is based.

The RAT's Mouse

A third category of nonessential information appears under the heading *The RAT's Mouse.* This signpost is a mixed metaphor—that is, this rat and this mouse are quite different from one another. This illustrated signpost introduces references that, by using a computer and the computer's mouse, can lead readers to particularly promising web sites on the same subject.

The reader should be aware, of course, that many web sites are, in fact, mouse-like. That is to say, they are there one instant and gone the next. At the time of publication, the web sites were all there. By the time you check, however, it's possible that a couple may be both nonessential and nonexistent.

Administering *The RAT*

One of the joys of *The RAT* is having other people take it. Parents, for example, may wish to make it a prerequisite for teens leaving home for the real world. It is important to remember—and of special interest to parents—that one need not be able to pass *The RAT* to administer it. Its purpose, after all, is to edify the young, not to mortify their elders. With the many cultural, educational, and technological advantages that today's younger generation has enjoyed, a more demanding standard for them seems only fair.

At the same time, those who are soon bound for the real world can use *The RAT* to turn the tables. Those who have taken *The RAT* can then use their knowledge and skills to challenge others—older brothers and sisters, for example—to take *The RAT*. In fact, parents and others who are old enough to think that they are quite knowledgeable about the real world may be particularly attractive targets for a challenge.

The mechanics of taking *The RAT* are quite forgiving. *The RAT* need not be taken in one session at a desk beneath a clock with a row of sharpened pencils in front of the test-taker. Taking *The RAT* may require some time, and some questions require props, such as a car or a stove. Testing may be spread over days or weeks or even longer. Sections may be taken in any order, and a section may be taken repeatedly.

The test may be taken at any age. College or high school students can get a head start on the process by beginning before their senior year. Alternatively, *The RAT* can be taken at other points at which a person is facing the real world—first time living away from home, first trip abroad, entering the military, bar mitzvah, going on sabbatical, returning from sabbatical, retirement. You get the idea.

The RAT is scored a bit like the SAT. Each correct answer is worth two points. The total number of points is added to a base of 200. Therefore, scores can range from 200 (no correct answers—a reliable sign that it is worth studying and trying again) to 800 (a perfect, highly suspect, score). Anyone who has taken *The RAT* only once and claims a perfect score of 800 should be tested politely but rigorously with a random sample of questions from *The RAT*. At the same time, any high score that is credible should be rewarded with special recognition and lavish prizes.

That said, let the testing begin.

The RAT

(Real-world Aptitude Test)

Welcome to *The RAT*, a modest tribute to Renaissance curiosity. By suggesting that the real world may present diverse challenges, *The RAT* may both educate and stimulate you. Should it, in fact, help you to manage and thrive in that world, it probably is underpriced.

To get credit for correct answers when taking *The RAT*, you must know, must know how to do, or must have satisfactorily done what is called for in each of the questions that follow. For convenience, the test is divided into categories of real-life skills and knowledge. You may tackle them in any order you choose.

At the risk of making a ridiculously obvious point, we note that the inclusion of a topic is not necessarily an endorsement by the author or publisher. Rather, it suggests that the subject is one about which it may be useful to be knowledgeable. Thus, a question asking how many ounces are in a jigger should not be taken as validation of mixed drinks any more than a question about athlete's foot should be viewed as a recommendation that you try to contract it.

Good luck! And remember, the answers are in the back.

A. THE BASICS

1.   MANAGING YOUR MONEY

1. **Money Management Plan.**   The most important tool in managing your own personal finances is a monthly plan that estimates your monthly income and the amounts for your monthly expenses. This basic financial planning tool, which need not be complicated, can help you avoid spending more than you are earning ("living beyond your means"). It is called a _____.

2. **Your Checking Account.**   Which of the following statements about checking accounts in banks is *true*?

   a. _____ Banks never pay you interest on checking accounts (because checking accounts are normally for convenience, not saving), but they may charge you a fee for such accounts.

   b. _____ Banks never charge you fees on checking accounts (because they are normally just a convenience for their customers), but they may pay you interest.

c. _____ Banks neither pay interest on checking account balances (because they are not savings accounts), nor do they charge fees on checking accounts (because banks get free use of those funds).

d. _____ Banks may pay interest on certain checking accounts *and* charge fees on certain checking accounts, sometimes both on the same account.

3. **Bounced Checks.**   If you write a check to a store for an amount that is more than the balance you have in your checking account, you will probably "bounce a check." Which of the following usually does *not* occur if you bounce a check?

a. _____ When the store deposits your check and it ultimately reaches your bank, your bank will return the check and refuse to pay it.

b. _____ The store to which you gave the bad check will ask that you pay again *and* charge you an additional fee.

c. _____ The store's bank, which has incurred the cost of processing your bad check, will charge you a processing fee.

d. _____ Your bank will charge you a fee for "overdrawing" your account.

4. **Bank Cards.**   Banks issue different types of bank cards. An "ATM" card allows you to withdraw cash from automatic teller machines (ATMs) and deducts the amount from your account. "Check cards" or "debit cards" allow you to charge purchases with your card, and the amount of the purchase is deducted electronically from your account balance. Which of the following statements about bank cards is *not* correct?

a. _____ Because ATM transactions are electronic, it is always cheaper to get cash by using an ATM card than by writing a check.

b. _____ Most banks have a daily limit on the amount of cash you can withdraw with an ATM card.

c. _____ Losing a check card is riskier than losing an ATM card because if the person who has your card knows your personal identification number (PIN), he or she may spend all of the money in your account.

d. _____ Using an ATM or check card in a foreign country is generally a cheaper way to get local currency than exchanging currency, which always involves a fee.

5. **Credit Cards.**   Correctly answer *True* or *False* for *each* of the following:

   a. _____ If you charge purchases on a credit card such as VISA, MasterCard, or Discover, you are, in effect, borrowing money from the company or bank that issued the card.

   b. _____ If you pay less than the full "new balance" on your monthly credit card statement, or if you pay the "minimum payment due," you will be charged interest on the unpaid balance.

   c. _____ Major credit card companies typically charge interest (a "finance charge") that is approximately twice the prime interest rate.

6. **Credit Card Debt.**   Assume that you accumulate $2,000 in charges on your credit card and that your credit card company charges a monthly finance charge of 1.5 percent (18 percent annually). If you never charge another item and pay a minimum payment of $40 a month every month, approximately how long will it take you to pay off your credit card balance?

   a. _____ Just under a year

   b. _____ Just over two years

   c. _____ Nearly five years

   d. _____ Nearly eight years

7. **Car Payments.**   If you take out a $13,500 car loan at 12.5 percent interest and repay the loan over 5 years, the total amount you will have paid (principal and interest) for the car at the end of 5 years is approximately:

   a. _____ $14,000.

   b. _____ $15,100.

   c. _____ $16,600.

   d. _____ $18,200.

8. **Your Paycheck.**   Most employers give you the option of having your paycheck go directly into your bank account rather than delivering it to you at the end of the pay period. Having your paycheck go directly to the bank instead of to you is called _____.

9. **Payroll Deductions.**   The total amount of money that you earn per month is your gross monthly income. From this total, your employer typically deducts certain amounts from your paycheck automatically. Which of the following is *not* a typical deduction?

    a. _____ Social Security taxes

    b. _____ Savings deduction

    c. _____ Medicare taxes

    d. _____ Estimated federal and state income taxes

10. **Taxes.**   Correctly identify at least *three* of the following terms that relate to your federal taxes:

    a. The date by which individual taxpayers are required each year to file their federal tax returns and to pay any taxes that are due is _____.

    b. The number of the federal tax form on which you must calculate and report your federal income tax is _____.

    c. The term that describes a tax system that requires high-income taxpayers to pay not only more tax but also at a higher tax rate than taxpayers who have lower income is _____.

    d. The downward adjustment that you can make to your income without having to itemize each of your tax deductions is _____.

YOUR SCORE: For the correct answers, see pages 97–105. Giving yourself two points for every question you answered correctly, your score for MANAGING YOUR MONEY is

0   2   4   6   8   12   14   16   18   20

2.   COOKING

1. **Cookbook.**   Name one good, general reference cookbook, *either* by its title *or* author _____ .

2. **Boiling Water.**   You know that water on the stove is boiling when
   a. _____ it has been on high heat for 12 minutes or more.
   b. _____ steam starts rising from the surface of the water.
   c. _____ air bubbles start forming on the bottom of the pot.
   d. _____ air bubbles start breaking the surface.

3. **Ways of Cooking.**   Correctly identify each type of cooking described below.
   a. Cooking in an oven with indirect heat: _____
   b. Cooking in an oven by exposing one side of the food at a time to high, direct heat: _____
   c. Cooking in a saucepan using a small amount of butter or cooking oil: _____

4. **Microwave Cooking.**   Select *one* of the two following questions and answer it correctly:
   a. Which one of the following does a microwave oven *not* do well?
      _____ i.   Pop popcorn
      _____ ii. Bake bread
      _____ iii. Re-heat leftovers
      _____ iv. Cook vegetables
   b. When using a microwave oven, which of the following types of containers should *not* be used?
      _____ i.   Plastic
      _____ ii. Metal
      _____ iii. Glass
      _____ iv. Cardboard

5. **Measurements.**   Correctly identify the abbreviations and the missing equivalent in at least *two* of the following equations for measurements commonly used in cooking:

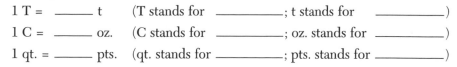

6. **Precise Recipes.**   It is most important to follow a recipe precisely when cooking which of the following types of foods?

   a. _____ Meats

   b. _____ Casseroles

   c. _____ Breads and pastries

7. **Preparing Salads.**   Which of the following is correct?

   a. _____ The two primary ingredients in a vinaigrette dressing are vinegar and soy sauce.

   b. _____ The dressing coats the salad better if the greens are dry rather than moist.

   c. _____ The dressing should be added to the salad well before serving so the greens can absorb the flavors of the dressing.

   d. _____ The purpose of "tossing" the salad is to get rid of excessive amounts of dressing.

8. **Basic Cooking Skills.**   Describe, and then demonstrate, how to do at least *two* of the following:

   a. Separate a raw egg.

   b. Cook two eggs "sunny side up."

   c. Prepare and cook either pancakes or French toast.

   d. Cook rice.

   _____

   _____

   _____

9. **Rotten Food.**   Describe *either* of the following:

    a. How to determine if food in your refrigerator has gone bad

    b. What to do once you determine that food in your refrigerator has, in fact, gone bad

    (This question should enable you to score an easy two points.)

    _____

    _____

10. **Coffee and Tea.**   Correctly answer *either* of the following:

    a. Which of the following is *not* an accepted way to make coffee?

    _____ i.   Drip

    _____ ii. Percolate

    _____ iii. Steep

    _____ iv. Press

    b. Which of the following is *not* a type of tea?

    _____ i.   Orange Pekoe tea

    _____ ii. Black tea

    _____ iii. Blue Mountain tea

    _____ iv. Green tea

EXTRA CREDIT: One Good Dish.   For an extra two points, demonstrate how to cook one great soup, one great entree, or one great dessert. (Your choice could become your signature dish.)

YOUR SCORE: For the correct answers, see pages 105–118. Giving yourself two points for each question you answered correctly, your score for COOKING is

0   2   4   6   8   12   14   16   18   20

3.   CARPENTRY

1. **Hammering.**   Give *two* tips or pointers on how to hammer a nail into a piece of wood.

    _____ and _____

2. **Nails.**   Nails that are best suited for exterior use out of doors are
    a. _____ common nails or brads.
    b. _____ six penny nails.
    c. _____ galvanized nails.
    d. _____ finishing nails.

3. **Nails vs. Screws.**   A nail has greater holding power than a similar-sized screw. _____ *True* or *False*?

4. **Screwdrivers.**   Screws that have two crossed slots (in the shape of a "+") require what type of a screwdriver? _____

5. **Screws in Wallboard.**   Name at least one way *or* one device used to anchor a nail or screw securely in a hollow wall (a wall made out of wallboard, plaster-board, gypsum, or plaster). _____

6. **Saws.**   Name *either* of the following:
    a. _____ Two types of handsaws, *or*
    b. _____ Two types of power saws

    _____ and _____

7. **Plywood.**   Although stronger than ordinary boards (natural sawn wood), plywood can warp, while boards do not. _____ *True* or *False*?

8. **Workbench Terms.**   Correctly identify at least *three* of the following terms that are defined below:

   a. The device used to loosen or tighten the drill bit in an electric drill is

   _____.

   b. The horizontal wooden pieces, normally placed on their edges, that support the wooden subflooring and the wooden floors of most houses are

   _____.

   c. The common term for a piece of lumber that is 1½" thick and 3½" wide is

   _____.

   d. A strong type of wood normally sold in sheets and made by gluing chips or shavings together is _____.

9. **Adhesives.**   To glue two pieces of wood together in a simple carpentry job, which of the following adhesives would typically be used?

   a. _____ Epoxy

   b. _____ Caulk

   c. _____ White glue (like Elmer's)

   d. _____ Putty

10. **Safety Rules.**   Name at least *two* safety rules to follow when using power tools.

    _____ and _____.

YOUR SCORE: For the correct answers, see pages 119–124. Giving yourself two points for each question you answered correctly, your score for CARPENTRY is

    0   2   4   6   8   12   14   16   18   20

4.   DOMESTIC SKILLS

1. **A Clothes Dryer.**   Certain fabrics, such as cotton, are most likely to shrink if

    a. _____ they are washed in hot water.

    b. _____ they are dried in hot air.

    c. _____ the dryer is allowed to continue running after the clothes are dry.

    d. _____ the dryer cycle is inadvertently set on "permanent press."

2. **Washing Clothes.**   Which of the following statements is *false*?

    a. _____ Bleach, which can be used to whiten clothes during washing, can take the color permanently out of clothes if it is accidentally dripped on them.

    b. _____ Washing dark clothing and white clothing in the same load can cause the color from the dark clothing to bleed into the white clothing.

    c. _____ Static electricity, which can cause pants to cling to socks or skirts to cling to panty hose, can be avoided by adding Bounce, or a similar product, to the wash.

    d. _____ Using more detergent than is recommended can cause soap bubbles to bubble up out of the washing machine.

3. **Washing Sweaters.**   The correct way to dry a wool sweater that you have just washed is

    a. _____ lay it out flat on a towel while it is still wet or damp.

    b. _____ hang it on a clothesline, pinned at the shoulders.

    c. _____ tumble dry in high heat in the dryer on the automatic cycle.

    d. _____ tumble dry in a dryer on the cool air cycle with a rubber ball or tennis shoe to keep it from creasing or wrinkling.

4. **Sewing on a Button.**   Describe and demonstrate how to sew a button on a shirt.

_____

_____

_____

5. **Cleaning Ovens.**   Which of the following statements about cleaning ovens is *not* true?

   a. _____ Some ovens are continuous self-cleaning, burning off any spills or spatters as you use the oven.

   b. _____ Some ovens have a self-cleaning cycle during which the oven is empty and the temperature rises to nearly 900 degrees.

   c. _____ Some ovens can be cleaned only by a qualified manufacturer's representative, normally when regular maintenance is performed.

   d. _____ All ovens can be cleaned manually by using warm soapy water and a sponge or cleaning pad.

6. **Candle Wax.**   When hot wax from a candle drips onto a candlestick or candle holder, the melted wax can best be cleaned by which of the following?

   a. _____ Wipe off the candlestick before the wax dries or hardens.

   b. _____ Reheat the wax by putting the candlestick into an oven on low heat until the wax softens.

   c. _____ Put the candlestick into the freezer so that the wax will freeze and can be peeled off more readily.

   d. _____ Wash the candlestick in a mild solution of household ammonia, in which candle wax is soluble.

7. **Household Items.**   Correctly match the items in column I with the domestic appliance or activity listed in column II. Place the letter of the item in the blank provided.

I		II
Bobbin	_____	a. Hot water heater
Flue	_____	b. Toilet
Pilot light	_____	c. Clothes dryer

(continued on next page)

I		II
Ammonia	_____	d. Sewing machine
Spray starch	_____	e. Fireplace
Plunger	_____	f. Ironing
Lint filter	_____	g. Window washing

8. **Painting.**   Which of the following statements about painting is correct?

   a. _____ Typically, walls are painted with semi-gloss paint, and wooden trim is painted with flat paint.

   b. _____ Brushes used to paint with latex paint can be cleaned with soap and water.

   c. _____ By painting with rollers rather than brushes, you can generally cover a greater surface with the same amount of paint.

   d. _____ Drops of oil-based paint can be cleaned up with either mineral spirits or turpentine, but not with paint thinner.

9. **Basic Skills.**   Demonstrate *either* of the following:

   a. _____ How to make a bed with hospital corners

   b. _____ How to iron a blouse or a collar shirt

10. **The Correct Tool(s).**   To remove a shower head or a faucet aerator to clean or replace it, which of the following is the correct tool or tools?

   a. _____ A screwdriver and a pair of pliers

   b. _____ A pair of pliers and a hammer

   c. _____ Just a pair of pliers or a wrench

   d. _____ A plumber

YOUR SCORE: For the correct answers, see pages 125–133. Giving yourself two points for each question that you answered correctly, your score for DOMESTIC SKILLS is

   0   2   4   6   8   12   14   16   18   20

5.   EMERGENCIES AND FIRST AID

1. **Small Emergencies.**   Name a remedy for at least *three* of the following
    small emergencies:

    a. Sunburn: _____

    b. Diarrhea: _____

    c. Blister: _____

    d. Kitchen burn: _____

    e. Poison ivy: _____

2. **Emergencies Caused by Small Creatures.**   Describe how to cope with at
    least *three* of the following creature emergencies:

    a. Bee sting: _____

    b. Tick: _____

    c. Jelly fish sting: _____

    d. Skunk spray odor: _____

3. **Spills on Carpets.**   Describe how to clean at least *one* of the following types
    of spills on a carpet or rug:

    a. Coffee: _____

    b. Red wine: _____

    c. Chewing gum: _____

    d. Chocolate: _____

4. **Minor Car Emergencies.**   Name at least *two* means of dealing with *either* of
    the following:

    a. Car keys locked in your car

    _____

    b. Frozen car door lock

    _____

5. **Snakes and Snakebites.**   Describe how to determine *one* of the following:

   a. A snake is poisonous

   b. A snakebite was by a poisonous snake

   _____

   _____

6. **Water Emergencies.**   Describe and demonstrate how to do *one* of the following:

   a. Perform artificial respiration on a drowning victim

   b. Float for long periods of time in rough surf

   _____

   _____

7. **Muscle Pulls.**   Four steps to help treat a muscle pull are contained in the mnemonic "RICE." Name what at least *two* of those four letters stand for.

   _____ and _____

8. **Natural Disasters.**   Name at least *two* possible protective measures to be taken in the case of (a) a tornado, (b) a hurricane, *or* (c) an earthquake.

   _____ and _____

9. **The Heimlich Maneuver.**   Describe when the "Heimlich maneuver" should be used, and demonstrate how it is performed.

   _____

10. **Intruders.**   Describe at least *one* prudent response if you believe that an intruder has broken into your house or apartment while you are there.

    _____

YOUR SCORE: For the correct answers, see pages 133–142. Giving yourself two points for each question you answered correctly, your score for EMERGENCIES AND FIRST AID is

0   2   4   6   8   12   14   16   18   20

6.   SAVING AND INVESTING

*When once asked to describe his most notable discovery, Albert Einstein
reportedly replied: "Compound interest. The miracle and magic of
compound interest."*—Tama McAleese, *Get Rich Slow* (Hawthorne,
N.J.: Career Press, 1995) 29.

1. **Interest-Bearing Accounts.**   Name at least *one* type of bank account or
bank-offered investment on which you earn interest: _____

2. **Federally Insured Accounts.**   Through federal agencies such as the Federal
Deposit Insurance Corporation (FDIC), the federal government provides insurance covering certain types of accounts up to a specified level (in 2000, the
amount was $100,000). This insurance protects depositors from bank failures,
for example. Which of the following types of bank deposits does FDIC insurance *not* protect?

   a. _____ Savings accounts

   b. _____ Investment accounts

   c. _____ Money market accounts

   d. _____ Certificates of deposit

3. **Compound Interest.**   (a) Define the term "compound interest" and (b) using
as an example an investment of $100 that earns 10 percent interest each year,
demonstrate how that investment would grow over three years with compound
interest.

   Definition: _____

   Year 1: $100   Year 2: $_____   Year 3: $_____   Year 4: $_____

4. **Doubling Your Money.**   How quickly you can double your money by
earning interest on savings or an investment depends on two variables: the
interest rate you are earning and the period of time during which you are
earning it. There is an important principle that allows you, by a simple arith-
metical formula, to determine how long it will take you to double your savings
or your investment at any given rate of interest. This principle is known as
_____.

5. **Types of Investments.**   Correctly name the type of investment in which you invest in a fund that, in turn, invests in a portfolio of between 30 and 300 different companies, thereby allowing you, through a single investment, to achieve investment diversity that may reduce your level of risk.

   _____

6. **Rate of Return and Risk.**   Generally speaking, the higher the potential rate of return on an investment (the annual increase in value as a percentage of your original investment), the higher the risk. Name one type of investment in which the potential rate of return is relatively modest but the level of risk is low, and one type of investment in which the potential return is higher but so is the risk of losing some or all of the money you have invested.

   Relatively low risk/return: _____

   Relatively high risk/return: _____

7. **Rate of Return and Inflation.**   If you have money in a savings account that earns 3 percent interest annually and the annual rate of inflation is 4 percent, the purchasing power of the money in your savings account, after one year, will have

   a. _____ increased.

   b. _____ decreased.

   c. _____ remained unchanged.

8. **Stock Market Terms.**   Correctly name at least *three* of the following terms or facts, each of which relates to the stock market:

   a. Slang term for a declining market: _____

   b. Slang term for a rising market: _____

   c. Stocks of large, well-established companies: _____

   d. Year of the great stock market crash, which led to the Great Depression:

   _____

   e. Money that profitable companies sometimes pay to their shareholders as earnings on their stock investment:

   _____

9. **The Dow.**   Daily stock market reports indicate the extent to which "the Dow" has gone up or down. "The Dow" refers to

   a. _____ the price of a share of the stock of Dow Chemical, a company that was selected for this purpose because it is a reliable indicator of the overall performance of the market.

   b. _____ "the Dow Jones Industrial Average" of the prices of 30 major industrial stocks that are considered to be a reliable indicator of the overall performance of the market.

   c. _____ the average gain or loss of the 500 largest stocks, named after Dow & Sons, the founders of the New York Stock Exchange.

   d. _____ an acronym for "Down or Worse," a bleak term that originated during the Great Depression when the market repeatedly fell in value.

10. **Retirement Accounts.**   Give the correct name of at least *one* account in which you can save for your retirement and avoid paying taxes on either the amounts you deposit or the amounts earned by your investment, or both, until you reach retirement age and begin making withdrawals from your account.

   _____

YOUR SCORE: For the correct answers, see pages 143–149. Giving yourself two points for each question you answered correctly, your score for SAVING AND INVESTING is

   0   2   4   6   8   12   14   16   18   20

7. SHOPPING

1. **Sales Days.** Which of the following is *not* a day on which stores traditionally have highly publicized sales?

   a. _____ The day after Christmas

   b. _____ The Fourth of July

   c. _____ The first day of summer

   d. _____ George Washington's birthday

2. **Online Shopping.** Name two advantages *or* two disadvantages of online shopping.

   _____ and _____

3. **Secondhand Stores.** Stores at which you can buy secondhand items that actually belong to individual owners but that the store agrees to sell in exchange for a percentage of the sales price are

   a. _____ consignment shops.

   b. _____ pawnshops.

   c. _____ thrift shops.

   d. _____ outlets.

4. **Returns.** Which of the following statements about returning merchandise that you have bought, but not worn or used, is *not* true?

   a. _____ The store may accept the merchandise but charge you a "return fee" of 5–10 percent.

   b. _____ The store may refuse to take back the merchandise, even if you have the sales receipt.

   c. _____ The store may take back the merchandise but refuse to refund your money, giving you only a "credit" to use at the store.

   d. _____ The store may refuse to accept the merchandise if you have worn it, removed the tags, not returned it in its original packaging, put your name in it, or left the receipt at home.

   e. _____ The store may accept the merchandise and agree to refund your money but only by sending you a check at a later date.

5. **Cars.**   As a general rule, you get the highest value for the money you spend if you

    a. _____ buy a car new.

    b. _____ lease a new car.

    c. _____ buy a late model used car.

    d. _____ buy a car that needs repairs.

6. **Electronics.**   When buying electronic equipment—stereos, VCRs, TVs, CD players—which of the following statements is *true*?

    a. _____ Large stores often can offer better prices because they can get bulk discounts for buying in large quantities.

    b. _____ By law, the "manufacturer's suggested retail price" is lowest price at which an item can be sold at a reputable store.

    c. _____ Extended warranties are sold by stores as a customer relations benefit for their customers, not because they are profitable.

    d. _____ It is unlawful for a salesperson to attempt to "bump" or to "step up" a customer to buying a more expensive product than the customer requested.

7. **Sales Taxes.**   If you buy an item for $160 and pay sales tax of 6 percent ($9.60), the sales tax will not be refunded if you return the item because a sale has taken place. _____ *True* or *False*?

8. **Efficient Grocery Shopping.**   As a general rule, your grocery shopping will be more efficient and more cost-effective if you

    a. _____ comparison shop by focusing on actual out-of-pocket cost, not unit cost.

    b. _____ shop before you eat so you can focus on only what you need.

    c. _____ avoid store brands since they are high-profit items that the store wants you to buy.

    d. _____ use a shopping list since most of your purchases are repeat purchases.

9. **Unbranded Medicines.** Over-the-counter medications that are sold under the name of the store or without a brand name are called _____.

10. **Grocery Store Techniques.** Which of the following do grocery stores *not* do to encourage more purchases by you?

    a. _____ Typically locate milk at the back of the store so you have to walk past many other products to get a carton of milk.

    b. _____ Use the term "lite" to promote products that have as little as 10 percent less fat than nonlite products.

    c. _____ Place items that are likely to appeal to children (sugary cereals, for example) on low shelves, closer to children's eye level.

    d. _____ Create large end-of-aisle displays to encourage impulse buying.

    e. _____ Line checkout counters with sweets and other small products to encourage impulse buying.

YOUR SCORE: For the correct answers, see pages 149–154. Giving yourself two points for each correct answer, your score for SHOPPING is

0 2 4 6 8 12 14 16 18 20

8.   EMPLOYMENT

1. **Job Information.**   Name at least *two* places where you can look for information about jobs.

    _____ and _____

2. **Resumes.**   In addition to your name and address, name *three* pieces of information that every resume should include.

    _____

    _____

    _____

3. **Interviews.**   Name at least *three* things that will create a favorable impression in a job interview.

    _____

    _____

    _____

4. **Minimum Wage.**   As of the year 2000, the federal minimum wage was
    a. _____ $4.15 an hour.
    b. _____ $5.15 an hour.
    c. _____ $6.15 an hour.
    d. _____ $7.15 an hour.

5. **Overtime.**   Salaried workers get paid overtime, but workers paid by the hour do not. _____ *True* or *False*?

6. **Workplace Terms.**   Correctly supply *either* of the two workplace terms defined below.
    a. The principle of U.S. law that holds that hiring must be done on a nondiscriminatory basis without regard to gender, age, race, religion, or sexual orientation is _____.
    b. Benefits that are paid to workers who are laid off from their jobs when, for example, a plant closes or a company is reorganized are _____.

7. **Benefits.**   Name at least *two* benefits that may come with a job in addition to your paycheck.

   _____ and _____

8. **Paycheck Deductions.**   For most jobs, employers hold back a portion of their employees' pay to cover their income taxes, whether or not their employees want them to do so. _____ *True* or *False?*

9. **Retirement Plans.**   Correctly name *either* of the following:

   a. The name of the government-operated retirement system to which all employees must contribute and from which all qualified retirees are entitled to collect benefits is _____.

   b. The name of at least one private retirement plan in which employees may choose to participate and for which the government grants certain tax benefits is _____.

10. **Tips.**   Tips are taxable income and must be reported fully as a part of your annual income. _____ *True* or *False?*

YOUR SCORE: For the correct answers, see pages 154–162. Giving yourself two points for each question you answered correctly, your score for EMPLOYMENT is

   0   2   4   6   8   12   14   16   18   20

B. THINGS WORTH KNOWING

9.   AUTOMOBILES

1. **Parts of a Car.** Correctly identify *either* of the following parts of a car:

    a. The small, replaceable parts that ignite the mixture of gasoline and air in the engine's cylinders, thereby causing combustion (parts that you don't want to get "gummed up") are ————————————————.

    b. The assembly that contains the car's gears and allows power to be transferred, at various rates, from the engine to the car's power wheels is

    ————————————————.

2. **Basic Operations.**   Select *either* of the following questions and answer it *True* or *False*.

    a. ——— Generally speaking, a car with rear-wheel drive will have better traction in rain, snow, or deep sand than a car with front-wheel drive.

b. _____ Antifreeze is used to prevent your gas line from freezing in cold weather.

3. **Basic Maintenance.** Which of the following statements relating to basic maintenance of a car is *not* true?

a. _____ Of the three grades of gasoline offered at most service stations, the highest octane gasoline (supreme, high-test, etc.) is more expensive because it gives you better gas mileage.

b. _____ If the air pressure in your car's tires is lower than the recommended pressure, it may adversely affect both your gas mileage and tire wear.

c. _____ You should avoid substituting water for windshield washer fluid during the winter because water freezes at a higher temperature and can freeze on your windshield.

d. _____ It is important to change the oil in your car periodically because dirty engine oil can damage engine parts.

4. **Flat Tires.** In changing a flat tire, which of the following should you *not* do?

a. _____ Put the car in gear and put the emergency brake on before changing the tire.

b. _____ Jack up the car before loosening the lugs.

c. _____ Jack up the car higher than needed to remove the flat tire.

d. _____ After you have replaced the flat with the spare tire, tighten the lugs by hand before lowering the car.

5. **Emergencies.** Correctly answer at least *two* of the following three questions dealing with automotive emergencies:

a. If you are on the road and run out of gas or have car trouble, what is one way to signal for help?

_____

b. If an indicator light or temperature gauge indicates that your car is overheating, or if you see steam coming out from under your hood, what is the first thing you should do?

_____

c. In using jumper cables to start a car with a dead battery, what is the fundamental rule to remember in connecting one battery to another?

_____

6. **Safety Tips.**   Correctly answer *either* of the following:

One rule of thumb to avoid tailgating is

_____

_____

Three precautionary steps you can take if you start to get sleepy when you are driving are

_____

_____

_____

7. **Stick-Shift Cars.**   With respect to cars that have a manual, or standard, transmission (a stick shift) rather than an automatic transmission, correctly answer *either* of the following, *True* or *False*.

a. _____ When downshifting from third gear to second gear with a stick shift, the car will slow down because the engine's revolutions per minute (RPMs) will decrease when you downshift.

b. _____ When the clutch is depressed, it is not possible to shift from one gear to another without grinding the gears.

8. **Cars and the Law.**   Correctly identify *two* of the following three terms:

a. The document issued by the state in which your vehicle is registered that certifies ownership of the vehicle (usually this document has spaces on the back for you to assign ownership rights should you sell the car) is

_____ .

b. Many states assign penalty units to drivers who receive tickets for moving violations. Accumulation of a sufficient number of these penalty units can result in your driver's license being suspended or revoked. These penalty units are _____ .

c. The immobilizing device that police sometimes attach to one of the four wheels of a car that is illegally parked or whose owner has unpaid parking tickets is _____.

9. **Engines—The Basics.** Correctly fill in all of the blanks of *either* (a) or (b), both of which involve basic elements of automobile engines.

a. Most automobiles have internal combustion engines. For combustion to occur—in an automobile or otherwise—three essential elements must be present. They are _____, _____, and _____.

b. In an automobile engine, gasoline is moved from the gas tank to the engine by a simple device called a _____(1)_____. The gasoline mixture is then injected into chambers where combustion takes place (most cars have four, six, or eight of these chambers), which are called _____(2)_____.

In these chambers, the fuel mixture is compressed by a snug-fitting engine part that moves back and forth within these combustion chambers, which is called a _____(3)_____. When the fuel mixture is ignited and combustion occurs, the power that is generated is transmitted to the wheels of the car through a series of shafts and gears, one of which is called the _____(4)_____. The gases and residue produced by the combustion process then escape from the engine through the _____(5)_____.

10. **Insurance.** Correctly identify at least *two* of the following terms relating to automobile insurance.

a. The type of insurance that provides protection in case you injure another person while driving your car is _____.

b. The type of insurance that covers damage to the vehicle itself in the event of an accident is _____.

c. For certain types of insurance coverage, such as comprehensive coverage for theft of possessions in a vehicle, the amount you must pay before the insurance coverage pays for the rest is _____.

YOUR SCORE: For the correct answers, see pages 162–175. Giving yourself two points for each question you answered correctly, your score for AUTOMOBILES is

0   2   4   6   8   12   14   16   18   20

10. COMPUTERS

1. **Computer Functions.** Correctly provide *each* of the following computer terms.

    a. The component that allows signals to be transmitted to and from a computer over a telephone line is _____.

    b. Sets of electronic instructions, or programs, that are installed in a computer and tell the hardware what to do, and when, where, and how to do it are _____.

    c. The computer function, equivalent to electronic typing, that is used to prepare letters, memos, and other documents is _____.

2. **Hardware.**   Name at least *two* components of a standard personal computer (PC) that are considered to be "hardware."

    _____ and _____

3. **Laptops.**   Which of the following statements about portable, or laptop, computers is *not* correct?

    a. _____ Although laptops are smaller than desktops, they are more expensive.

    b. _____ Liquid crystal display (LCD) screens that are common on laptops are thinner than monitor screens and use more electricity.

    c. _____ Lithium-ion batteries are more expensive than nickel metal hydride (NiMH) batteries but are both longer-lasting and lighter.

    d. _____ Laptops have no mouse.

4. **Units of Data.**   Arrange in the correct order the following measures of amounts of information that computers can store, from the smallest unit to the largest.

    Megabyte   _____

    Gigabyte   _____

    Byte   _____

    Kilobyte   _____

5. **Complex Programs.** Whether a particular computer can run a complex program or a complex game depends primarily on whether the computer has sufficient

   a. —— processor speed.

   b. —— memory.

   c. —— processing power.

   d. —— networking capacity.

6. **Data.** Name two ways you can save data *or* two ways you can lose data on a computer.

   _____

   _____

7. **Floppy Disks.** Data stored on a floppy disk can be lost if the disk is touched by a magnet. _____ *True* or *False*?

8. **Computer Acronyms and Symbols.** Give the correct terms for at least *three* of the following four common computer acronyms or symbols:

   a. ROM _____

   b. CPU _____

   c. A: _____

   d. GUI _____

9. **Computer Terms.** Correctly supply at least *four* of the following defined terms:

   a. The mouse function that normally displays a list of commands on the screen from which you can select is _____.

   b. A type of computer manufactured by Apple that is easy to use and excellent for desktop printing, but generally incompatible with most other PCs is _____.

   c. The term used to describe restarting your computer by pressing Ctrl-Alt-Delete, which causes your log-in process to start over is

   _____.

    d. A high-quality storage device that has the capacity to hold approximately six times as much data as a CD-ROM and that can hold a full-length movie is _____.

    e. A device that can read graphics and text and enter them into a computer is

    _____.

10.   **The Internet.** Which of the following statements about the Internet is *true*?

    a. _____ The accuracy of information available through the Internet is regulated by the FCC.

    b. _____ Confidential information that is transmitted by e-mail over the Internet is secure because, unlike telephone lines, the Internet cannot be tapped by eavesdroppers or other unauthorized parties.

    c. _____ As a consumer, you have the same protections when engaged in electronic commerce (buying products over the Internet) as you do in a store.

    d. _____ You may explore any web site you find free of any charge other than the monthly charge that you pay the browser service to which you subscribe.

    e. _____ None of the above statements about the Internet is true.

YOUR SCORE: For the correct answers, see pages 175–182. Giving yourself two points for each question you answered correctly, your score for COMPUTERS is

0 2 4 6 8 12 14 16 18 20

11.   THE BIBLE

"No one in the English-speaking world can be considered literate
without a basic knowledge of the Bible." E.D. Hirsch, Jr., Joseph F.
Kett, James Trefil.—*The Dictionary of Cultural Literacy* (Boston:
Houghton Mifflin Company, 1988) 1.

1. **The First Five Books of the Bible.**   Which of the following statements is
    correct? The first five books of the Bible

    a. _____ tell the story of Jesus of Nazareth.

    b. _____ are also the first five books of the *Koran,* the holy book of Islam.

    c. _____ also constitute the *Torah,* which is the sacred text of Judaism.

    d. _____ were written in Latin during the Roman Empire.

2. **Books of the Old Testament.**   Name at least *five* books of the Old
    Testament.

    _____, _____,
    _____, _____, and
    _____.

3. **Prophets.**   The prophets of the Old Testament foretold the coming of the
    Messiah. Name at least *three* Old Testament prophets.

    _____, _____, and
    _____.

4. **The Exodus.**   The book of Exodus describes the escape of the Israelites from
    Egypt. Correctly answer *two* of the following:

    a. Before the Israelites' escape from Egypt, God visited plagues on Egypt.
       Name at least *three* of the ten plagues:

       _____, _____, and
       _____.

    b. The meal that celebrates the Israelites' escape from Egypt is

       _____.

c. The commitment made by God to the Israelites was carried to the promised land in a wooden container overlaid with gold. Name both the commitment and the container.

_____ and _____

5. **The Ten Commandments.**   Name *five* of the ten commandments that Moses received from God.

_____

_____

_____

_____

_____

6. **Biblical Pairs.**   Identify at least *three* of the following well-known Biblical pairs:

a. The king of Judah and the woman he married after sending her husband to be killed in battle are

_____ and _____.

b. Sons of Adam and Eve, one of whom killed the other, are

_____ and _____.

c. The blind biblical figure, whose supernatural strength was derived from his long hair, and his lover, who cut his hair while he slept, are

_____ and _____.

d. The twin cities of evil, known for their licentiousness and sin, are

_____ and _____.

e. Two famous mountains, one on which Moses received the Ten Commandments and one on which Noah's ark came to rest, are

_____ and _____.

7. **The Languages of the Bible.**   Which of the following is *correct* about the primary languages in which the texts of the Old and New Testaments of the Bible were originally written?

   a. _____ The Old Testament in Aramaic, the New Testament in Hebrew.

   b. _____ The Old Testament in Roman (Latin), the New Testament in Greek.

   c. _____ The Old Testament in Hebrew, the New Testament in Greek.

   d. _____ The Old Testament in Greek, the New Testament in Aramaic.

8. **The New Testament.**   The second of the two major sections of the Bible, the New Testament, concerns the life and teachings of Jesus. Which *one* of the following statements about the New Testament is *false*?

   a. _____ Jesus was a Jew.

   b. _____ During Jesus's life, Israel was ruled by Rome.

   c. _____ Many of the books of the New Testament are letters written by Jesus to cities where Christianity had taken root.

   d. _____ All twelve of Jesus's disciples were men.

   e. _____ When he was crucified, Jesus was only in his 30s.

9. **The Teachings of Jesus.**   Correctly answer *two* of the following:

   a. The first four books of the New Testament, which were written by the disciples of Jesus and describe the life of Jesus, are collectively known as the _____.

   b. Stories that Jesus used as vehicles for his teachings—such as the story of the Good Samaritan—are called _____.

   c. A central tenet of Christianity as set forth in the scriptures of the New Testament is that those who believe in God and accept the teachings of Jesus shall be rewarded with _ _____ _.

10. **The Letters of Paul.**   A number of the books of the New Testament are letters from the apostle Paul to churches in cities that Paul visited on his missionary journeys. Among these letters were letters to the Corinthians, Galatians, Ephesians, Philippians, Colossians, and Thessalonians. All of these towns and cities are located in one of which *two* of the following modern-day countries?

    a. _____ Egypt

    b. _____ Jordan

    c. _____ Syria

    d. _____ Iraq

    e. _____ Macedonia

    f. _____ Turkey

    g. _____ Greece

    h. _____ Italy

YOUR SCORE: For the correct answers, see pages 182–188. Giving yourself two points for each question you answered correctly, your score for THE BIBLE is

0   2   4   6   8   12   14   16   18   20

12. GEOGRAPHY

1. **Time Zones.**   You are in California and are about to call someone in Paris. In Paris it is

   a. _____ 9 hours earlier.

   b. _____ 9 hours later.

   c. _____ the same time as it is in London.

2. **Populous Countries.**   Name *three* of the four most populous countries on Earth.

   _____

   _____

   _____

3. **The Earth.**   Which of the following statements about Earth is *false*?

   a. _____ More than two-thirds of the earth's surface is covered with water.

   b. _____ The ice cap that covers the North Pole is over land, and the ice cap that covers the South Pole is over water.

   c. _____ The circumference of Earth at the equator is about 25,000 miles.

   d. _____ When it is summer in Italy, it is winter in South Africa.

4. **Africa, Asia, and Europe.**   Either a. name twelve countries in Africa, twelve countries in Asia, or twelve countries in Europe, *or* b. give the names and capitals of six African countries, six Asian countries, or six European countries.

   Note: In your definition of Europe, include the British Isles, Scandinavia, countries of the former Yugoslavia, and countries that were western republics of the former Soviet Union. In your definition of Asia, include the subcontinent of Asia, Asia Minor, the Middle East, and countries that were former republics in the central and eastern regions of the former Soviet Union.

   _____   _____   _____

   _____   _____   _____

   _____   _____   _____

   _____   _____   _____

5. **Cities, Rivers, and Islands.**   Correctly name *one* of the following:

   a. Four of the ten largest metropolitan areas of the world

   b. Four of the ten longest rivers in the world

   c. Four of the ten largest islands (excluding Australia) in the world

   _____   _____

   _____   _____

6. **Canada and the Former Soviet Union.**   Name four of the ten provinces of Canada *or* four of the fifteen former republics of Soviet Union.

Canada	*Former Soviet Union*
_____	_____
_____	_____
_____	_____
_____	_____

7. **The Continental United States.**   With respect to the continental United States (excluding Alaska and Hawaii), correctly name *two* of the following four:

   The northernmost state: _____

   The easternmost state: _____

   The westernmost state: _____

   The southernmost state: _____

8. **The Globe.**   Which of the following statements about the globe is *not* correct?

   a. _____ On a globe or a map, latitudes, not longitudes, measure degrees north or south—that is, distance from the equator.

   b. _____ The "tropics" is a zone on the globe between two lines that run parallel to the equator known as the Tropic of Capricorn and the Tropic of Cancer.

   c. _____ You cross the international date line and it becomes the next day when you travel east from Japan to Hawaii.

   d. _____ The Prime Meridian, from which time zones are measured, is a vertical line that runs through England.

9. **Mountains and Deserts.**   Correctly answer *either* of the following.

   a. The highest mountain in Africa is

   _____ i.   Mount McKinley.

   _____ ii. Mount Everest.

   _____ iii. Mount Kilimanjaro.

   b. The largest desert in the world is

   _____ i.   the Sahara, in Africa.

   _____ ii. the Gobi, in Asia.

   _____ iii. the Arabian, in the Middle East.

10. **The Americas.**   Name eight countries in South America *or* eight countries in Central and North America; then name the capitals of five of the countries.

   Countries   *Capitals*

   _____   _____

   _____   _____

   _____   _____

   _____   _____

   _____   _____

   _____   _____

   _____   _____

   _____   _____

EXTRA CREDIT: For two points, give both the question and the correct answer to at least one good geography trivia question. (It may be a question that you have made up.)

YOUR SCORE: For the correct answers, see pages 188–202. Giving yourself two points for every question you answered correctly, your score on GEOGRAPHY is

   0   2   4   6   8   12   14   16   18   20

13.   ELECTRICITY

1. **Sources of Electricity.**   Electricity can be generated from

    a. _____ coal.

    b. _____ moving water.

    c. _____ nuclear reactions.

    d. _____ wind.

    e. _____ sunlight.

    f. _____ all of the above.

2. **Household Current.**   Household electricity that flows to appliances through wall sockets is

    a. _____ analog current.

    b. _____ digital current.

    c. _____ alternating current.

    d. _____ direct current.

3. **Defective Wiring.**   An unintended connection between two live wires (such as the two separate strands of standard lamp cord) that can overload a circuit, cause electrical shock, or cause a fire is called a _____.

4. **Circuitry Safety Devices.**   One of the safety devices in the wiring system of a house or apartment that automatically shuts off the flow of electricity when a circuit gets overloaded or an appliance has an electrical malfunction is

    _____.

5. **Light Bulbs.**   Although an incandescent lightbulb (the round, screw-in-type bulb) burns hotter than a fluorescent lightbulb (the long, tube-type bulb) of similar wattage, it is cheaper than a fluorescent bulb. _____ *True* or *False*?

6. **Old Wives' Tales.**   Which of the following is an *untrue* "old wives' tale"?

   a. _____ Lightning never strikes in the same place twice.

   b. _____ Rubber shoes can help prevent electrical shock.

   c. _____ The coating on the inside of fluorescent bulbs is toxic.

   d. _____ Copper wire, although less expensive, is a better conductor than aluminum wire.

7. **Currents and Plugs.**   Which *one* of the following statements is *false*?

   a. _____ Most European wall plugs do not fit American wall sockets, and vice versa.

   b. _____ The electrical current produced by a car battery is direct current, while the electrical current in wall sockets is alternating current.

   c. _____ The round, third prong on the plug on many appliances permits a greater amount of electricity to flow to the appliance.

   d. _____ The electrical voltage in a typical household electrical line in most European countries is 220 volts, in contrast to 110–120 volts in the United States and Canada.

8. **Electrical Hazards.**   Which of the following does *not* present an electrical hazard?

   a. _____ Playing outdoor sports during an electrical storm

   b. _____ Operating a hair dryer while in a bathtub

   c. _____ Installing a light switch without turning off the electricity

   d. _____ Changing a broken lightbulb with the power on but the wall switch off

9. **Electrical Safety.**   Correctly name *either* of the following:

   a. A proper technique for putting out an electrical fire

   b. The proper first aid response for high-voltage electrical shock

   _____

   _____

10. **Electrical Terms.**   Correctly match each of the terms in column I below
with the proper corresponding description in column II.

I

II

Tungsten   ———

a. A metal alloy used, because of its low
melting point, to connect metal electrical
components

Voltage   ———

b. A metallic element used, because of its high
melting point, as a filament in light bulbs

Rheostat   ———

c. A unit of measurement for the flow of elec-
trons (electric current) through a circuit

Solder   ———

d. A unit of measurement for the force of the
electric power pushing and causing an electric current

Ampere   ———

e. A device that, by regulating the flow of
current in a circuit, can be used to dim a
light

YOUR SCORE: For the correct answers, see pages 202–207. Giving yourself two
points for every question you answered correctly, your score for
ELECTRICITY is

0   2   4   6   8   12   14   16   18   20

14. SPORTS

1. **Championships.** Correctly fill in all of the blanks for *two* of the following three:

    a. The four grand slam tournaments of professional tennis.

    _____   _____

    _____   _____

    b. The three races in horse racing's Triple Crown.

    _____   _____

    _____

    c. The four majors of the men's PGA golf tour.

    _____   _____

    _____   _____

2. **Individual Sports.** Correctly name *each* of the following terms used in individual sports.

    a. In golf, the term for completing a hole in one stroke more than "par" is

    _____ .

    b. In tennis, the term for describing a 40–40 tie score is _____ .

    c. In sailing, the left side of the boat as you face forward is _____ .

    d. In track, the 26.2-mile foot race that originated in ancient Greece is

    _____ .

3. **Team Sports.** Correctly name *each* of the following terms that are used in team sports.

    a. In basketball, a field goal scored from outside the semicircle that is drawn 23 feet from the basket is _____ .

    b. In football, two points scored by tackling the other team's ball carrier in his own end zone is _____ .

    c. In baseball, as you look out from home plate, the infield player whose position is just to the left of second base is _____ .

    d. In soccer, the infraction that occurs when an offensive player is farther downfield than the ball and all other opposing players except the opposing goalie is _____ .

4. **Professional Sports Teams.**   Correctly name, using both the location name and nickname (e.g., Mudville Sluggers), at least 4 professional teams in any *one* of the following professional sports: basketball, football, baseball, hockey.

   _____   _____

   _____   _____

5. **Sports Common outside the United States.**   Correctly identify each of the following sports that are popular in parts of the world *other* than the United States:

   a. A game popular in England and other Commonwealth countries that is played with a small leather ball and two flat wooden bats by opposing teams of 11 players who typically are dressed in white is _____.

   b. The sport that is known as "football" in most of the world except the United States is _____.

   c. A game played on ice with a heavy metal or stone disk that is slid toward a target circle by players who affect the speed and direction of the disk by sweeping the ice with brooms is _____.

   d. A type of football that originated in England, played with a ball that is slightly more rounded than an American football, by up to fifteen players per side who tackle other players but do not wear pads is _____.

6. **The National Pastime.** With respect to the game of baseball, which has been called the "national pastime" of America, correctly answer *two* of the following:

   a. Name either three members of the Baseball Hall of Fame who played for the New York Yankees *or* three of the first five members who were selected in 1936 as the top five players of the post-1900 era.

   _____   _____

   _____

   b. Name one way to make a double play in baseball other than through a ground ball double play.

   _____

   c. Name the first African American to play in the major leagues.

   _____

7. **Women Athletes.** Correctly match the women athletes listed below with the sports in which they excelled.

    _____ Mary Lou Retton and Nadia Comaneci

    _____ Billie Jean King and Serena Williams

    _____ Wilma Rudolph and Marion Jones

    _____ Sonja Henie and Kristi Yamaguchi

    a. track
    b. golf
    c. tennis
    d. soccer
    e. ice skating
    f. swimming
    g. gymnastics
    h. skiing

8. **The Olympics.** Name a city or country in which one of the three most recent Winter Olympics *or* one of the three most recent Summer Olympics was held.

    _____ .

9. **The World Cup.** Name *one* of the countries that has won the Men's World Cup or the Women's World Cup of soccer in the last ten years.

    _____ .

10. **Cardiovascular Endurance.** Which of the following activities does the *least* to improve your cardiovascular endurance or your aerobic capacity?

    a. _____ Bicycling

    b. _____ Weight lifting

    c. _____ Swimming

    d. _____ Walking

YOUR SCORE: For the correct answers, turn to pages 207–216. Giving yourself two points for each question you answered correctly, your score for SPORTS is

0   2   4   6   8   12   14   16   18   20

15.   IMPROVISING

We are frequently faced with situations that can be dealt with easily if we have the correct tool, material, or accessory. Often, however, the right tool or material is not immediately available, and we have to improvise to meet the challenge at hand in a more creative way.

The following are daily situations in which improvisation is often required. Giving yourself two points for each correct answer, up to a maximum of 20 points, identify a satisfactory method of improvising for each of the following.

1. **Measuring.**   Measure a distance of a few feet precisely when you do not have access to a ruler or tape measure.

   _____

2. **A Missing Button.**   Compensate for a button that has come off something you are wearing in a place that you do not want to leave unbuttoned.

   _____

3. **Jar Lids.**   Open a stuck lid on a jar.

   _____

4. **Screwing in a Screw.**   Screw in a screw without a screwdriver.

   _____

5. **Shining Shoes.**   Shine leather shoes, a leather handbag, or a leather briefcase without shoe polish or leather cream.

   _____

6. **Polishing Silver.**   Polish silver or a piece of silver jewelry when you have no silver polish.

   _____

7. **Getting Wrinkles Out.**   Get wrinkles out of a suit or dress, for example, after it has been packed.

   _____

8. **Collar Stays and Panty Hose.**   Deal with either lost collar stays or a run in panty hose.

   _____

9. **Spots.**   Remove a food spot on clothing.

   _____

10. **Starting a Fire.**   Start a fire without matches.

   _____

11. **Staying Dry in a Sudden Rain Shower.**   Stay dry in a sudden rain shower when you have no umbrella or raincoat.

   _____

12. **Drying a Just-Washed Item of Clothing.**   Quickly dry an article of clothing you have just washed when you do not have access to a clothes dryer.

   _____

13. **Windshield Ice.**   Clean frost or ice off your windshield without an ice scraper.

   _____

14. **Bad Breath.**   Freshen your breath without using mouthwash, toothpaste, or chewing gum.

   _____

YOUR SCORE: For the correct answers, turn to pages 217–222. Giving yourself two points for each question you answered correctly, your score for IMPROVISING is

   0   2   4   6   8   12   14   16   18   20

C. THINGS IT IS RISKY NOT TO KNOW

16. SEX

1. **Conception.**   For a woman with a menstrual cycle that averages between 26 and 30 days, on how many days of her average menstrual cycle can she safely assume that she can have unprotected sex without risk of becoming pregnant?

    a. _____ 27 days

    b. _____ 20 days

    c. _____ 11 days

    d. _____ 3 days

2. **Masturbation.**   Frequent masturbation often has adverse physical consequences. _____ *True* or *False*?

3. **Sex Terms.**   Correctly identify at least *three* of the following terms:
   a. Sex between members of the same family is _____.
   b. The term, derived from one of the evil cities of the Old Testament, used to refer to intercourse between males or, in some contexts, oral sex is _____.
   c. The principal male sex hormone produced in the testicles of men and often associated with aggressive behavior is _____.
   d. Abdominal discomfort frequently experienced by females during menstruation is _____.

4. **Birth Control.**   Which of the following is the most reliable form of birth control?
   a. _____ Condoms
   b. _____ Birth control pills
   c. _____ Diaphrams
   d. _____ Withdrawal before orgasm

5. **Unwelcome Sex.**   Which of the following statements about unwelcome sex is *not* correct?
   a. _____ Unwelcome sex with a date—even if you and your date are regular sexual partners—may constitute the crime of rape.
   b. _____ Repeated, unwelcome sexual comments by a coworker may sometimes constitute sexual harassment, even without any touching or physical contact.
   c. _____ In most states, sex with someone under the age of 16 constitutes "statutory rape," even if the younger person consents.
   d. _____ When a female supervisor or manager insists on having sex with a male subordinate, she may be guilty of rape.

6. **Pregnancy.**   Which of the following statements is *true*?
   a. _____ Pregnancy cannot occur if the male does not reach orgasm.
   b. _____ Pregnancy cannot occur if the male takes a hot bath within 15 minutes before having sex.
   c. _____ Pregnancy cannot occur if the female douches after having sex.
   d. _____ Pregnancy cannot occur while a female is menstruating.

7. **AIDS.**   Name at least *two* ways of avoiding the potentially lethal disease of AIDS.

    _____ and _____

8. **STDs.**   Name at least *two* sexually transmitted diseases (STDs) in addition to AIDS that may be transmitted through sexual intercourse.

    _____ and _____

9. **Abortion.**   In *Roe* v. *Wade*, the Supreme Court's landmark decision on abortion, the Court ruled that a woman has a constitutional right to have an abortion up to what point of her pregnancy?

    a. _____ Within the first week

    b. _____ Within the first month

    c. _____ Within the first 3 months

    d. _____ At any time during her pregnancy

10. **Responsibilities of an Unmarried Father.**   If an unmarried woman becomes pregnant, gives birth, and chooses not to put the child up for adoption, which of the following is/are the legal responsibilities of the father, even if he is *not* married to the mother of the child?

    a. _____ The father has no responsibilities to the mother or child.

    b. _____ The father has to marry the natural mother.

    c. _____ The father has to provide financial support to the natural mother.

    d. _____ The father has to share custody of the child.

    e. _____ The father has to provide financial support for the child.

YOUR SCORE: For the correct answers, turn to pages 223–231. Giving yourself two points for each question you answered correctly, your score for SEX is

0   2   4   6   8   12   14   16   18   20

17. DRUGS

1. **Acetylsalicylic Acid.**   Acetylsalicylic acid is the chemical term for
    a. _____ aspirin.
    b. _____ coffee.
    c. _____ LSD.
    d. _____ the active ingredient in hashish (marijuana).

2. **Analgesics.**   Which of the following is *not* an analgesic, over-the-counter painkiller?
    a. _____ Ibuprofen
    b. _____ Percocet
    c. _____ Aspirin
    d. _____ Acetaminophen

3. **Generic Drugs.**   Generic drugs, which generally sell for less than brand-name drugs, cannot be sold under brand names that are protected by another manufacturer's trademark, but they may be chemically identical to their brand-name counterparts. _____ *True* or *False*?

4. **Drugs and Their Uses.**   Correctly match at least *five* of the drugs or medications listed in column I with the associated terms listed in column II.

I		II
Valium	_____	a. antibiotic (bacterial infections)
Ritalin	_____	b. muscle strength
Viagra	_____	c. muscle relaxant
Amoxicillin	_____	d. acne
Benadryl	_____	e. sexual function
Retin-A	_____	f. hyperactivity
Anabolic steroids	_____	g. allergies

5. **Steroids.**   Which of the following statements about anabolic steroids is *not* correct? Anabolic steroids

   a. _____ can increase weight, strength, athletic performance, and endurance.

   b. _____ in men can cause shrinking of the testicles, breast development, and hair loss, and in women can cause masculinization of the body, acne, and hair loss.

   c. _____ if abused can have irreversible short-term effects and long-term effects, including heart disease, liver tumors, cancer, and death.

   d. _____ although less expensive, cortial and estrogenic steroids are no less subject to abuse than anabolic steroids.

6. **Addictive Drugs.**   Which of the following drugs is *not* addictive?

   a. _____ Caffeine

   b. _____ Nicotine

   c. _____ Dramamine

   d. _____ Codeine

7. **Illicit Drug Use.**   Which of the following statements about illicit drug use in the United States in 1999 is *not* correct?

   a. _____ The number of people engaged in illicit drug use in the United States in 1999 was approximately 40 percent lower than in 1979.

   b. _____ In the age group 18–25, those who smoke cigarettes are approximately four times more likely to use illicit drugs as those who don't.

   c. _____ Approximately 45 million Americans (approximately 16 percent of the population) engage in binge drinking (5 or more drinks on 5 or more days during the past 30 days).

   d. _____ The use of illicit drugs among whites is less than half the rate of illicit drug use among Hispanics, blacks, Asian Americans, Native Americans, and multiple-race Americans.

8. **Marijuana.**   Which of the following statements about marijuana is *not* true?

    a. _____ Marijuana is the most common illicit drug for Americans between the ages of 12 and 17.

    b. _____ Marijuana can impair memory, concentration, coordination, and knowledge retention.

    c. _____ The effects of ingesting marijuana frequently last up to 24 hours.

    d. _____ If used during pregnancy, marijuana can cause birth defects.

9. **Drug Facts.**   Which of the following statements about drugs is factually not accurate?

    a. _____ Crack, a popular, chemically altered form of cocaine, is in a form that looks like pellets of salt or soap and is typically smoked.

    b. _____ AIDS can be transmitted by drug users who share needle syringes.

    c. _____ Quaaludes, alcohol, "downers," and barbiturates are all depressants that slow down the body's vital functions.

    d. _____ Heroin and cocaine are both made from cannabis, a plant that is also a legitimate source of hemp, which is used to make rope.

10. **Hallucinogens.**   Which of the following statements about hallucinogens—drugs that cause hallucinations and alter perceptions of time, smell, and touch—is *not* true?

    a. _____ Acid and red or green dragon (names for LSD), angel dust and loveboat (names for PCP), mescaline, and psilocybin are all hallucinogens.

    b. _____ Withdrawal symptoms from taking hallucinogens can include tremors, disorientation, and lethargy.

    c. _____ "Designer drugs," such as Ecstasy and PCE, can be stronger than the drugs they imitate and may cause irreversible brain damage.

    d _____ Large doses of hallucinogens can cause convulsions, heart failure, or ruptured blood vessels in the brain.

YOUR SCORE: For the correct answers, turn to pages 232–235. Giving yourself two points for each question you answered correctly, your score for DRUGS is

0   2   4   6   8   12   14   16   18   20

18.   ALCOHOL ABUSE

A. Generally

1. **Alcohol Content.** Of the following, which contains the most alcohol?
    a. _____ A beer
    b. _____ A glass of wine
    c. _____ A shot or mixed drink
    d. _____ They all have approximately the same amount of alcohol.

2. **The Effects of One Drink.**   On average, the length of time it takes a person to oxidize and eliminate the effects of one drink is
    a. _____ 45 minutes.
    b. _____ 1½ hours.
    c. _____ 3 hours.

3. **Treacherous Drinks.**   Name at least *three* types of drinks that, because of their smoothness or pleasant taste, increase the risk of drinking too much and of causing intoxication.

    _____   _____

    _____

4. **Nonalcoholic Drinks.**   Name at least one nonalcoholic beer *and* one non-alcoholic bar drink.
    Nonalcoholic Beer   *Nonalcoholic Bar Drink*

    _____   _____

5. **Saying No.**   Name at least *three* reasons you might give if you want to say no to friends who are urging you to have a beer or a drink.

    _____   _____

    _____

6. **Reducing the Effects of Drinking.**   Name *three* ways in which the effects of drinking can be reduced to some extent.

   _____   _____

   _____

7. **Long- and Short-term Effects of Drinking.**   Name *either*:
   a. Three possible short-term effects of excessive drinking

   _____   _____

   _____

   b. Three possible long-term effects of excessive drinking

   _____   _____

   _____

8. **Alcohol Content.**   Which of the following has the lowest concentration of alcohol, and which has the highest?
   a. _____ Beer
   b. _____ Grain alcohol
   c. _____ Whiskey
   d. _____ Wine

B. Drinking and Driving

9. **Alcohol and Traffic Deaths.**   Correctly answer *either* of the following:
   a. The percentage of traffic deaths that are alcohol-related is
      _____ i.   5 percent.
      _____ ii. 25 percent.
      _____ iii. 50 percent.
   b. The percentage of single-car traffic deaths after midnight that are alcohol-related is
      _____ i.   25 percent.
      _____ ii. 50 percent.
      _____ iii. 90 percent.

10. **Getting a Drinking Driver to Stop and Let You Out.**   What are *three* things you could say to a friend who has been drinking and is driving fast that might persuade him or her to stop and let you out of the car?

_____

_____

_____

YOUR SCORE: For the correct answers, turn to pages 236–242. Giving yourself two points for every question you answered correctly, your score for ALCOHOL ABUSE is

0   2   4   6   8   12   14   16   18   20

19. CARDS AND GAMBLING

1. **A Deck of Cards.** Which of the following statements about cards is correct?

   a. _____ Spades outrank hearts, and diamonds outrank clubs.

   b. _____ Kings, queens, and jokers are the three face cards in a deck.

   c. _____ The highest card in each suit is the ace, the lowest is the one.

   d. _____ The dealer deals first to the person on her right and, continuing counterclockwise, deals to herself last.

   e. _____ A deck of cards is cut to change the sequence of cards and shuffled to ensure that the cards on the bottom and top of the deck are changed.

2. **Classic Card Games.** Answer *either* of the following:

   a. Name one classic social card game and generally describe its basic rules.

   b. Name one children's card game and generally describe its basic rules.

   _____

   _____

   _____

3. **Solitaire.** Name and demonstrate how to play at least *one* type of solitaire.

   _____

4. **Poker.** Name at least *one* type or game of poker and describe its basic rules.

   _____

   _____

   _____

5. **The Lottery.** Which of the following statements about lotteries is *not* true?

   a. _____ Lotteries are now legal in most states, and a lottery ticket can be purchased for a nominal amount, usually $1.

   b. _____ In most states, lotteries are now public lotteries, which are run and controlled by the state and are free of corruption.

c. _____ A higher percentage of money taken in from the sale of lottery tickets is paid out in winnings than the percentage of money played in slot machines is paid out in slot machine winnings.

d. _____ The current value of a lottery jackpot of "$10 million," that is paid in equal installments over 20 years is actually less than $10 million because the lottery, not the winner, gets the benefit of the time value of the money.

6. **The Odds of Winning the Lottery.**   Assume that to play California Super Lotto, you must pick one of six numbers, from 1 to 51, for six sets of numbers. To win the Super Lotto, the six numbers that you select (or that a computer selects for you) must match the six winning numbers. The odds of your six numbers matching the six winning numbers and your winning the Super Lotto are approximately

a. _____ 1 in 36.

b. _____ 1 in 306.

c. _____ 1 in 3,443,000.

d. _____ 1 in 18,009,000.

7. **Casino Gambling.**   Correctly identify *three* of the following four statements as *True* or *False*:

a. _____ In casino gambling, the odds for all of the games favor "the house," not the gambler.

b. _____ In casinos, because skilled players are able to "beat the odds," the actual win percentage of the house is typically lower than the mathematical odds of the house's winning.

c. _____ Casinos often offer free food, drinks, or entertainment as an inducement to customers to gamble.

d. _____ In casino gambling, time is usually on your side in the sense that the longer you play, the better you are likely to do.

8. **Blackjack.**   Of all of the games played in casinos, Blackjack is the most popular and is also the game at which an educated player, over time, has the greatest odds of winning. _____ *True* or *False*?

9. **Casino Games.**   The popular casino game that is played with standard six-sided dice on a long, rectangular, felt-covered table and that includes both a dealer and a "stickman" is called _____.

10. **Gambling Facts.**   Consider the accuracy of each of the following statements.

    a. The terms "raise" and "ante" are betting terms used in card playing, but the term "trump" is not a gambling term.

    b. If you have flipped a coin four times and each time it has landed "heads," the chance that the next time you flip the coin it will land "tails" is only 50-50.

    c. If you bet on a horse to finish second and it finishes first, you still win; but if you bet on a horse to finish first and it finishes second, you do not win anything.

    Of these three statements that appear above,

    a. _____ all are true.

    b. _____ some are true and some are false.

    c. _____ all are false.

YOUR SCORE: For the correct answers, turn to pages 242–250. Giving yourself two points for each question you answered correctly, your score for CARDS AND GAMBLING is

0   2   4   6   8   12   14   16   18   20

D. THINGS TO GIVE YOU AN EDGE

20. INTERNATIONAL FUNDAMENTALS

1. **Crossing International Borders.**   Many countries require, in addition to your passport, an official, written authorization to *enter* their territory. This authorization is called

    a. _____ a tariff.

    b. _____ a customs declaration.

    c. _____ a health certificate.

    d. _____ a visa.

2. **Fahrenheit and Centigrade.**   If the outside temperature is 20 degrees Celsius, what is the temperature in degrees Fahrenheit? _____

3. **International Phrases.**   Correctly say or write at least one common word or phrase—such as "hello," "good-bye," "thank you"—in *three* other languages:

   _____   _____

   _____

4. **Driving Abroad.**   Name at least *two* countries in which cars are driven on the left side of the road:

   _____   _____

5. **Foreign Languages.**   Correctly identify *one* of the following:

   a. The language spoken by the greatest number of people in the world is

      _____.

   b. The second most common language spoken in the world (also the predominant language of international business and international aviation) is

      _____.

   c. The traditional language of international diplomacy is _____.

6. **Time Differences.**   What is the time difference between the city where you live and *one* of the three cities listed below?

   a. London   _____ hours

   b. Vancouver   _____ hours

   c. Moscow   _____ hours

7. **International Travel.**   Answer *either* of the following:

   a. A tip for minimizing jet lag when traveling across time zones is

      _____.

   b. A medication that is effective for motion sickness *or* a medication that is effective for diarrhea is _____.

8. **Foreign Currencies.** Correctly answer *either* of the following:

   a. If the U.S. dollar is "strong," it is relatively more expensive to travel abroad than when the dollar is "weak." _____ *True* or *False*?

   b. Name the principal unit of currency of at least three foreign countries.

   _____   _____

   _____

9. **Violating Local Law.**   If, while traveling in a foreign country, you violate one of its laws,

   a. _____ you cannot be arrested if you show your passport.

   b. _____ you may be detained and deported from the country, but you may not be punished.

   c. _____ you may be arrested and punished in accordance with local law.

   d. _____ you may be arrested and punished, but the U.S. embassy can prevent any punishment that would be unreasonable under U.S. law.

10. **Neighboring Countries.**   Name *either* the Prime Minister of Canada *or* the President of Mexico.

    _____ .

YOUR SCORE: For the correct answers, see pages 250–259. Giving yourself two points for each question you answered correctly, your score for INTERNATIONAL FUNDAMENTALS is

   0   2   4   6   8   12   14   16   18   20

21.   ETIQUETTE

1. **Expressing Thanks for Having Been a Guest in Someone's Home.**
    You have been a guest in someone's home, perhaps for a weekend or a holiday meal. Name at least *two* appropriate ways of expressing your thanks for the hospitality and for having been a guest in another person's home.

    _____

    _____

2. **Sneezing.**   While having dinner with friends, you feel a sneeze coming on. Name *two* of the several things you might do to be courteous to (and considerate of) the others at the table.

    _____

    _____

3. **Formal Meals.**   Correctly respond to at least *two* of the following:
    a. Describe or demonstrate how to set a complete place setting for a meal, including knife, fork, and spoon; dinner plate; salad plate or bread-and-butter plate; glass; and napkin.

    _____

    _____

    b. Name at least *one* rule of thumb for deciding which piece of silverware to use for which course at a formal dinner.

    _____

    c. Correctly identify the side from which plates of food are correctly served and the side from which plates are cleared at the end of the meal.
        Plates are served from the _____, cleared from the

    _____ .

4. **Etiquette Books.**   Name the author or title of *one* current etiquette reference book.

    _____

5. **Introductions.**   Describe or demonstrate how to make a proper introduction when the two people to be introduced are an older person and a younger person, such as your parent and a friend.

_____

_____

6. **Proposing a Toast.**   Name at least *two* rules of thumb to follow when proposing a toast. Demonstrate by proposing a toast to a friend or colleague.

_____

_____

7. **Etiquette Conventions.**   Correctly answer at least *three* of the following:

   a. Traditionally, which arm should a man offer to a woman? _____

   b. When dining, what is a universally recognized signal that you have finished eating? _____

   c. On which lapel or side of your chest should you wear a name tag?
   _____

   d. How do you properly respond to a formal (printed or engraved) invitation? _____

8. **Etiquette Anachronisms.**   Historically, a number of traditional etiquette rules have required that men behave solicitously toward women. Of the following traditional rules, which ones are now considered sexist or anachronistic and no longer necessary to good manners, as opposed to those that are still considered good etiquette rules for men to follow. (*Hint:* The correct answer includes more than one of the following.)

   a. _____ Standing aside before getting off an elevator so that female passengers may exit first

   b. _____ Standing when a female enters the room

   c. _____ Opening a door for a female

   d. _____ Walking on the outside (the curb side) when walking with a female on a sidewalk

   e. _____ Helping seat a female at dinner by standing behind her chair and sliding the chair in behind her as she sits down

9. **Hi-Tech Etiquette.**   Technological advances have introduced new opportunities for behaving rudely. For *each* of the new technologies listed below, describe one practice that is, or should be considered, rude or impolite.

    a. Call waiting   _____

    b. The Internet   _____

    c. Cellular phones   _____

10. **Invitation Terms.**   Correctly identify *both* of the following terms, which are often used on invitations, particularly formal ones.

    a. The term used on formal invitations to indicate that guests should wear a suit, cocktail dress, or business attire is _____ .

    b. The term used on written invitations to indicate that you should call or write the host or hostess to say whether or not you accept the invitation and will attend is _____ .

YOUR SCORE: For the correct answers, see pages 259–272. Giving yourself two points for every question you answered correctly, your score for ETIQUETTE is

        0   2   4   6   8   12   14   16   18   20

22. MULTICULTURAL BASICS

1. **Cultural Rituals.**   Correctly identify at least *two* of the following terms:

    a. The Jewish ritual by which 13-year-old boys assume religious obligations and symbolically enter manhood is _____.

    b. The annual Islamic pilgrimage to the holy city of Mecca, in which more than 2 million people participate each year is _____.

    c. The Christian ceremony, characterized by the sprinkling of or immersion into water, by which a Christian is dedicated to and initiated into the Christian faith is _____.

2. **Ethnic Groups.**   Correctly identify the national ethnic group in the United States that is

    a. the largest ethnic population in the city of Chicago.

    b. predominantly Catholic.

    c. originally from the country that gave us the dance, the mazurka, and the sausage, kielbasa.

    d. of the same national origin as Pope John Paul II.

    _____

3. **Holidays.**   Correctly name at least *two* of the following special observances or holidays:

    a. The carnival-like celebration observed in New Orleans, and other cities that marks Shrove Tuesday, the last day before the beginning of Lent, is

    _____.

    b. The Islamic period of daytime fasting that coincides with the ninth month of the Islamic year is _____.

    c. The African-American Christmastime celebration, the name of which is based on the Swahili term for "first harvest," is _____.

4. **Judaism.**   Correctly identify *three* of the following defined terms relating to Judaism:

   a. The Jewish New Year is _____.

   b. The head covering worn by Conservative or Orthodox Jewish men is _____.

   c. The term that describes food, or food preparation and cooking, that conforms to traditional Jewish dietary laws is _____.

   d. An Orthodox Jewish sect, the male members of which typically wear black clothing and beards, is _____.

5. **National Cultural Habits.**   Correctly answer at least *three* of the following as *True* or *False*:

   a. _____ Tea, referred to in many parts of the world as chai, is the dominant hot beverage in China, England, and Brazil.

   b. _____ In most Spanish-speaking countries, the evening meal generally is eaten at an earlier hour than it is in North America and northern Europe.

   c. _____ In conservative Arab countries, it is a criminal offense for male friends to hold hands while walking or talking.

   d. _____ In both the Far East and Canada, smoking is less common than in the United States.

6. **Famous Authors.**   The following recognized and honored authors—Toni Morrison, Maya Angelou, Alex Haley, and Langston Hughes—are all members of what ethnic or cultural group? _____

7. **Music and Dance.**   For at least *three* of the following, correctly name the culture—country or group—that is associated with the type of music or dance named.

   a. Tango: _____

   b. The song, "Tis a Gift to Be Simple": _____

   c. Yodeling: _____

   d. The hora: _____

   e. Mariachi bands: _____

8. **Expressions.**   Identify the culture or country with which each of the following terms or expressions is associated. For two points, correctly answer *five* of the six questions.

   a. *G'day mate,* commonly used as a greeting: _____

   b. *Gesundheit* (pronounced "guh-ZOONT-height"), used to wish good health to someone who has just sneezed: _____

   c. *Gambei* (pronounced "gahm-BAY"), a term used to propose a toast that roughly corresponds to the U.S. term "bottoms up": _____

   d. *Chutzpah* (pronounced either "HOOT-spuh" or "KHOOT-spuh"), a term used to describe fearless audacity: _____

   e. *C'est la vie* (pronounced "say-la-vee"), a term of cheerful acceptance that whatever will be, will be: _____

   f. *Enshallah,* which, translated literally, means "God willing": _____

9. **Islamic Culture.**   Correctly identify at least *three* of the following definitions relating to Islamic culture.

   a. The holy city to which the annual Islamic pilgrimage is made and toward which Muslims face when praying is _____.

   b. The buildings that are places of worship in Islam are _____.

   c. The holiest day of the week for Muslims, which is also the second day of the "weekend" in most Arabic countries, is _____.

   d. The accessory, in some respects equivalent to the Catholic rosary, that many Muslims carry and use in conjunction with prayer is _____.

10. **Rude Gestures.**   Name at least *three* different gestures or other physical actions that are considered rude in some cultures or societies.

   _____   _____

   _____

YOUR SCORE: For the correct answers, see pages 273–279. Giving yourself two points for each question you answered correctly, your score for MULTI-CULTURAL BASICS is

   0   2   4   6   8   12   14   16   18   20

23. AMERICANA

1. **The National Anthem.** Stand and sing (or recite) from memory the first verse of "The Star-Spangled Banner."

    _____

    _____

    _____

    _____

    _____

    _____

2. **Demographics.** Which *one* of the following statements is *true*?

    a. _____ African-Americans account for less than 10 percent of the population of the United States.

    b. _____ There are more women than men in the United States.

    c. _____ More than 300 million people live in the United States.

    d. _____ The median age in the United States is just under 30.

3. **U.S. Currency.** Identify what is pictured on the following pieces of U.S. currency by correctly filling in at least *six* of the following blanks. (*Hint:* You may recall that the front of the bill generally portrays people; the back, usually places.):

	Front	*Back*
$1 bill	_____	_____
$2 bill	_____	_____
$5 bill	_____	_____
$10 bill	_____	_____
$20 bill	_____	_____
$50 bill	_____	_____
$100 bill	_____	_____

4. **The National Debt.**   The per capita national debt of the United States—the amount of government debt that is outstanding for every woman, man, and child—is approximately:

    a. _____ $2,000.

    b. _____ $9,000.

    c. _____ $20,000.

5. **State Capitals.**   Name the capitals of at least 25 of the 50 states of the United States.

Alabama	_____	Alaska	_____
Arizona	_____	Arkansas	_____
California	_____	Colorado	_____
Connecticut	_____	Delaware	_____
Florida	_____	Georgia	_____
Hawaii	_____	Idaho	_____
Illinois	_____	Indiana	_____
Iowa	_____	Kansas	_____
Kentucky	_____	Louisiana	_____
Maine	_____	Maryland	_____
Massachusetts	_____	Michigan	_____
Minnesota	_____	Mississippi	_____
Missouri	_____	Montana	_____
Nebraska	_____	Nevada	_____
New Hampshire	_____	New Jersey	_____
New Mexico	_____	New York	_____
North Carolina	_____	North Dakota	_____
Ohio	_____	Oklahoma	_____
Oregon	_____	Pennsylvania	_____
Rhode Island	_____	South Carolina	_____
South Dakota	_____	Tennessee	_____
Texas	_____	Utah	_____
Vermont	_____	Virginia	_____

| Washington | _____ | West Virginia | _____ |
| Wisconsin | _____ | Wyoming | _____ |

6. **Presidents.**   Name, in order, the first five U.S. Presidents, the most recent five U.S. Presidents, *or* any other five consecutive Presidents.

_____

_____

_____

_____

_____

7. **Mission to the Moon.**   The first successful manned expedition to the moon was achieved by America. Correctly name *one* of the following:

a. The astronaut who first walked on the moon: _____

b. The space craft or space program that took the astronaut to the moon:

_____

c. The year that the first lunar landing occurred: _____

8. **Supreme Court.**   Name *either* the first woman *or* the first African-American appointed to the United States Supreme Court.

_____

9. **The Constitution.**   Identify at least *three* of our 26 constitutional amendments and describe generally what each of the three provides.

_____	_____
_____	_____
_____	_____

10. **Ancestral Groups.**   America is a country of immigrants, who came from approximately 200 different countries or "ancestral groups." According to the last census, which of the following is *not* one of the four countries or groups that accounted for the largest number of ancestors of Americans:

    a. _____ Ireland

    b. _____ England

    c. _____ Africa

    d. _____ Poland

    e. _____ German

YOUR SCORE: For the correct answers, see pages 279–287. Giving yourself two points for each question you answered correctly, your score for **AMERICANA** is

0   2   4   6   8   12   14   16   18   20

E. IMPROVING YOUR QUALITY OF LIFE

24. DANCING

PEANUTS ®   By Charles M. Schulz

PEANUTS reprinted by permission of UFS, Inc.
First Printed: May 5, 1958.

1.   **Famous Tap Dancers.**   Name one great tap dancer, male or female, dead or alive.

_____

2. **Movie Dance Scenes.**   Name at least *three* movies with great dance scenes or sequences.

   _____

   _____

   _____

3. **Dancers and Dance Groups.**   Correctly answer at least *two* of the following:

   a. The Irish dance troupe whose energetic style combines elements of folk dancing, jigs, clogging, and athletic dance is _____.

   b. The chorus line, famous for its synchronized dancing, that performs at Radio City Music Hall in New York City is _____.

   c. The performer who popularized the step known as the "moonwalk" is

   _____.

4. **Ballet.**   Name one famous ballet *or* one famous ballet dancer.

   _____

5. **Dance Directors.**   The person who writes the dance and creates the dance steps in a musical or in a ballet is called the _____.

6. **Dance Rhythm.**   Listen to some dance music and pay attention to its beat. Then do each of the following in time to the music:

   a. Clap your hands.

   b. Tap one or both feet.

   c. Shift your weight back and forth from one foot to the other.

   Ask someone who has a sense of rhythm to decide if you have earned two points.

7. **Dance Position.**   Describe, and then demonstrate, ballroom dance position.

   _____

8. **Ballroom Dancing.**   Correctly answer *each* of the following.
   i. In ballroom dancing,
      a._____   the man follows the woman's lead.
      b._____   the man leads and the woman follows.
      c._____   the man and woman coordinate their steps, but neither one leads the other.
   ii. In ballroom dancing, it is almost always true that
      a._____   the man begins with his left foot, and the woman begins with her right foot.
      b._____   both the man and the woman begin with their left feet.
      c._____   it varies with the dance, depending on the step and the rhythm.

9. **Dances.**   Correctly name at least *two* of the following dances:
   a. A country-western line dance done in which dancers without partners, all facing the same direction, follow a uniform pattern of steps that includes sliding to the left and right, rocking forward and backward, and then pivoting; often danced to a song of the same name, it can be done to any 4/4 country-western song or to funk music: _____

   b. A two-step that includes a slight bounce and is danced with a partner; popular in the southwest United States, this dance is often danced to songs by Boozoo Chavis, such as *Paper in My Shoe* and *Johnie Billie Goat*:
   _____

   c. A Latin line dance that became instantly popular in the United States in about 1995; normally "danced" solo or by individuals all facing the same direction, the movements involve hands, arms, and hips but no foot movement; recorded by Los Del Rio, this dance first became a popular hit in Spain: _____

   d. Originating in the 1920s along with Dixieland jazz, this dance may be performed solo, in a group, or with partners who may be facing one another or may be side-by-side; dancers bend their knees, pivot on their feet, and swing both arms to music in 4/4 time with a syncopated rhythm; this dance was popularized by the Ziegfield Follies and incorporated into the *Varsity Drag*: _____

10. **Latin Dances.**   Name *either*:

   a. The romantic Latin dance that was popularized in, and largely identified with, Argentina: ⸻

   b. Two other Latin dances: ⸻

YOUR SCORE: For the correct answers, see pages 287–293. Giving yourself two points for each question you answered correctly, your score for DANCING is

0   2   4   6   8   12   14   16   18   20

25. FRIENDS AND ACQUAINTANCES

1. **Handshakes.**   Name *three* elements of a good handshake.

                                        _____

    _____

    _____

2. **Talking to People You Don't Know.**   Name at least *one* technique that is effective in helping to strike up a conversation with someone whom you don't know.

3. **Remembering Names.**   Name at least *two* techniques for remembering names.

4. **The Art of Good Conversation.**   Name *three* keys to being a good conversationalist.

5. **Making Yourself Likable.**   Name at least *three* simple things you can do that, as a general rule, will tend to make other people like you.

6. **Friendships.**   In friendships, it is generally the case that "like" attracts "like." _____ *True* or *False*?

7. **Characteristics Valued by Friends.**   Surveys have shown that a certain characteristic is considered by most people to be the most important element for a close friendship. What is it?

    a. _____ Sense of humor

    b. _____ Willingness to listen

    c. _____ Loyalty

    d. _____ Ability to share emotional concerns

8. **The Sociology of Friendships.**   One of the decades in life in which people generally have the most time for friends is when they are in

    a. _____ their 20s.

    b. _____ their 30s.

    c. _____ their 40s.

    d. _____ their 50s.

9. **Undermining Relationships.**   Name at least *two* types of behavior that can be destructive to friendships or tend to weaken them.

    _____

    _____

10. **Building Friendships.**   Name at least *three* types of behavior that are effective in building or strengthening friendships.

    _____

    _____

    _____

YOUR SCORE: For the correct answers, see pages 293–300. Giving yourself two points for each question you answered correctly, your score for DEALING WITH PEOPLE is

       0   2   4   6   8   12   14   16   18   20

26. NUTRITION

1. **Snack Foods.** Name *three* healthful snack foods.

   _____   _____

   _____

2. **Fat.** Most nutritionists recommend that an average-sized adult consume approximately how many fat grams during the course of a day?

   a. _____ 65 fat grams

   b. _____ 115 fat grams

   c. _____ 225 fat grams

   d. _____ 315 fat grams

3. **Sources of Fiber.** Name *two* foods that are good sources of fiber.

   _____   _____

4. **High Blood Pressure.** High blood pressure, or hypertension, is often associated with diets containing high levels of what substance? _____

5. **Food Groups.** Of the following food groups, from which do most nutritionists recommend that you eat the largest number of daily servings?

   a. _____ Vegetables

   b. _____ Breads, cereals, rice, and pasta

   c. _____ Fruits

   d. _____ Meats, poultry, fish, dry beans and peas, eggs, and nuts

6. **Nutrients.** Carbohydrates and proteins are two of the six types of nutrients. Name *one* of the other four. _____

7. **Meats.** Name *either* of the following:

   a. Three low-fat meats

   b. Three high-fat meats

   _____   _____

   _____

8. **Variations on a Theme.**   Sucrose, dextrose, glucose, and lactose are all different types of what? _____

9. **Colas.**   The average 12-ounce can of cola contains the equivalent of about how many teaspoons of sugar?

    a. _____ 2

    b. _____ 4

    c. _____ 6

    d. _____ 9

10. **Nutritious Foods.**   Name *three* of the ten most nutritious common foods.

     _____   _____

     _____

YOUR SCORE: For the correct answers, see pages 301–306. Giving yourself two points for every question you answered correctly, your score for NUTRITION is

0   2   4   6   8   12   14   16   18   20

27. MUSIC

1. **Music Personalities.**   Answer *either* of the following:

   a. The four members of the Beatles:

   _____   _____

   _____   _____

   b. Two internationally renowned violinists:

   _____   _____

2. **American Music.**   Name at least *two* types of music that originated in the United States.

   _____   _____

3. **Musicals.**   Name one musical, the person who wrote either the words or music, *and* at least one song from the show.

   a. Name of the musical: _____

   b. Composer or lyricist: _____

   c. One song from the show: _____

4. **Instruments.**   Name at least *three* instruments in *three* of the following four families of instruments.

   a. Percussion instruments

   b. Brass instruments

   c. Woodwind instruments

   d. Stringed instruments

   _____   _____

   _____   _____

   _____   _____

   _____   _____

   _____   _____

   _____   _____

5. **Jazz Musicians.**   Who of the following was *not* a jazz musician?

    a. _____ Louis Armstrong

    b. _____ Dizzy Gillespie

    c. _____ Jerry Garcia

    d. _____ Dave Brubeck

6. **Singing Parts.**   Choral groups, choirs, and quartets typically sing in four parts, ranging from higher-pitched to lower-pitched voices. Name the four parts in a male chorus, a female chorus, *or* a mixed chorus.

    _____   _____

    _____   _____

7. **Composers.**   Name *two* Western (not Asian) musical composers who did not live in the 20th century.

    _____   _____

8. **Music Terms.**   Correctly name at least *one* of the following terms related to music:

    a. A singer who does not quite hit the correct note but instead sings slightly below the true pitch is said to be singing _____.

    b. On a piano, the note considered to be the middle note that is often used as a reference point for locating other notes is _____.

    c. The term used to describe singing, by a group or a vocalist, that is not accompanied by a piano or other musical instruments is _____.

    d. The type of rhythm achieved by stressing a beat that is normally an unaccented beat is _____.

9. **Music Miscellany.**   Correctly fill in the blanks in a, b, *or* c.

    a. Two of the three musicians about whom the song *American Pie* was written are _____ and _____.

    b. The name of the composer famous for his Viennese waltzes is

    _____.

    c. A type of popular music that originated among African-American inner-city youth in the 1980s that incorporated elements of rap, funk, and bits of melodies or rhythms taken from other recordings is _____.

10. **Lyrics.**   You should know the lyrics of at least one song that you can sing in the shower. Either recite the lyrics or sing at least one complete chorus of the song from memory.

_____

_____

_____

_____

_____

_____.

YOUR SCORE: For the correct answers, see pages 306–312. Giving yourself two points for each question you answered correctly, your score for MUSIC is

0   2   4   6   8   12   14   16   18   20

28.   FAMILY FACTS

1. **Names.**   Name one of the following facts about *either* your family name (last name, or surname) *or* your given name (first name).

    a. The country from which the name came is _____.

    b. The language from which it came is _____.

    c. It means, either in English or in another language, _____.

2. **Key Dates for Your Parents.**   Name *either* the birth dates (day, month, and year) of both of your parents *or* the date on which they were married.

    _____

3. **Your Mother's Names.**   Name your mother's middle name *and* her last name when she was born.

    _____   _____

4. **First Cousins.**   Name *all* of your first cousins.

    _____

    _____

    _____

5. **Second Cousins.**   The most accurate definition of a "second cousin" is

    a. _____ any child of a first cousin.

    b. _____ a generic term used to refer to anyone with whom you are related, but less closely than a first cousin.

    c. _____ your first cousin's first cousin.

    d. _____ the child of one of your parents' first cousins.

6. **The Old Country.**   Name *one* foreign country from which someone in your family tree originally came.

    _____

7. **Grandparents.**   Give the full names of your grandparents on both sides of your family, even if you never knew some of them.

    _____   _____

    _____   _____

8. **Your Grandparents' Home Towns.**   Name the cities or towns where *three* of your grandparents grew up or lived most of their lives.

    _____   _____

    _____

9. **Family Health History.**   Knowing your family health history is important. Which of the following statements about family health histories is *not* correct?

    a. _____ Certain diseases, such as hemophilia and cystic fibrosis, can be transmitted genetically from one generation to another.

    b. _____ Although your family line is known as your "bloodline," your blood type is determined randomly, not genetically.

    c. _____ If you have a parent or grandparent who died before age 60, the cause of death may be relevant to you because you may be genetically predisposed to having a similar condition.

    d. _____ If you have a parent or grandparent who died before age 60, the cause of death may be relevant to you because of behavioral or lifestyle patterns that may have been a contributing factor to early death.

10. **Your Family Tree.**   Draw your family tree, covering at least *three* generations, including your own generation and your parents' brothers and sisters. A simple family tree going back three generations might look like the following.

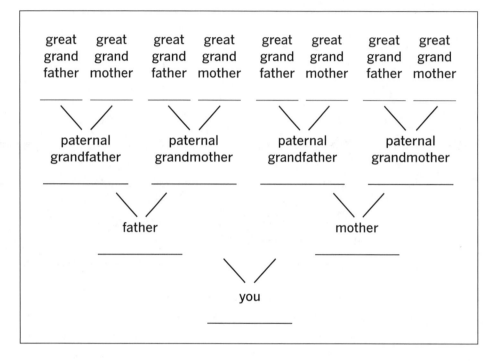

YOUR SCORE: For the correct answers, see pages 312–315. Giving yourself two points for each question you answered correctly, your score for FAMILY FACTS is

0   2   4   6   8   12   14   16   18   20

29.   THE FINE ARTS

1. **Classical Music.**   Name one piece of classical music that you can recognize when it is played, *and* name its composer.

    Piece: _____

    Composer: _____

2. **Plays.**   Name *either* two plays written by William Shakespeare *or* two plays written by 20th century playwrights.

    _____

    _____

3. **Film Classics.**   Name *either* of the following:

    a. One black-and-white movie that is considered a film classic.

    _____

    b. The titles, in the order they were released, of the famous trilogy of films directed by George Lucas in which we were introduced to "the Force," Yoda, and R2D2.

    _____   _____

    _____

4. **Art Museums.**   Of the following world-famous art museums, correctly identify the cities in which at least *three* of them are located.

Museum	City
Uffizi	_____
Metropolitan Museum of Art	_____
Louvre	_____
Tate Gallery	_____
Hermitage Museum	_____
National Gallery	_____
Musée d'Orsay	_____

5. **Sculptors.**   Correctly match the following famous sculptors with the work or style for which they are renowned.

Alexander Calder	_____	a. David
Auguste Rodin	_____	b. Reclining Figure
Henry Moore	_____	c. Suspended mobiles
Michelangelo	_____	d. The Thinker

6. **Impressionist Painters.**   Painters of the French Impressionist School, who lived and worked in the late 1800s and early 1900s, portrayed light and its effects in their painting and were able to "make" color through brushstrokes rather than by just mixing colors on a palette. By doing so, they made a historic break with representational (lifelike) painting. Which of the following was *not* a famous French impressionist:

   a. _____ Claude Monet

   b. _____ Auguste Renoir

   c. _____ Rembrandt van Rijn

   d. _____ Edgar Degas

7. **Symphony Orchestras.**   Name *two* renowned symphony orchestras.

   _____   _____

8. **Personalities in the Arts.**   Which of the following statements is *not* true?

   a. _____ Leonardo da Vinci, who painted the famed Mona Lisa in the 16th century, also designed human flying machines.

   b. _____ Vincent van Gogh, a contemporary and friend of Paul Gauguin with whom he was having a fight, cut off his own earlobe and gave it to a prostitute.

   c. _____ Pablo Picasso, whose famous work entitled *Bull's Head* was made solely with a bicycle seat and a bicycle handlebar, did most of his best work in a monastery, where he died at a tragically young age.

   d. _____ Andy Warhol, a renowned 20th-century artist, achieved fame painting such common objects as cans of Campbell's soup.

9. **Architecture.**   Name *either* of the following:

   a. The three classic styles of columns found in the architecture of traditional public or formal buildings

   b. Three famous 20th-century architects

   _____

   _____

   _____

10. **Ballet and Opera.**   Give the name, composer, and a one-line summary of the story of *either* one famous ballet *or* one famous full-length opera.

   Title :   _____

   Composer: _____

   Story Line: _____

YOUR SCORE: For the correct answers, see pages 316–325. Giving yourself two points for every question you answered correctly, your score for THE FINE ARTS is

   0   2   4   6   8   12   14   16   18   20

30. PRINCIPLES AND PRIORITIES

You will quickly recognize that, compared to others, this section might be considered "a gut." This is because there are many right answers to each of the questions, and for many of the questions, if you think it's a right answer, it is.

One of the purposes of this section is to encourage you to think carefully about the questions asked. If you consider each question thoughtfully and come up with answers as requested, you can score well. In fact, this section may be your best shot at a perfect score—yet another sign of *The RAT*'s civility, compared to other similarly named tests.

Enough procrastination. Get on with this section. Notwithstanding the opportunity it gives you to boost your overall performance on *The RAT*, it may not be as quick and easy as you may anticipate.

1. **Making Important Decisions.**   List at least *three* questions you should usually ask yourself, *or* three things you should do, before making an important decision.

   _____

   _____

   _____

2. **Traits of Successful People.**   Name at least *two* traits or characteristics of people who are successful *or* who have achieved a high level of excellence in what they do.

   _____   _____

3. **Fabulous Books.**   If you were going to be alone for an extended period of time and could take just *three* books with you, which ones would they be?

   _____   _____

   _____

4. **Personal Goals.**   Name *three* goals for yourself for the next year, the next three years, *or* the next five years.

   _____   _____

   _____

5. **A Poem.**   Know, or learn, one poem (or one segment of a long poem, or several lines from a play) by heart, and recite or write it from memory.

    _____

    _____

    _____

    _____

    _____

    _____

    _____

    _____

    _____

    _____ .

6. **An Older Friend.**   Give at least *two* advantages of having a friendship with a person who is two to three times your age.

    _____

    _____

7. **Learning from Mistakes.**   Learning from mistakes requires that you recognize the mistakes you have made. Identify at least two significant mistakes you believe you made in the last year, why they were mistakes, and how you would have acted differently if you had it to do over. (*Wrong answers on tests you have taken do not qualify as correct answers for this question.*)

    _____

    _____

    _____

8. **Listening.**   Give three characteristics of good listening *or* three techniques for being a good listener:

    _____

    _____

    _____

9. **Role Models.**   Answer *one* of the following:

    a. Name two people to whom you are not related who have influenced your life significantly.

    b. Name a person whom you believe to be one of the three greatest people of the 20th century and, in one sentence, why.

    c. Name the individual whom you would most like to be like, and why.

    _____

    _____

10. **A Principle for Life.**   Name at least *one* principle to which you would like to adhere during your lifetime.

    _____

YOUR SCORE: For the "correct answers," see pages 326–337. Giving yourself two points for each question you answered correctly, your score for PRIORITIES AND PRINCIPLES is

0   2   4   6   8   12   14   16   18   20

The Answer Section

Welcome to the Answer Section. In the pages that follow, you will find at least one correct answer for every question asked (each correct answer is worth two points), additional tidbits of information in the Merely Informative boxes, and references to lots of other books and web sites.

As noted in the questions, some of them require that you correctly provide more than one piece of information to get credit for a correct answer. Some require you to perform some task. A few correct answers are wholly within your own control, so they are easy to get right.

If you believe that there are important correct answers that are not included here, make a note of them; we would like to hear about them. We would even like to hear about good questions and answers not included or useful subjects not covered by *The RAT*. Send your ideas to the publisher, or note them on our web site at **www.TakeTheRat.com**.

But, before you get too carried away, let's see how you do on the 300 answers that follow. Good luck!

A. THE BASICS

1.   MANAGING YOUR MONEY—ANSWERS

> Neither a borrower nor lender be:
> For loan oft loses both itself and friend;
> And borrowing dulls the edge of husbandry.
>
> —*Hamlet,* Act I, Scene 3
> Polonius's advice to his departing son, Laertes

1.   **Money Management Plan.**   The answer is *budget.*

Your monthly budget is uniquely personal to you and your circumstances. However, good budgets share some common features. Here are some rules of thumb that financial experts offer:

a. Your budget should balance—that is, your revenue, or income, should equal or exceed your expenses. If it does not, you are operating *in the red* and are going into debt.

b. Start with your total monthly income; that is the upper limit of your budget. (Budgets obviously can be annual or weekly or biweekly or on any other basis. Monthly usually makes sense because rent and car payments, utility bills, and the like, generally are payable each month.)

c. Many financial advisers recommend that you *pay yourself first*. This means that you should put some portion of your earnings, even if only a small amount, into a savings or investment account. Regular savings grow surprisingly fast, and building a financial cushion will give you flexibility and, over time, security.

d. Start with your *fixed expenses*. Regular expenses like apartment rent, food, car payments, and the like, are nondiscretionary—you generally can't change these obligations in the short run. Plan your budget around them.

e. Plan on credit card bills if you use a credit card. Your budget should allow you to pay off those charges each month.

f. Allow for unanticipated, nonrecurring expenses, such as car repairs, trips, and uninsured medical costs.

An individual budget—yours will reflect your own situation—typically includes your monthly net income from all sources (after taxes and other deductions from your pay); all fixed monthly expenses (rent, car payments, savings, etc.); and all variable expenses (clothes, entertainment, investments). Your budgeted expenses should not exceed your budgeted income. Developing a sound budget is an important first step; sticking to it is a challenge that presents itself every month.

2. **Your Checking Account.**   The answer is *d*; banks may do both.

Banks may pay you interest on your checking account, but at the same time charge you fees on the same account.

The types of fees that banks may charge include a monthly service fee for maintaining the account; a per-check fee for each check you write during a month over a specified number of checks; fees for new checks; and fees for making wire transfers, ordering travelers' checks, or bouncing a check. Some or all of these fees may be avoidable, depending on the bank, particularly if you maintain an average minimum balance in your account, or if you also have savings or money market accounts that meet specified minimum balances. Sometimes banks waive monthly fees for students or new customers.

3. **Bounced Checks.**   The answer is *c*; the only party that may not charge you a fee is the store's bank.

All of the others are likely to happen. In most cases your bank will refuse to honor the check and will return it to the store with the notation "Insufficient funds." The store will require you to pay for the merchandise again and may well charge you a fee for writing a bad check. And your bank also may charge you a service charge for writing a check without having sufficient funds to pay the face amount of the check. The fee may be $25, or more, for each bad check.

4. **Bank Cards.**   The answer is *a*; it is the only statement that's not true. Withdrawing cash from an ATM is *not* always cheaper because sometimes you have to pay a fee for using an ATM.

Whether you have to pay to use an ATM generally depends on what bank owns and operates the machine. If you withdraw cash from an ATM run by the bank with which you have an account and from which you received your ATM card, there is usually no charge for withdrawing cash. In that situation, using a card is cheaper than writing a check (you typically have to pay for your checks).

However, if you use your card to make a withdrawal from another bank's machine, you likely will be charged a fee. An ATM service fee can range from 75 cents to $1.50 for each ATM transaction. As a result, this is a pretty expensive way to get cash. Although it is quick and easy, it is far more expensive than writing a check since the cost of a single check is quite low.

Note, however, that getting cash in another country using an ATM, whether or not you pay an ATM fee, is generally cheaper than exchanging U.S. currency for foreign currency, something for which you are likely to be charged a considerably larger fee.

Most banks do have a daily limit on the amount of cash you can withdraw with an ATM card. Losing a check card is riskier than losing an ATM card because the person who finds a check card may be able to use it to charge merchandise up to the amount in your account (often the only security check is a comparison by the sales clerk of the signature on the card and the buyer's signature), whereas a person who finds an ATM card can use it to withdraw cash only if he or she also knows your PIN.

Merely Informative
Check or Debit Cards

Because charges made on check cards are deducted immediately (electronically) from your checking account, they have certain advantages over regular credit cards:

- Your bank account balance is automatically adjusted within two or three days of the time of sale, so you are less likely to accumulate a credit card balance that is larger than your account balance.
- You avoid the fees and interest charges that credit card companies usually charge.
- Stores that take check cards often allow you to charge more than the amount of the purchase and will give you the difference in cash (like a withdrawal from your account).
- If you try to charge more on your check card than you have in your account, your charge will be refused (unless your account provides "overdraft protection," which essentially means that the bank will lend you the amount of any overdraft).

Disadvantages of a debit card compared to a credit card include the following:

- A credit card, by definition, allows you to charge purchases, regardless of whether you have money in the bank to cover the charge (depending on your point of view, this may be an advantage or a disadvantage).
- Credit cards allow you to make charges that you may pay off over time.
- Credit cards may be used without a PIN.

---

5. **Credit Cards.**   The answers are

   a. *True.* It is entirely appropriate to think of a credit card charge as a loan from the credit card company to you. If you use your card only as a convenience and pay your total card balance on time each month, you can avoid being charged anything for that so called loan.

   b. *True.* If you pay less than the full balance on your credit card (if you pay the "minimum payment due" or some other amount), or if you don't pay the full amount by the due date, you will be charged interest on the unpaid balance. You may even be charged interest on recent purchases you have made but that have not yet appeared on your statement.

c. *True.* Almost all credit card companies charge a high rate of interest. Credit card companies typically calculate the interest, or finance charge, on a monthly basis. Thus, the not uncommon finance charge of "only one and a half percent" translates into an annual interest rate of 18 percent.

Merely Informative
Credit Card Charges

Credit card companies make money by charging each of the following:

a. annual membership fees,

b. interest on unpaid balances,

c. late payment fees, and

d. in some circumstances, interest from the date a charge is made until date of payment.

Typically, credit card companies express their annual interest rates as "prime plus." Thus, a credit card company charging "prime plus 10" charges a rate that is the prime rate (for example, 8.5 percent) plus 10 percent, or an annual rate of 18.5 percent.

Credit card interest rates tend to be among the highest interest rates lawfully charged consumers. For example, if the prime rate is 7 percent, it is not uncommon for mortgage rates to be about 8 percent; home equity loan rates to be about 9 percent; car loans to be about 12 percent; personal loan rates to be about 14 percent; and credit card interest to be about 18 percent.

---

6. **Credit Card Debt.** The answer is *d*, nearly eight years.

Merely Informative
Credit Card Interest

At a monthly interest rate of 1.5 percent, or 18 percent annually, in the first year most of your payments go to pay off interest. Little of your $40 per month goes initially to pay off the amount you owe (your principal balance), so your balance declines slowly at first. In the example used in this question, at the end of 12 months, your balance has been reduced less than $150, even though you have paid $480 to the credit card company. Continuing to pay $40 a month, you pay for five years and two months before your $2,000 balance has been cut in half.

At this rate, your credit card balance is not paid off completely until you have paid $40 a month for seven years, eleven months. You will then have paid a total of $3,765 dollars for your $2,000 in purchases. This repayment schedule does not count annual fees, minimum service charges, late payment fees, or any additional purchases you have charged on your card.

As this example shows, credit card interest can be deceptively expensive, and carrying a credit card balance from month to month can be one of the most expensive ways of buying merchandise. This is why financial advisers typically advise clients who are struggling with debt to get rid of credit card debt first, either by paying it off as quickly as possible or by consolidating it into a home equity loan, for which interest payments are generally tax-deductible. Interest paid on credit card debt is not tax-deductible.

7. **Car Payments.**   The correct answer is *d*, $18,200.

This example highlights an underappreciated fact about consumer debt—namely, how interest payments can add to the total cost of a purchase, compared to saving for a purchase and paying cash. In this example of a five-year car loan, you would end up paying about $4,700 in total interest, or about one-third more in dollars, than you would have paid if you had paid cash.

Borrowing simply lets you buy sooner—before you have the money for the purchase. However, by borrowing, you put yourself on a mandatory repayment schedule for an extended period of time, and you pay more for the purchase than you otherwise would.

See More Where This Came From page 104.

8. **Your Paycheck.**   The answer is *direct deposit.*

Many employers have arrangements with their banks that allow your paycheck to be deposited automatically and directly to your account rather than delivered to you. This saves you the step of having to cash or deposit the check yourself.

You also may be able to arrange with your bank to have a specified portion of your paycheck automatically transferred into a separate savings or investment account. For this to happen, you would have to work out the arrangements with your bank.

9. **Payroll Deductions.**   The answer is *b*, savings deduction.

Like it or not, employers automatically deduct from your gross paycheck Social Security taxes, Medicare taxes, and estimated federal and state income taxes, unless you have no legal obligation to make payments or you have already paid the maximum for a particular required contribution. Employers do not routinely make deductions for savings.

Merely Informative Withholding

The term *withholding* refers to amounts that are automatically deducted, or withheld, from your paycheck by your employer. The amount withheld for taxes is calculated on the basis of your annual pay and on the number of tax exemptions you will be entitled to claim when you file your taxes. Your employer pays the withheld amounts to the government. Over the course of the entire year, the amounts withheld should cover your total tax obligation, unless you have additional sources of income.

If the state where you live imposes a state income tax, you may have an amount withheld for state taxes as well as for federal taxes. You also may choose to have other voluntary deductions from your paycheck, such as contributions to your retirement fund or to charity.

---

10. **Taxes.**   The correct tax terms are

   a. *April 15.* This is the deadline each year for filing your income tax return and paying any federal taxes still due. If April 15 falls on a Saturday or Sunday, the deadline becomes Monday. Some post offices stay open late on April 15 and tend to be congested as midnight approaches.

   b. *1040.* This is a number with which you will become familiar. Form 1040 is the standard form for individual tax returns. If your tax return is simple, you may use the short form. More complicated tax returns involve other forms, but most taxpayers don't worry about filing other forms until they have to use them.

c. *A progressive tax system.* The United States has had a progressive income tax for most of the twentieth century (the sixteenth constitutional amendment, which authorized the income tax, was ratified in 1913). How steeply progressive it has been has varied, with marginal tax rates in the highest brackets reaching as high as 94 percent at one time. The maximum individual tax rate in 2000 was 39 percent, although the loss of certain otherwise available deductions effectively increases the upper rates.

An alternative to a progressive tax is a proportional, or *flat* tax under which all taxpayers pay the same percentage of their taxable income. With a flat rate, higher-income individuals would pay more taxes, but not increasingly higher tax rates.

d. *The standard deduction.* The standard deduction allows taxpayers to take an arbitrary deduction from their taxable income regardless of whether their actual deductions equal that amount. By using the standard deduction, taxpayers can avoid having to itemize deductions and can get the benefit of the arbitrary amount. When you reach the point where your actual deductions exceed the standard deduction, you will have to itemize (list) all of your actual deductions. However, it will be worth it.

More Where This Came From

Beth Kobliner. *Get a Financial Life.* New York: Fireside, 1996. This book includes chapters on "Debt and the Material World," "Basic Banking," and "Living the Good Life in 2030," and references to 100 financial web sites.

Kenneth Morris and Alan Siegel. *Guide to Understanding Personal Finance.* New York: Lightbulb Press, 1992. Published by the *Wall Street Journal*, this is an excellent, concise reference on financial topics—banking, credit, taxes, investment, etc.

Marc Robinson. *Credit Basics.* Alexandria, Virginia: Time Life Books, 1996. This is a short primer on credit and debt.

The RAT's Mouse

Use a computer mouse to check the following web sites for more information on managing your money:

- **www.techtv.com/moneymachine/** Lots of information about spending, various accounts, investing, tips, etc.
- **www.state.ma.us/consumer/Pubs/credsecr.htm** Twelve credit card secrets that banks don't want you to know
- **www.creditcardfreedom.com/** Includes debt strategies, credit card reviews, tips
- **www.leaseguide.com/** Leasing a car vs. buying a car, payment breakdowns, how to get a good deal

2.   COOKING—ANSWERS

Wash your hands!!

1. **Cookbook.**

There are countless cookbooks, many of them excellent. The following are a few comprehensive classics:

The Joy of Cooking
The New York Times Cookbook
The Good Housekeeping Step-by-Step Cookbook
The Way to Cook by Julia Child
Betty Crocker's New Cookbook—Everything You Need to Know How to Cook
How to Cook Everything by Mark Bittman
The Silver Palate Cookbook

A few of the more famous authors:

Julia Child
Betty Crocker
"Two Fat Ladies" (Jennifer Paterson and Clarissa Dickson Wright)
Paul Prudhomme
Martha Stewart

Among the many other possibilities:

The Starving Students' Cookbook by Dede Hall
The 5 in 10 Cookbook (5 ingredients in 10 minutes or less) by
   Paula Hamilton
Microwave Cooking by Nitty Gritty Productions

For Jewish dishes and recipes, see Joan Nathan's *Jewish Cooking in America* (1998) and *The Jewish Holiday Kitchen* (1988).

2. **Boiling Water.**   The answer is *d*.

Water has begun to boil when air bubbles begin to rise and break the surface of the water. In physical terms, water boils when it is placed over direct heat and it reaches the temperature at which it vaporizes. Steam escapes because the vapor pressure of the liquid equals the atmospheric pressure.

When water boils vigorously, the water becomes agitated and bubbles come to the surface rapidly, sometimes spilling water over the edge of the pot. If this happens, you should turn the heat down a bit, preferably without splashing scalding water onto your hand.

Steam will begin to rise from the surface of the water, and small air bubbles will begin to form on the bottom of the pot before the water boils. What happens after twelve minutes, if anything, will depend on how much water you have on the stove, how hot the burner is, and at what altitude you're cooking (water boils faster at higher altitudes).

3. **Ways of Cooking.** The answers are

   a. *Baking.* Cooking in an oven, usually between 250 and 400 degrees. Pretty simple.

   b. *Broiling.* Broiling involves exposing high heat, usually 3–4 inches from the heat source. (Accidentally turning on the broiler in the oven when you mean to bake something is an excellent way to burn the food you are cooking beyond recognition.)

   c. *Frying or Sautéing.* Fast, hot cooking done in an open pan using a small amount of butter or oil is frying or sautéing. (Food that is sautéed is usually thin or minced and should be kept moving and be seared to prevent loss of juices. Food sometimes is floured or breaded before it is sautéed.)

To make a sauce after food is sautéed, add wine, chicken stock, or water to the pan to deglaze the tasty tidbits stuck to the pan; then stir, add salt and pepper, and pour over food.

Frying is essentially the same as sautéing, but usually implies the use of more oil. Deep frying involves immersing the food in hot oil. Frying, discussed in the Nutrition section, produces a much higher fat content than if the food is grilled or broiled.

4. **Microwave Cooking.**

    a. The answer is *ii.* Bread doesn't do well in the microwave.

    Microwaves work very well, however, on many foods. Microwave popcorn does very well. Heating up leftovers is one of the premier uses of a microwave oven. Vegetables can also be cooked nicely in microwaves (but read the instructions on how to microwave them first).

    In addition, soups, stews, and pasta dishes all can be prepared successfully in a microwave. A microwave also softens ice cream nicely (8–10 seconds is usually enough; more than that has the results you might expect).

    b. The correct answer is *ii.* **Never** put metal in a microwave. Metal bowls, metal cookware, spoons, foil containers, even tinfoil—none is microwave friendly.

    Sealed dishes are also a serious mistake. A paper container covered with plastic wrap, for example, should have holes punched in the plastic wrap to allow hot air to escape (holes made with a fork are fine).

    Glass is generally safe to use in microwaves, and microwaves do not melt most plastics. Many frozen food containers will indicate whether they are microwave safe.

5. **Measurements.**   The correct equivalents and abbreviations are

    1T (tablespoon) = 3t (teaspoons)
    1C (cup) = 8 oz. (ounces) or 15T (tablespoons)
    1qt. (quart) – 2 pts. (pints) or 32 oz. (ounces)

6. **Precise Recipes.**   The answer is *c*, breads and pastries.

    If you stray slightly from the proportions or the directions in making casseroles or meats, the taste of the casserole may vary slightly or the meat may be slightly overdone or underdone. If you don't follow the recipe for breads or pastries precisely, however, the results can be more serious. The bread won't rise, for example, or the pie dough may not look or taste like a piecrust.

7. **Preparing Salads.**   The answer is *b*.

Salad dressings adhere better to the greens if the greens are dry. This great principle led to such inventions as the salad spinner, or crisper, a round plastic device with a handle on top into which washed greens can be placed and spun around at great speed, not unlike a small amusement park ride, until all of the moisture has been thrown off by centrifugal force.

Vinaigrette is made with oil and vinegar (3:1 is a commonly recommended ratio), together with salt, pepper, and other seasonings. Dressing the salad in advance is to be avoided because the greens wilt or become soggy. And salads are tossed, not to get rid of extra dressing, but rather to mix the dressing well into the salad.

8. **Basic Cooking Skills.**

a. *Separating raw eggs*. Many recipes call for egg whites, egg yolks, or both. This may require that you separate the yolk from the white of one or more raw eggs. Apart from buying and using an egg separator, here's how to separate raw eggs:

Method # 1—the traditional method:

*   Use two small bowls.
*   Crack the eggshell by tapping the egg firmly on the edge of the bowl that will hold the egg whites.
*   Tip the cracked egg so that the smaller half is pointing slightly up, and pull the shell apart, allowing some egg white to spill into the bowl but keeping the egg yolk in the bottom part of the shell.
*   Pour the egg yolk in the bottom part of the shell into the other half of the shell, letting more egg white slip off into the bowl.
*   Pour the yolk back and forth another time or two, until most of the egg white has run off into the bowl.
*   Put the yolk in the other bowl and discard the shell.

Method # 2—the fun, less elegant method:

- Wash your hands very well.
- Break the egg into your hand, keeping your fingers only slightly apart so that the yolk won't slip through.
- Gently roll the yolk back and forth in your hand, letting the egg white run through your fingers into the bowl but keeping the yolk in your hand.
- Drop the yolk into other bowl.
- Voila! A little messy, but it works. But you may not want to use this method in front of any fastidious members of your family.

Merely Informative
Breaking an Egg with One Hand
(This is primarily for showing off)

- Hold an egg in your hand, palm facing down.
- Tap the egg firmly against edge of bowl.
- With your thumb and index finger, gently pull the shell in one direction; with your other three fingers, gently pull the shell in the other direction.
- The egg will slip out into the bowl.

With practice, you'll get no eggshell in the egg. This stunt impresses real cooks. Save it for occasions when you can get maximum impact.

Doing this trick correctly requires that the separated egg whites and yolks be free of eggshells and that the separated egg whites contain *no* yolk. (If egg white is contaminated with yolk, the egg whites won't do some of the things for which they are most famous, such as whipping up into a the kind of froth that some recipes call for.)

b. *Cooking Eggs Sunny Side Up*

- Put a small amount of butter or margarine in frying pan (or spray pan with oil); heat the pan to medium.
  - Break eggs one at a time into the pan (breaking them first into a small bowl and slipping the eggs into the pan from a saucer will reduce yolk breakage).
  - Reduce heat and cook the eggs slowly.
  - Sunny side up: don't flip the egg over (to cook the egg white on top, cover the pan; trapped steam will cook the top).

    (*Eggs over Easy.* Proceed as two eggs sunny side up; then gently turn the eggs over with a spatula (so as not to break the yolk) and cook them a little more. (If you break a yolk, you will learn that it cooks much more quickly than an unbroken one.)

c. (1) *Making Pancakes.* The easiest way to make pancakes and waffles is to buy a pancake mix (Bisquick, Hungry Jack, etc.) and follow the directions on the box.

  - Heat pan or griddle (it needs to be hot enough so that if you put a drop of tap water on the pan, it will dance, sizzle, and disappear quickly) and lightly coat it with butter, margarine, or oil.
  - Mix the batter according to instructions on the box of pancake mix.
  - Pour the batter onto the griddle. Using a large spoon or small measuring cup, pour the batter to form about three 4" pancakes (crowding pancakes or letting them run together will make them harder to turn; making pancakes in the form of legible letters or recognizable animals takes practice).
  - Cook the pancakes until small air bubbles form and break on their top edge. Using a spatula, peek underneath; when they're golden brown, turn them over and brown the other side.
  - Remove and serve at once. Serve with butter or margarine and syrup, strawberry jam, or lemon and powdered sugar.

Merely Informative
Flipping a Pancake

Real chefs can flip a pancake or an egg. To flip a pancake or fried egg using only the pan (no utensils), make sure there is enough butter in the pan to allow the pancake to slide freely. Sliding the pancake by using a back-and-forth motion, flip the pancake with a quick flick of the wrist as it is about to slide out of the pan, catching it in the pan as it flips over and lands on its other side.

A few things to remember:

- If any part of the pancake sticks to the pan, it won't flip nicely.
- Successfully flipping the pancake includes catching it on the way down, not just flipping it out of the pan.
- Flip only one pancake at a time.
- When just practicing, you can use the same pancake over and over.
- If your pancake comes down folded or lands somewhere other than back in the pan, you should not count your attempt as a success.

    c. (2) *Making French Toast.*

- Make batter: Blend 2 beaten eggs, 1/2 cup of milk, 1/4 teaspoon of salt, and 1/2 teaspoon of vanilla (1/2 teaspoon of sugar or 1/4 teaspoon of cinnamon are optional) in a shallow bowl.
- Heat a pan or griddle (until hot enough that a drop of water dances on the surface) Coat the surface with butter, margarine, or oil.
- Batter bread. Cut 6 slices of day-old bread in half and dip each one into the batter, coating each side.
- Place the slices in the pan and brown them evenly on both sides. Serve with syrup, lemon and powdered sugar, fruit, or jam.

    d. *Cooking Rice.*

- Add 1 teaspoon of salt to 3 1/2 cups of water, and bring the water to a boil.
- Add 2 cups of rice, stirring once or twice.
- Immediately turn the burner to low; cover the pot and cook for 20 minutes.
- Although the rice should be perfect, you may want to fluff it a bit with a fork. Leave it covered, and it will stay hot for about 20–25 minutes.

If you want to produce variations, you may use chicken broth instead of water (omit the salt), add diced vegetables or mushrooms at the beginning, or add spices. Cooking instant rice is even easier—just follow the directions on the box. The results are faster, but not as good.

9.   **Rotten Food**.   This is a question for which the right answers may prove useful. Read carefully. (This should be an easy two points.)

   a. *How to tell.* There are several indicators that food in the refrigerator has gone bad; many are not particularly scientific. For example, if your refrigerator smells as though something in it is rotten, or something in it may have died, it probably contains food that has gone bad.

   A logical way to follow up on this clue is to smell individual items of food. If you come across something that smells really bad, you may have solved the mystery. Remember, though, that something that has caused your whole refrigerator to smell bad may smell even worse up close, particularly if it's in a container. Small, cautious sniffs are a good approach.

   Another clue is foreign growth on an item of food. Green or gray fuzz on cream cheese, for example, is a clue. Sour milk just doesn't smell the same as fresh milk, and milk is never meant to be lumpy. Meats that begin to change color from red to gray or green are also suspect. Fresh vegetables kept indefinitely in a plastic bag in the vegetable drawer of a refrigerator can become rancid or decay over time. If a fresh vegetable has become mushy in its plastic bag or has started to become a liquid, you may just want to skip smelling it.

   In short, foods that have collected mold or mildew, or have a different appearance or aroma from when they were purchased, probably have gone bad. By poking around in your refrigerator every now and then it is possible to find old food that has not yet become rancid, and you can throw it away then. Cooking food that has gone bad will not make it okay.

   b. *What to do.* This part is not too hard to master either. If your first answer about what to do was to get rid of the rotten food, that was a very good answer. If, however, you move the bad food from the refrigerator to the garbage can in the kitchen, then the garbage can, or perhaps the entire kitchen, will smell bad. Running it through the disposal or placing it in the outside garbage in a tightly wrapped plastic bag may be a better idea.

As for your smelly refrigerator, the conventional solution is to use baking soda, which absorbs odors. Put an open box or a few tablespoons of baking soda in a small dish in your refrigerator for a few days. You can buy baking soda at the grocery.

Cleaning the refrigerator is also helpful. If you unload it in the process, you may spot some items that are becoming overripe and you can get rid of them. You may be pleased to know that soft drinks, pickles, and jams rarely go bad.

10. **Coffee and Tea.**

   a. The answer is *iii—steep.* Tea is steeped. Coffee can be prepared in a drip coffee pot, percolator, or French press.

   b. The answer is *iii—Blue Mountain tea.* Blue Mountain is, in fact, a type of coffee. All the other colored teas are legitimate.

Merely Informative
Brewing Coffee or Tea

As noted above, coffee can be freshly brewed a variety of ways—with a drip coffee pot, percolator, "French press," or more exotic coffeemakers. Perhaps the most common (certainly in hotel and motel rooms) is the drip grind coffee pot. It is also one of the easiest. The following instructions are for brewing six 6 oz. cups of coffee in a drip-style coffeemaker:

- Fill a carafe with water to the 6-cup mark, and fit a paper filter into the basket.
- Measure 1 teaspoon coffee for each cup (6 teaspoons). (Use 1–2 teaspoons per cup if you like stronger coffee.)
- Pour water into the top of the coffeemaker and turn on the coffeemaker.
- Serve when the water has stopped dripping, but within 20 minutes (if you leave the coffee for 20 minutes or more, it will begin to taste overcooked.

Tea, perhaps the most common beverage in the world, may be brewed using either tea bags or leaf tea. If you're using tea bags, simply put the tea bag or bags in a pot or cup of water. If you use leaf tea (chopped up tea leaves, as you may have guessed), you can keep the leaves out of your tea either by putting the

continued on next page

loose tea in something that serves the same purpose as a tea bag or by pouring the tea into a cup through a strainer.

Water that is boiling, or close to boiling, is best for tea. The longer you leave the tea in the hot water, the stronger it will become. You will notice that tea drinkers don't say that they are "soaking" their tea bag; rather, they "steep" their tea. If tea is steeped too long, it may turn bitter.

EXTRA CREDIT: One Good Dish.

Knowing how to cook one great dish can get you proudly through crises ranging from a camping trip to a dinner party. The following are possibilities. Be aware, however, that some of the following dishes shamelessly use short-cuts (mixes, prepared sauces, soup mixes, etc.) rather than making everything from scratch, the virtues of which you may also want to learn to appreciate.

a. *One Great Soup*

A good soup, which can serve as an entree, is healthy, relatively easy to make, cheap, filling, great when you're cold or sick, simple to freeze and reheat, and easy to make in large quantities.

Soup #1: Chicken Noodle Soup (homemade). A soup that tastes good and has legendary powers to cure what ails you.

- 2–3 lbs. chicken breast (dark meat can be included, but it is more fattening and harder and more time-consuming to separate from the bone)
- 3 quarts canned chicken broth
- 2 cups water
- 2 cups rice (uncooked) or 1/2 pound pasta (uncooked)
- Vegetables and seasonings:
    - 3–4 carrots cut in thick rounds
    - 1 medium onion, sliced
    - 1 small bunch parsley, chopped
    - 1 bay leaf
    - 3 stalks celery (with or without leaves), chopped
    - (No salt: canned broth has sufficient salt)
    - Optional: fresh herbs such as tarragon, oregano, thyme

1. In a 6-quart Dutch oven, simmer all ingredients, except the rice or pasta, for 45 minutes.
2. Remove the chicken from broth and let it cool. Remove the skin and bones, cut the meat into bite-sized morsels, and set it aside.
3. Strain the broth and remove any vegetables you don't want in the soup.
4. Taste the broth for flavor; if it's not rich enough, simmer it with lid off for 5 or 10 minutes and taste it again.
5. Add rice or pasta. Cook rice in broth for 25 minutes. If you're using pasta, cook it for 10 minutes uncovered.
6. Add chicken, cook 5 minutes more. Taste and serve.

Soup #2: Cuban Black Bean Soup with Rice

- 1 cup raw rice
- 2 cups water
- 1/2 teaspoon salt
- 1 can Goya Black Bean Soup
- 1/4 cup chopped onions
- Olive oil and vinegar

1. Bring water and salt to a boil; add the rice; reduce heat to low; cover, and cook for 20 minutes.
2. Heat the black bean soup.
3. In individual soup bowls, place 1/2–1 cup of cooked rice and top with black bean soup.
4. Add chopped onions, oil, and vinegar to taste.
5. Serve with French bread and green salad or cold orange wedges.

b. *One Great Entree*

Entree #1: Pasta Shells and Cheese

- 1 package frozen, stuffed pasta shells
- 1 24–36 ounce jar of spaghetti sauce
- 8 ounces grated mozzarella cheese
- Fresh or store-grated Parmesan cheese

1. Heat the oven to 350 degrees.
2. In a 9" × 13" glass Pyrex dish, pour approximately 1 cup of spaghetti sauce to cover the bottom.
3. Fill the pan with a single layer shells (about 15–18 shells).

4. Pour about 2 cups of sauce over shells (cover each shell), and sprinkle mozzarella over the shells.
5. Cover the dish with foil and bake for 40 minutes.
6. Uncover and cook for 5 minutes more.
7. Sprinkle with Parmesan cheese.
8. Serve 2–4 shells per person.

Entree #2: Pot Roast with Vegetables

• 1 large Reynolds Oven Cooking Bag (found in most grocery stores)
• 3–4 pounds beef rump roast or boneless beef chuck roast
• 1/2 cup flour
• 1 package Lipton Onion Soup mix
• 1 can cream of chicken or cream of mushroom soup
• 4–6 medium potatoes, quartered
• 3–4 carrots, cut into thick rounds

1. Shake flour into the bag.
2. Add all the remaining ingredients to bag and mix slightly.
3. Follow directions on cooking bag box.
4. After 2–2 1/2 hours, remove the roast, and serve with gravy and vegetables.

Entree # 3: Charcoal-grilled Hamburger

The following makes three burgers:

• Charcoal grill (either natural charcoal or gas)
• 1 pound ground round
• Salt and pepper

1. Light the fire (charcoal takes 15 minutes or more to get hot).
2. Put ground round in a bowl; add 1/2 teaspoon salt and 1/2 teaspoon pepper; mix well.
3. Form ground round into three burgers.
4. Put the burgers on the grill; cook about 5 minutes on each side for medium (if too rare, put them back on); if desired, add cheese slices *after* one side is cooked and you have turned the burgers.
5. Serve on warmed or toasted buns or English muffins.

c. *One Great Dessert*

Great Dessert #1: Cherries-to-Die-For (cherry crisp)

- 1 small box (7–8 oz.) yellow cake mix
- 1 can cherry pie filling
- 1 stick butter or margarine (not low-fat margarine)
- 8 ounces pecan halves or pieces

1. Preheat the oven to 375 degrees.
2. Pour cherry pie filling into an 8" or 9" glass pie plate.
3. Spread dry cake mix on top of the pie filling.
4. Sprinkle pecans over the top of the cake mix, and cover with slices of butter or margarine.
5. Bake for 35–40 minutes until deep golden brown.
6. Serve warm or at room temperature (great with vanilla ice cream).

Great Dessert #2: Angel Food Cake with Raspberries and Whipped Cream

1. Make* or buy 1 angel food cake.
2. Whip 2 cups whipping cream (or use Cool Whip), adding 1/4 cup of powdered sugar.
3. Frost the cooled cake with whipping cream, and sprinkle with raspberries (or serve cake plain and pass the whipped cream and raspberries).

*It's simple to make an Angel Food cake from Duncan Hines Angel Food Cake Mix. Just follow the instructions.

Great Dessert #3: Hot Fudge Sauce, Served over Ice Cream

Over a good ice cream, pour hot fudge sauce, made as follows:

- 1 can (15 ounces) sweetened condensed milk
- 2 squares (2 ounces) unsweetened chocolate
- Dash of salt
- 1/2 cup water
- 1/2 teaspoon vanilla

1. Combine all the ingredients in a four-cup glass measure.
2. Microwave 2–3 minutes; stir well. Makes two cups.

More Where This Came From

A comprehensive cookbook that is also a good standard reference source is an essential kitchen staple. Each of the following is excellent and is available in paperback:

Betty Crocker's New Cookbook—Everything You Need to Know How to Cook. New York: Hungry Minds Inc., 1996.

365 Quick Tips. Cook's Illustrated Magazine. Boston Common Press, 2000.

Better Homes and Gardens—New Cook Book. Jennifer Darling (ed.). Des Moines, Iowa: Meredith Books, 1996. Includes 58 pages on "basics."

The Everything Cookbook, by Jaycox, Jaycox, and Lawson. Holbrook, Massachusetts: Adams Media Corporation, 2000.

Joy of Cooking, by Irma S. Rombauer and Marion Rombauer Becker. Plume, 1997.

The RAT's Mouse

If you want to find out more by using a computer to check some informative web sites, you might use your mouse to check the following:

- **www.epicurious.com/e_eating/e02_basics/main.html** "Awesome" has been used to describe this site; "guide to the nuts and bolts of cooking"; easy-to-follow recipes with illustrations; tips on how to stock your kitchen and bar; reference section

- **www.minutemeals.com** Tips and recipes for quick meals; pick by category; ask the minute cook

- **www.pastarecipe.com** Lots of pasta recipes, as you may have guessed; friendly site

- **www.cookinglight.com** Healthy recipes; weekly features; healthy living; good site

- **www.southernfood.about.com/food/southernfood/library/info/blcooks.html** Go to "Cooking Basics" and then "Cook's Tools" for a glossary of cooking terms and food names, common substitutions, liquid measurement conversion, temperature charts, tips; also includes recipes for holiday specials, regional foods, kid-friendly foods

3.   CARPENTRY—ANSWERS

1. **Hammering.**   Here are some possibilities:
   - Begin by holding the nail with the thumb and index finger of the hand that is not holding the hammer.
   - Tip the nail slightly away from you (at about a 10 degree angle).
   - Lightly tap in the nail until it stands by itself.
   - Hold the hammer at the base of the grip (for better leverage).
   - When hammering in the nail, first bring the hammer back toward your ear, then hit the nail squarely on its head.
   - Don't swing hard; let the weight of the hammer do the work for you.

   There are several ways to tell if you haven't put these pointers into practice effectively: Hammering your thumb instead of the nail is one. Other indicators are nails that have been hammered in at an unintended angle; nails that have been bent or knocked over partway through so that the upper part of the nail is embedded horizontally into the wood; or a properly driven nail that is surrounded by circular indentations in the wood, memorializing the number of times that your hammer missed the nail altogether. If any of these features remind you of your own hammering, you may wish to spend a little extra time working on the pointers listed above.

2. **Nails.**   The answer is *c*, galvanized nails.

   Galvanized nails are coated with zinc so they will not rust. Therefore, when they are used on the exterior of a house, in a fence, or in some other outdoor application, rain or other moisture will not cause them to rust.

3. **Nails vs. Screws.**   *False.*

   A screw has greater holding power than a comparably sized nail because screws have threads that grip the wood. A nail can often be pulled out of a piece of wood with a claw hammer; however, if two pieces of wood have been attached with a screw, you usually have to unscrew the screw to separate the wood.

   For many uses, a nail is more than strong enough; nailing is generally faster than putting in a screw; and nails are cheaper than screws.

   Screws are not meant to be hammered into wood. If you nonetheless do nail a screw into wood, you will have defeated the purpose of the threads on a screw and might as well have used a nail, which would have been easier and cheaper.

Merely Informative
Which Way to Screw, or to Unscrew

Ever struggle to remember which way you turn the screwdriver to unscrew a screw, or to screw it in? Struggle no more. Just remember:

"Lefty-Loosey, Righty-Tighty"

That's it. To loosen or unscrew a screw, turn the screwdriver to the left. To tighten or drive the screw in, turn it to the right. This may not be something you want to say out loud in a group of carpenters, but you need wonder never again.

---

4. **Screwdrivers.** *Phillips screwdrivers.*

The tip of a Phillips screwdriver is obviously designed to fit Phillips head screws. A Phillips screwdriver grips a Phillips head screw better and is less likely to slip than is the case with a regular, slotted screwdriver and slotted screw. It is also less likely to strip the screw head. As a result, it is usually easier to get force or leverage with a Phillips screwdriver. In addition, drill bits that are shaped like the tip of a Phillips screwdriver or a straight slot screwdriver can be inserted in a power drill to give you, in effect, a power screwdriver (but they require greater attention to make sure the drill bit driver doesn't slip out of the screw head).

Merely Informative
Screwdrivers' Multiple Uses

Straight-slot screwdrivers "are, more than any other tool, used for purposes other than what they were designed for . . . . They are used as levers to open paint cans . . . as chisels when a proper wood chisel isn't available . . . as scrapers . . . to pry open an infinite number of stuck items . . . as punches to pierce or penetrate many different materials."
—Norm Abram. *Measure Twice, Cut Once.* New York: Little Brown and Company, 1966.

5. **Screws in Wallboard.** Because wallboard is generally not as solid as wood, and because there may be nothing behind it but an occasional stud, a nail or screw may be unstable. A nail or screw planted in a hollow wall may pull right back out of the wall with just a little use or stress. There are, however, a number of ways that a nail or screw may be secured in a hollow wall.

Name one way *or* one device to securely anchor a nail or screw for a correct answer.

   a. *Nail or screw into a stud (the vertical piece of wood with which builders typically frame out walls).* (Finding studs is a separate art form for which there are home methods—tapping lightly with a hammer until you get a less hollow sound, indicating the presence of a stud—and technological aids—most hardware stores will sell you a "stud finder.")

   b. *Use a wall anchor or plastic plug.* These are installed in wallboard by first drilling the correct size hole in the wall (the size of the shaft of the anchor) and then inserting the anchor or plug snugly. The screw is then screwed into the anchor or plug, which expands as you drive in the screw, ensuring a snug fit for the anchor and the screw.

   c. *Use a toggle bolt or a molly bolt.* Toggle bolts and molly bolts are designed to go through the wallboard and then to open up small braces or wings that press against the back of the wallboard to hold the screw securely.

There are many *different wall fasteners—plugs, expansion bolts, anchors, toggles, mollies, etc.* They should be matched to the particular application, the weight of the load, and the like. Ask the person at the hardware store who knows everything there is to know about wall fasteners.

More Where This Came From

Or, *see* "Who Is Molly Bolt?" which is Part I in Susie Tompkins' *I Can Fix That*. New York: Harlequin Books, 1996.

6. **Saws.** In fact, there are several types of both handsaws and power saws.

   a. *Types of handsaws* include:

   - rip saw (to cut boards lengthwise, with the grain);
   - cross-cut saw (to cut across the grain, as in cutting across a 2" × 4");
   - back saw (saw with a short, rectangular blade, used in miter boxes);

- hacksaw (for cutting metal);
- keyhole saw (also a "compass" saw, with a thin blade and pointed tip, good for cutouts and curves); and
- coping saw (u-shaped frame, narrow blade; for cutting curved or intricate lines).

b. *Types of power saws* include:

- jigsaw, or "sabre saw" (portable; drives a thin blade up and down vertically; ideal for curves, circles, and cutouts);
- circular saw (a portable power saw with a circular blade that spins rapidly and can be used, depending on the blade selected, for cross-cutting or long, straight cuts);
- table saw (the same principle as a circular saw except that the revolving circular blade is permanently mounted on a table or bench);
- radial arm saw (found in workshops and used for major jobs);
- bandsaw (a permanent saw that operates with a vertical blade); and
- power miter saw (for angled cuts used in joining pieces of wood).

7. **Plywood.**   *False.*

   With respect to warping, the opposite is true. A regular piece of lumber can warp, as you can see if you carefully look around the next time you're at a lumberyard. If you use a regular piece of lumber (a 1" × 10" plank, for example) as a bookshelf, it can sag under the weight of the books.

   Plywood, by contrast, is less likely to warp or sag. The reason is that plywood is made of several thin layers of wood glued together. Because the grain of each layer runs in a different direction from the next layer, plywood tends to be stronger and less likely to warp.

   Plywood does have its disadvantages: it is heavier than sawn lumber of the same dimension; the edge of plywood shows the layers and is therefore not a clean edge; and plywood comes in large sheets rather than as boards.

   As a result, lumber and plywood each has its own best uses.

8. **Workbench Terms.**   The defined terms are as follows:

   a. *A chuck.* This is the little elbow-shaped (or t-shaped) metal piece, one end of which has a little circle of teeth or gears. A chuck is most commonly used when it is new because it is easy to lose, which is a problem since it is essential for changing the drill bits on many electric drills.

b. *Joists.* What's harder is to keep straight are the differences among joists, studs, rafters, beams, and headers. This, on the other hand, may be something you don't need to know.

c. *A 2" × 4" (a "two-by-four").* The common terminology for dimension lumber is not precise. The stated lengths are generally correct; however, the thickness and width of a 1" × 2", for example, are a little less than 1" and 2".

d. *Composition board or chipboard.* Sheets of composition board are used in a variety of construction applications. Chipboard is strong and less expensive than plywood; however, it is considerably heavier than plywood and does not have the same strength characteristics.

9. **Adhesives.** The answer is *c*, white glue.

The most common adhesive for gluing pieces of wood together is white glue, a glue like Elmer's Glue, sometimes also called wood glue. Although this glue is water soluble, it is otherwise a strong, easy-to-apply glue for most carpentry projects.

Merely Informative
Carpenter's Glue

A first cousin to white glue is yellow glue, sometimes known as Carpenter's glue. It is a bit stronger, somewhat more heat-resistant, and sets up faster. And unlike white glue (polyvinyl), yellow glue (aliphatic resin) doesn't normally require that the two pieces of wood be clamped together.

---

10. **Safety Rules.** If not used carefully and prudently, power tools can cause serious injury. Here are a few of the most important safety rules to follow when working with power tools.

   • When using any power tool, wear *goggles.*
   • When not using a power tool or when adjusting it (changing a blade, installing a larger drill bit, etc.), *unplug* the tool.
   • When using a power saw, be sure to position the electrical cord that runs from the saw to the power source so that you don't inadvertently cut it while using the saw.

- Don't use any power tool in or around water.
- When operating any power tool, make certain that you have good, solid footing and that your legs and arms are well clear of the tool and its likely path.
- Remove any loose-fitting clothing or jewelry that might get caught up in a power tool.
- Don't operate power tools around young children or pets.
- Don't talk to anyone else while you are using a power tool.

More Where This Came From

Black & Decker, The Complete Guide to Home Wiring. Minnetonka, Minnesota: Creative Publishing International, 1998. (One of a series.)

Basic Carpentry. Menlo Park, California: Sunset Books, 1989. (One of the Sunset series, it is a useful general reference for carpentry. *Basic Home Repairs* from the same series is also handy.)

Measure Twice, Cut Once. New York: Little, Brown and Company, 1996 by Norm Abram is an elegant and informative small book on carpentry wisdom.

I Can Fix That, by Susie Tompkins. New York: Harlequin Books, 1996. [For chattier information see Section Three, "I Can Fix That—Nailed," Part Two of which is "Counting Your Fingers." Section Three also includes tips on "What to Do When They Won't Unscrew" (p. 101) and "How to Drill a Hole in the Ceiling without Taking a Plaster Shower" (p. 102).]

 *The RAT's Mouse*

- **www.bhg.com/homeimp/carpentry.html** Information on carpentry basics, a guide to tools, selecting power tools
- **www.homedepot.com** The "fix it" section has tips on fixing decks, floors, etc.

4. DOMESTIC SKILLS—ANSWERS

1. **A Clothes Dryer.**   The best answer is *b*, drying clothes in hot air.

    Cotton may shrink if it is dried in a dryer set at a high temperature. Shrinkage can be avoided by drying at a cooler temperature or by removing clothes from the dryer before they are completely dry.

    Although certain cotton fabrics are generally susceptible to shrinkage, washing cotton in hot water is less likely to shrink the fabric, nor will extra time in the dryer, *if* the dryer is on a cool setting. Permanent press cycles are cooler than regular drying cycles.

    To help the drying process, shake clothes before putting them into dryer. If dry clothes sit for a period of time in a hot dryer after it has shut off, they will become extremely wrinkled. If that's not the look you desire, remove them promptly and fold them. For many casual clothes, that will eliminate the need for ironing.

2. **Washing Clothes.**   The answer is *c*. You add a sheet of Bounce in the *drying process*, not the washing cycle.

    A few drops of undiluted bleach directly on a piece of colored clothing can ruin it. Mixing colors can produce new, unintended colors, the most conspicuous perhaps being the pink garments that often emerge from a wash containing red and white items. A little too much detergent generally will not cause the suds to bubble over, although putting clothes detergent in your dishwasher can.

Merely Informative
Tips for Using Washing Machines

Follow instructions under lid or on the coin box, but also know the following laundry rules:

- Separate clothes according to color; four color piles give the absolute best results: *white, dark* (primarily black and navy), *red,* and *colored* (whites with color or pastels)
- Pour detergent, usually 1 cup per full load, into empty machine.

continued on next page

DOMESTIC SKILLS

- Select washing temperature (rinsing is almost always cold); use hot water only for extremely dirty cottons).
- Add one color of clothing to machine, loosely packed. (Clothes that are crammed into the machine will not have room to agitate properly and will not get clean.)
- Put large items in first and small items (socks, etc.) on top.
- Turn machine on.
- Add chlorine bleach carefully after machine is *full* of water and is agitating (add 1 cup or less to *white* load).

3. **Washing Sweaters.**   The answer is *a*, lay it out on a towel while it is still wet or damp.

   If a wet sweater is hung on a clothesline while it is wet, it's likely to stretch. Drying on high heat will shrink the sweater, maybe dramatically. Tumble drying with a ball or tennis shoe is a technique that can be useful when you are drying something that needs to be fluffed up, like a sleeping bag or down coat.

4. **Sewing On a Button.**   If you know how to use a sewing machine, you can sew a button on in a matter of seconds. Otherwise, the traditional method of sewing by hand requires the following:

   - Find a sewing needle that feels comfortable—not too small (you have to be able to see the hole) and not too large (no darning needles).
   - Find thread that matches the color of the thread used on the other buttons; cut off a length of about 18 inches.
   - Thread the needle: lick the end of the thread so you can twist it to a fine point; guide it through the eye of the needle, and pull it through so both ends of the thread meet.
   - Tie the ends together twice (two knots).
   - Position button on fabric.
   - Bring needle up from underside of fabric, coming up through one of the button's holes (check out the other buttons to see if you should go back and forth or form an "x" with the thread); poke needle back through hole, come up again through another hole, go back down . . . ; repeat three or four times, ending on the underside.

- Cut needle from thread.
- Separate threads and tie them close to the fabric two or three times; cut threads short.

According to *The Little Know-How Book* (see More Where This Came From), "No craft is more necessary or profound" than sewing. Pages 34–35 also give similar step-by-step instructions for sewing on a button.

You get two points for a correct answer to this question if the button you have sewn on is snug to the fabric and doesn't fall off during the first two wearings.

5. **Cleaning Ovens.**   The answer is *c*, which is *not* true. Most ovens don't require regular maintenance by the manufacturer.

Alas, manual cleaning will work for virtually any oven. In addition to sudsy water and elbow grease, there are various commercial products to assist in the process of cleaning an oven—including ones you spray on, leave for a specified period of time, and then wipe off. One secret is to wipe up any spills in an oven quickly before they dry out or get baked onto an inside surface of the oven—being careful to avoid touching the oven coils or otherwise burning yourself.

Many ovens have self-cleaning features, most of which rely on the heat of the oven to burn off any residual spills or food particles. Temperatures can, in fact, get up to 900 degrees.

6. **Candle Wax.**   The correct answer is *c*, put the candlestick in the freezer!

This technique works because when candle wax freezes, it becomes brittle and can be peeled or flicked off the candlestick more easily.

The other solutions are not recommended. Removing dripping wax at the table as you go is impractical because the wax melts continuously and hardens almost immediately. Reheating the wax, along with the candlestick, might remove the wax but it also might damage or destroy the candlestick and almost certainly would lead you back to the previous question because you would then have to clean the candle wax off the inside of the oven. And the ammonia solution? Just a bogus answer—it doesn't particularly work with candle wax.

7. **Household Items.**   The answers are

Bobbin	*d.* Sewing machine
Flue	*e.* Fireplace
Pilot light	*a.* Hot water heater
Ammonia	*g.* Window washing
Spray starch	*f.* Ironing
Plunger	*b.* Toilet
Lint filter	*c.* Clothes dryer

Merely Informative
Plunging a Toilet

Here are a few tips for plunging a toilet:

- If the toilet starts to overflow, reach down behind the toilet and turn off the water valve.
- Get the plunger.
- Place the plunger over the flush hole; hold it firmly and plunge up and down vigorously 10–15 times. There will be very little water in the bowl at this point.
- Turn the water valve back on and flush the toilet. If it starts to overflow, turn the water off again and repeat the previous steps or keep plunging while the bowl is filling. Flush.

---

8. **Painting.**   The answer is *b*. You can clean latex paint off both hands and brushes with soap and water.

For *a*, the opposite is true. Walls are usually painted with a flat paint, and wooden trim is commonly done in semi-gloss or high-gloss. Rollers can be faster than painting with brushes, but usually use more paint. Oil base paints—whether dripped on the floor or on your hands—do not clean up with soap and water; mineral spirits, turpentine, or paint thinner all work to clean up drops of oil-based paint.

Merely Informative
1. Prepare to Paint
2. Paint

Preparation is half of the job of painting. The more time you spend on this part of your project, the better it will look, the longer the paint will last, and the faster the painting will go.

- To prepare the wall surface or wood surface, first clean it with detergent to remove dirt, peeling paint, cobwebs, etc.
- Fill in any cracks or small imperfections with spackling compound for walls or wood filler for wood, applying with a putty knife.
- When dry, lightly sand rough spots and wipe with a damp cloth to remove dust, if necessary.
- Cover floor adjacent to area to be painted with newspapers or a drop cloth.
- Tape any areas that must be avoided (door locks, for example) with masking tape.
- Shake can of paint well, or open with a screwdriver and stir.
- If using a roller, pour paint into paint pan and roll the roller in the pan until it is coated.
- Start rolling.
- Some helpful rules of thumb: Paint from the top down, beginning with the ceiling; on the walls, do the edges first (a 2-inch angled brush or a foam rubber "brush" can be helpful in getting at corners or trim); blend the edges later with overlapping strokes of the roller.
- Clean up spills immediately (latex paint cleans up with a damp cloth).
- *Tip:* Want to take a break or let a first coat dry before applying a second? Keep your brushes or roller from drying out by covering them with plastic wrap or putting them in a plastic bag.
- Clean brushes or rollers while the paint on them is still wet (again, latex paint is much more hassle-free than oil-based paints); rinse and dry.
- Nonchalantly tell your friends that you did the painting yourself.

9. **Basic Skills.**

    a. *Hospital corners.*

    Hospital corners are great for four reasons:

    *   they look good;
    *   they actually keep the corners of the sheets tucked in;
    *   once you get the knack of hospital corners, making a bed becomes quick and easy; and
    *   knowing how to do a hospital corner can earn you two full points on this question.

    Here's how: If your bottom sheet is a fitted sheet, use hospital corners only on two corners of the top sheet at the foot of the bed. If you don't have a fitted bottom sheet, use hospital corners on all four corners of the bottom sheet, as well.

    *   Tuck in the bottom end of the sheet evenly all the way across the foot end of mattress.
    *   At the side, by the foot end of the bed, pick up the bottom edge of the sheet about 12 inches from end of bed, lift it straight up, and place it on top of the mattress.
    *   You have created a large triangle; tuck in the lower end of the triangle under the mattress; then let the side of the sheet fall back down; the untucked portion will then hang at an angle from the corner of the bed.
    *   Tuck the hanging part of the sheet in at the corner and at the side.
    *   Repeat at the other corner(s).

    You get two points for this if you do a hospital corner and its look approximates the illustration shown on the next page.

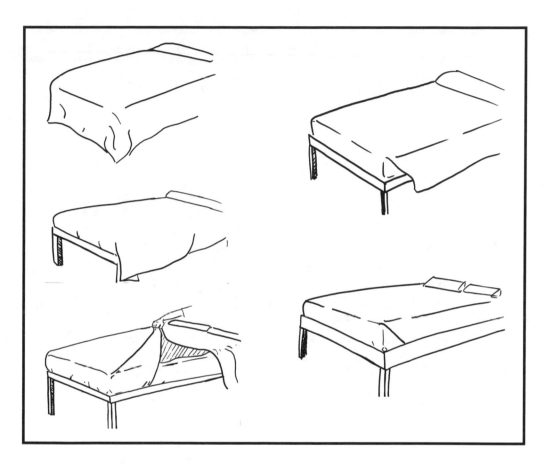

b. *Ironing a collar shirt or a blouse.*

- Ideally, remove shirt from the dryer before it is completely dry; alternatively, spray the shirt with water or spray starch, or use an iron that has a built-in sprayer. In any event, wrinkles will iron out more readily if the shirt is slightly damp.
- Set iron to proper temperature: natural fibers (cotton, linen) can be ironed at higher temperatures than synthetic fibers (polyesters and nylon, which will *melt* if ironed at too high a temperature—not a pretty sight).

- To minimize the extent to which you rewrinkle parts of the shirt you've just ironed, you might try ironing parts of the shirt in the following sequence:
  - the yoke (the shoulders and the part below the collar in the back)
  - the collar (wrongside first)
  - sleeves
  - cuffs (insides and out)
  - sides
  - back
- Keep moving. If you rest the iron for too long on one spot it will burn or scorch the garment or the ironing board cover. When you're pausing, set the iron up on its end so the hot, flat portion of the iron is not on any surface. When you've finished, turn the iron off.

The Little Know-How Book, on pages 98–100 (see More Where This Came From), describes not only how to iron a shirt but also the concept of "winter ironing," which is the practice of ironing only those portions of the shirt that protrude from the sweater under which it is worn. The author appropriately treats this practice with the scorn that any accomplished ironer would.

You get two points for successfully ironing a shirt if, after doing so, you can find another person who answers your question, "Does this shirt look ironed?" by answering yes.

10. **The Correct Tool(s).**   The answer is *c.* A shower head or faucet aerator can usually be removed with just a pair of pliers or a small wrench (plus a towel to cover the shower head to prevent scratching). Screws are not involved; a hammer is of no help; and a plumber is not the right answer, because a plumber is neither necessary nor a "correct tool."

Cleaning a faucet aerator:

- Unscrew outer 1/4" rim of faucet nozzle.
- Carefully remove rim and all the parts that come out with it .
- Place parts on a clean, uncluttered surface in the order they were removed, taking care not to reverse or mix up the order.
- Find the small, round screen; check it to see if it can be cleaned. If it can, clean it with water or a toothbrush, if necessary, and put all the parts back together in the correct order.
- If the screen cannot be cleaned, then you need a new aerator. It is safest to take the old one to the hardware store to match the size and type.

> ## More Where This Came From
>
> *Talking Dirty with the Queen of Clean.* New York: Pocket Books, 1998, by Linda Cobb, is filled with guidance on household and everyday cleaning challenges.
>
> *10,001 Hints & Tips for the House.* Orlando Florida: DK Publishing, 1998, by Cassandra Kent, offers over 2,000 solutions to daily problems.
>
> *Household Hints & Handy Tips.* Pleasantville, New York: Reader's Digest, 1994, is one handy reference.
>
> *The Big Book of Life's Instructions.* New York: Stonesong Press, 1995, by Sheree Bykofsky & Paul Fargis, has one section devoted to "Home."
>
> *The Little Know-How Book,* by Bob Scher, has instructions for making your bed, sewing on a button, ironing a shirt, and plunging a toilet.

The RAT's Mouse

For more, via your computer's mouse, check the following:

- **www.goodhousekeeping.com** Go to "Your Home Remedies" for lots of tips.
- **www.hints-n-tips.com** A site with hints and tips on a wide range of topics, including the household.
- **www.surf.co.uk** Look for "idiot's guide to laundry."

5. EMERGENCIES AND FIRST AID—ANSWERS

1. **Small Emergencies.**   For most small emergencies, there are effective remedies. Those listed below are correct responses.

    a. *Sunburn.* Sunburn, usually a first-degree burn caused by overexposure to the sun, is generally soothed by cool or cold water. A cream containing aloe can also provide relief. Aspirin or ibuprofen will alleviate the pain and inflammation of sunburn. It is generally *not* a good idea to rub sunburned areas, peel off dead skin if your skin begins to peel, or pierce blisters if the sunburn has been severe enough to form skin blisters. If sunburn is severe, seek medical attention rather than attempting to treat it yourself.

EMERGENCIES AND FIRST AID

Merely Informative
Preventing Sunburn

Prevent sunburn by using sun block, one of the great advances of modern civilization. Most suntan lotions indicate the SPF rating of the product. The higher the SPF rating, the greater the level of protection. An SPF rating of 4 is relatively low; an SPF of 15 or higher is generally recommended; sun block with a rating of 30 or more will filter out almost all of the sun's harmful burning rays. Unless they say otherwise, most suntan lotions wash off if you go swimming and must be reapplied.

Hats with brims also help protect against sunburn. Remember that you can get sunburned on cloudy days, and that snow and water reflect burning rays.

---

b. *Diarrhea.* The first concern with diarrhea is dehydration. Diarrhea can be treated by drinking water, diluted juices, or sports drinks. Breads, grains, potatoes, and rice are okay to eat; fatty foods, alcohol, and coffee should be avoided. Imodium is an over-the-counter medication; Lomotil is a strong prescription medication. Persistent diarrhea or dysentery, a more serious variant, requires medical attention.

c. *Blister.* Blisters caused by friction from rubbing of the skin (as, for example, when wearing new boots or shoes, wearing loose socks, using an axe without wearing gloves, etc.) produce a bubble filled with fluid under the outer layer of skin. Further friction on the blister can be reduced by isolating the blister by using a moleskin donut, a Band-Aid, "2d Skin," or duct tape over a bandage. If the blister has broken, or is drained by puncturing it with a sterilized needle or knife point, the "roof" of the blister should be left in place, antibiotic ointment applied, and bandaged.

d. *Kitchen burn.* A kitchen burn from grease or a hot pan is generally treated like any other burn. For most mild burns, the American Medical Association First Aid Guide suggests, if the skin is not broken, immersing the burned area in *clean cold running water,* applying a *cold compress,* or towel, to the affected area, and loosely placing a pad, handkerchief, or cloth over the burned area (to keep air away from it).

e. *Poison ivy.* Poison ivy—which can produce itching, redness, tiny blisters, or even headaches or fever—can be treated by washing the affected area thoroughly with soap and water and then by applying calamine lotion or another commercial product for treating poison ivy. To avoid spreading the substance that causes these symptoms, be sure to wash under your finger-nails and to clean or cut away clothing against which poison ivy has rubbed.

Merely Informative
Avoiding Poison Ivy

Poison ivy may be identified, and thus avoided, by its distinctive characteristics:

- three shiny leaflets growing out of a common stem;
- a reddened stem where the three leaflets begin and;
- relatively smooth, as opposed to jagged, leaf edges.

It can appear as a plant, bush, or vine and is usually among the first to change color in the fall.

In avoiding poison ivy, if you brush up against either poison oak or poison sumac, you haven't made much progress.

---

2. **Emergencies Caused by Small Creatures.**

   a. *Bee sting.* First, remove the stinger if it is still in your skin by scraping it away with a fingernail, toothpick, or other firm object (don't use tweezers, which could squeeze out more venom). Second, wash the sting area with soap and water. Third, wrap ice in a towel or cloth and apply it to the sting. Fourth, apply calamine lotion.

      Note: Bee stings can sometimes cause a severe allergic reaction, known as anaphylaxis, which is characterized by difficulty in breathing, bluish or grayish skin color, and shock. A severe allergic reaction to a bee sting can be treated with an epi-pen (epinephrine) or requires emergency medical attention.

   b. *Tick.* Since ticks embed themselves in your skin, they may be difficult to remove. Some first aid guides suggest suffocating a tick by covering it with petroleum jelly or mineral oil. If that does not cause the tick to release at once, wait a half-hour and then remove it with tweezers, gently grabbing the tick as close to its front (mouth) as possible.

Merely Informative Ticks

Ticks bites should be avoided because ticks can transmit Lyme disease, Rocky Mountain spotted fever, or Colorado tick fever. None of these is something you want to have. Occasional tick checks during a hike is one preventive measure as well as a social diversion.

---

c. *Jelly fish sting.* If there are any tentacles on the skin, lift them off with a comb or a knife (rubbing them off can cause more venom to be released). Rinse the sting area with seawater and soak in vinegar or rubbing alcohol for a half-hour. Some books recommend applying shaving cream or baking soda paste, shaving the area, and reapplying vinegar or alcohol.

d. *Skunk spray odor.* The best home antidote to skunk spray is tomato juice, in substantial quantities. Perhaps you can visualize the treatment process.

3. **Spills on Carpets.**

Here are some general principles:

- Move as quickly as possible; act while a liquid is still a liquid before a spill becomes a stain.
- Blot up as much of the liquid as possible; use absorbent paper towels or a white terry cloth towel; blot, don't rub.
- Work from the outside in to reduce the chances of leaving a ring.

As to the specifics . . .

a. *Coffee.* After blotting up as much coffee as possible, sponge with cold water and blot again with a sponge or towel. If more is needed, a paste of water and detergent can be applied, blotted, and rinsed off.

b. *Red wine.* Similar to coffee. Blot, blot; sponge with water and blot. Apply salt to the area, sponge with cold water, and blot dry.

c. *Chewing gum.* If ground into the carpet, pack the area with ice or frozen containers until the gum hardens and can be picked or scraped off the carpet surface.

d. *Chocolate.* Scrape off as much as possible and then sponge off the area with cool water. Since a chocolate stain is likely to contain grease—as in a stepped-on brownie—the next step may be to apply a solvent that works on grease, such as dry cleaning fluid. Finish by sponging with cool water and blotting dry.

More Where This Came From

For more detail and discussions of a greater variety of types of stains, see *Household Hints and Handy Tips*. Pleasantville, NY: Reader's Digest, 1994.

The Big Book of Life's Instructions. New York: Stonesong Press, 1995, by Sheree Bykofsky & Paul Fargis (See "Remove Stains," at pp. 218–222).

Talking Dirty with the Queen of Clean. New York: Pocket Books, 1998, by Linda Cobb, pp. 64–68.

4. **Minor Car Emergencies.**

   a. *Car keys locked in your car.* We'll skip over the best solutions—using the spare key that you always carry or that you keep in a magnetized box hidden in a special place on the underside of your car.

   Now you are forced to consider coat hangers and other devices such as a Slim Jim to try to reach into the inside of your car door to release the lock or open the door from the inside. This can be facilitated, of course, if you have left one of your windows open a crack. Some door locks are easier than others. Power door locks are a problem.

   More reliable solutions may be calling a policeman (likely to have experience with this problem), a locksmith (they do this for a living), your auto dealership (which may be able to locate the code for your key and make you a new one), or emergency roadside assistance (happy to assist for a fee or the cost of a club membership).

   b. *Frozen car door lock.* There are a variety of potential remedies for this condition, some better than others.

   Let's start with the obvious ones. If the lock on the driver's door is frozen, try the lock on the passenger side. If that works, you can attribute your success to whatever type of technological cleverness you choose.

   Otherwise, one family of remedies involves raising the temperature of the lock to the point that ice melts or the lock otherwise operates. If you are close enough to an electrical power source, a hair dryer can be used to warm up the lock. If the lock is in a raised door handle, pouring hot water on the handle may work.

Another philosophy is to heat the key so that when it is inserted into the lock, it warms and unfreezes the lock. An obvious problem with this solution is that any technique that heats the end of the key that goes in the lock will also heat the other end of the key, which is in your hand. Holding the key with something that serves the same purpose as a potholder to keep from burning your hand may work, but this is not a preferred solution.

Finally, sometimes while you're gathering up whatever equipment you plan to use, the outside temperature rises enough that the lock melts on its own, giving you another opportunity to claim credit creatively.

5. **Snakes and Snakebites.**

a. *Poisonous Snakes.* Three of the four poisonous snakes found in America— rattlesnakes, copperheads, and water moccasins—are pit vipers. Each has a triangular-shaped head, slit-like eyes (like a cat's), and a depressed "pit" between its nostrils and eyes. Each bites with a pair of retractable fangs. The distinctive sound of the rattle at the end of its tail can serve as a warning that a rattlesnake is nearby. The fourth poisonous snake, a coral snake, is brightly colored with red, yellow, and black bands, and it has a black snout. A member of the cobra family, the coral snake is typically found in the United States only in the Southeast and in southern Texas.

b. *Bites by Poisonous Snakes.* One can determine whether a snakebite was from a poisonous by any of the following:

- recognizing that the snake that bit you is a poisonous snake;
- two small puncture wounds about a half-inch apart, caused by the snake's fangs;
- severe burning sensation at the bite site;
- rapid swelling;
- discoloration or blisters around the bite (within a few hours);
- nausea, vomiting, sweating, weakness;
- blurred vision; or
- shock.

Merely Informative
Poisonous Snakes in North America

Rattlesnakes account for about two-thirds of all venomous snakebites in America. A pit viper can strike an object a half-body length away from its head. The inside of the mouth of a water moccasin (cottonmouth) is white. Water moccasins can swim, and can be belligerent if annoyed. Coral snakes need to chew their victims to secrete their deadly venom.

First aid measures include

- moving away from the snake (snakes can bite twice or be accompanied by a companion),
- keeping the victim calm,
- washing the bite area with soap and water,
- getting prompt medical attention.

If you have a Sawyer extractor, you should use it as quickly as possible.

First aid books tend to advise *against* using "cut-and-suck" techniques, cold packs, tourniquets, or electric shock.

6. **Water Emergencies.**

a. *Artificial respiration or Rescue breathing.* For drowning victims who are not breathing, mouth-to-mouth resuscitation is a common first aid technique and should be administered immediately. For a victim lying on his or her back,

- tilt the head back;
- pinch the victim's nose shut;
- seal your lips around the victim's mouth, and
- give two slow breaths for 1–1½ seconds each, and then repeat.

If a victim is not breathing *and* has no pulse, cardiopulmonary resuscitation (CPR) is necessary. Administering CPR, a vital emergency skill, requires prior training. In either event, call 911 immediately for emergency medical assistance.

b. *Floating in rough water for long periods.* If surf or water is at all rough, floating on your back for any extended period of time may be difficult. However, you can float for extended periods of time by using what is sometimes called the "dead man's float."

The dead man's float is accomplished by treading water momentarily, taking a breath, and then, holding your breath while floating face-down in the water with both your arms and your legs hanging down, limp in the water. In this position, your shoulders, upper back, and back of your head are at or above the surface of the water, and you are holding your breath with your face down in the water.

When you need to take a breath, you lift your head up, tread water momentarily, take a breath, and then resume your face-in-the-water position. In this position, you simply float with waves or other rough water until you need to take your next breath. If you relax and just hang limply in the face-down position, you can remain afloat for long periods of time, even in rough water.

7. **Muscle Pulls.**

RICE. The "RICE Routine," as described in both the *AMA Pocket Guide to Emergency First Aid* and the *National Safety Council's First Aid Handbook,* refers to steps you should take to treat minor sprains, strains, and muscle pulls. "RICE" stands for the following:

a. *Rest*—stopping what you were doing will prevent further injury, stop further bleeding in the tissues, and help reduce swelling.

b. *Ice*—applying an ice pack for 20–30 minutes every 3 hours for the first couple of days will reduce pain, swelling, and bruising.

c. *Compression*—wearing an elastic compression bandage will provide support and help limit swelling and bruising.

d. *Elevation*—keeping the injured part of your body elevated above the level of your heart will reduce pressure on the tissues, swelling, and bruising.

8. **National Disasters.**

a. *Tornadoes.* Safety measures include:

- *Get inside* a sturdy building; not a tent, car, or motor home.
- Go to the basement or lower level of the building you are in.
- If there is no basement or cellar, *go to the center of the house, stay away from windows, and get under a sturdy table.*
- As a tornado approaches, close all the doors and windows facing the storm and open all of those on the opposite side.

- If you're outside and can't reach a building, *lie down* in a ditch or low area and cover your head with your hands.

b. *Hurricanes.* Common precautions include:
- *Evacuate* if you are in a coastal or low-lying area that is subject to either rising tides or flooding.
- *Stock up on flashlights, batteries, and candles;* you may find yourself without electrical power.
- Make sure you have a supply of *food and water* in case you are stranded.
- *Store extra water* for drinking and cooking in a clean bathtub in case your water service is disrupted.
- Have a *battery-operated radio or TV* so you can keep up with weather or other emergency reports.
- *Board up windows* if necessary.
- Secure or *store loose objects* that are outside.
- *Avoid driving or going outdoors* where the odds of encountering flying glass, debris, or lightning are generally higher than if you remain indoors.

c. *Earthquakes.* Earthquakes are the opposite of tornadoes in that you want to *get outside* in the event of an earthquake.
- Outside, *stay away from power lines,* buildings, lampposts, etc.
- If you can't get outside, *get under a solid desk or table.*
- *If you are driving, stop.* However, try not to stop on a bridge, by a tall building, or under trees, power lines, or large signs.
- *Do not* seek refuge in underground cellars, subways, or tunnels.

9. **The Heimlich Maneuver.**   The Heimlich maneuver is a first aid technique designed to assist someone who is choking and unable to breathe. A common cause of choking is a piece of partially chewed food that is caught in a person's windpipe. The steps in performing the Heimlich are these:
- Stand behind the victim.
- Reaching around the victim with your arms, make a fist and place the thumb side of your fist just below the victim's navel.
- Grabbing your fist with your other hand, thrust your fist inward and slightly upward with a strong motion (this motion will force air up and out of the victim's lungs).

- Repeat this motion until the object lodged in the victim's airway is dislodged.

10. **Intruders.**   According to the experts, if you hear an intruder in your apartment or house, among the steps you might prudently take are the following:
    - If the door to the room that you are in has a lock, lock it.
    - Call 911 or your local emergency number.
    - Turn on lights.
    - Loudly say, "John, I think I hear somebody in the house" (whether or not there is a "John" with you).
    - If you have an intercom, use it to ask who's there.
    - Go to the window and yell, "fire" (people are more likely to help if you yell, "fire," than if you yell, "burglar").

More Where This Came From

Some of the preceding information is drawn from the following references, all of which are excellent:

Backcountry First Aid and Extended Care. Merrillville, Indiana: ICS Books, Inc., 1994, by Buck Tilton (an excellent, compact, no-nonsense guide)

Pocket Guide to Emergency First Aid and *Pocket Guide to Sports First Aid.* New York: Random House, 1993, both published by the American Medical Association.

First Aid Handbook. Boston: Jones and Bartlett Publishers, 1995, published by the National Safety Council.

The RAT's Mouse

- **www.gorp.com/gorp/health/main.htm** The Great Outdoor Recreation Page, which has guidance on staying healthy and keeping safe in the great outdoors; discusses wilderness emergencies, survival, medicine
- **www.fema.gov/library/winterf.htm** A good fact sheet for winter driving
- **www.healthy.net/asp/templates/article.asp?** A good site on first aid for poison ivy

6.   SAVING AND INVESTING—ANSWERS

1. **Interest-Bearing Accounts.**   There are several correct answers:
    - Savings account
    - Money market account
    - Certain checking accounts, such as "NOW (Negotiable Orders of Withdrawal) accounts"
    - Certificates of deposit (CDs)

2. **Federally Insured Accounts.**   The answer is *b*, investment accounts.

    Checking, NOW, savings, and money market accounts, and certificates of deposit are all insured by federal agencies. Insurance is typically up to a maximum of $100,000 per depositor. Joint accounts are insured up to $200,000.

    Investment accounts, which many banks now offer, are not insured. This is in part because investment accounts, which allow depositors to invest in stocks or mutual funds, are not simply deposits, but are, by definition, investments that carry with them some degree of investment risk. Nor are Treasury securities (such as Treasury bills or savings bonds) insured, although they are backed by the full faith and credit of the federal government.

3. **Compound Interest.**

    Compound interest is interest that is paid on a sum of money or an account balance, and then added to it. The next payment of interest is then paid on the new balance, which consists of both the original amount in the account plus the interest payment that was added to the account balance. The following year, interest is paid on the current balance, which has been increased again by another interest payment.

    Take the example of a bank account with $100 in it that earns 10 percent interest, "compounded annually." At the end of the first year, the $100 will have earned interest of $10. Adding the $10 of interest to the $100 account brings the account balance to a total of $110. Earning compound interest, the account earns interest in the second year of $11, bringing the account balance to $121. Through compound interest, the balance of the account continues to grow year by year. At an annual compound interest rate of

10 percent a year, the account will have doubled from $100 to $200 in just over 7 years.

Thus, the answers to the second part of this question are

Year 2: $110   *Year 3: $121*   *Year 4: $133.10*

4. **Doubling Your Money.**   The answer is *The Rule of 72*.

What is the "Rule of 72"? It is, first, one of the most useful and intriguing financial concepts you can learn. With this rule, you can quickly tell how long it will take a bank account or an investment to double in value if the interest it earns is compounded.

Here's the rule: *To determine how long it will take your money to double if the interest you earn is compounded, simply divide the rate of interest you are earning into 72. The answer tells you—in years—how quickly your money will double.*

If, for example, you are earning 6 percent interest, compounded, your investment will double in 12 years. If, however, you are earning 9 percent, your $100 investment will become $200 in 8 years. With a 10 percent return, you will double your investment in 7.2 years. If you can consistently earn 12 percent interest, you will double your money in just 6 years.

When this formula is applied to long-term investments—such as for retirement or your kid's education—you can see that compound interest is, as Einstein said, magical. It is one of the most powerful concepts in financial planning.

For example, a $1,000 investment made at age 20 that earns 8 percent compound interest will have grown, by age 65, from $1,000 to $2,000 (age 29), to $4,000 (age 38), to $8,000 (age 47), to $16,000 (age 56), to $32,000 (age 65). If that investment earned 12 percent (a figure that many mutual funds have achieved in many years), that same $1,000, by age 65, would be worth more than $179,000. And that's just one year's investment!

If that $1,000 investment were put in a retirement account, that growth would have been tax-free.

Merely Informative
Three Ways to Accumulate
a Million Dollars by Age 65

In the book, *Kiplinger's Money-Smart Kids,* Washington: Kiplinger Books, 1993, author Janet Bodnar lists three ways to become a millionaire by age 65. Assuming a 10 percent return on your investments, do any of the following:

  a. deposit $2,000 each year for 41 years, beginning at age 24;
  b. deposit $2,000 each year for 7 years, beginning at age 17; or
  c. deposit $2,000 once, at birth.

All of these examples play off the power of compound interest. It is because of this that beginning to save or invest at a young age can create such value over time. The earlier you begin, the more opportunities for your money to double and redouble, as the Rule of 72 demonstrates.

---

5. **Types of Investments.**   The answer is *a mutual fund.*

Mutual funds are one of the most popular types of stock investments. They are generally safer than investing in any single stock because your risk is spread over the number of stocks the mutual fund owns. Although a single stock can go up in value dramatically, it can also fall dramatically. Because mutual funds spread their investment risks over a number of different stocks, they tend to be less volatile than individual stocks and are generally considered to be safer investments, particularly if the stocks are in companies in different sectors of the economy.

Merely Informative
Mutual Funds

Each mutual fund is managed by one or more fund managers. They manage the fund and charge shareholders some fee for that service. The performance of the mutual fund depends, in part, on the skill of the fund manager. When investing in stocks, there are no risk-free investments, even when your risk is spread over a number of companies through a mutual fund. Nonetheless, mutual funds are considered to be safer than investing in individual stocks.

---

6. **Rate of Return and Risk.**

Investments that have relatively low risk and a relatively low rate of return are *insured savings accounts, money market accounts,* and *certificates of deposit; government savings bonds; highly rated corporate bonds.*

By contrast, most common stocks may produce a higher rate of return, but they also entail relatively higher risk than insured saving accounts and bonds. *Speculative investments that entail high risk include "penny stocks," investments in start-up companies, "junk bonds," and derivatives (investments in which you put up only a portion of the total investment amount for which you are obligated).*

Merely Informative
Reducing Investment Risk

Investment advisors suggest several common ways to reduce investment risk. Here are a few:

*   Insured Savings Accounts. Invest only in bank accounts that are insured by the federal government. Savings and money market accounts in most banks and savings and loans (S&Ls) are insured by a federal agency known as the the Federal Deposit Insurance Corporation (FDIC). Most insured bank accounts are thus very safe investments. However, they tend to pay relatively low rates of interest, so they do not offer the promise of higher rates of return. In fact, in some years, they may not keep up with inflation (See next question).
*   Government Bonds. Invest in U.S. government savings bonds or Treasury bills. These investments are backed by the full faith and credit of the federal government and are considered the safest of all investments.
*   Corporate Bonds. Invest in highly rated bonds. Bonds are, in essence, loans that you make to a corporation or a municipality at a stated rate of interest. Corporate bonds are rated according to the level of perceived risk. Unless the company issuing the bonds encounters such severe financial distress that it is forced to restructure or default on its debt, it will make required payments, including interest, on its bonds. Historically and on average, however, bonds have not produced as high a level of return as common stocks.

continued on next page

- Diversify your investments. The most common technique for reducing investment risk is to diversify investments. For example, a diversified portfolio may include stocks, bonds, and money market funds. Within the stock (or "equity") investments, investments may be spread among different companies, different types of companies, different industrial sectors, even different countries.

7. **Rate of Return and Inflation.**   The answer is *b*, decreased.

   The purchasing power of your investment actually will have declined. This is because the general cost of good and services—the effect of the rate of inflation—will have risen more than the value of your savings. Thus, although your $100 may have grown to $103, this amount will buy slightly less than what $100 would have bought a year earlier.

Merely Informative Real Rate of Return

The term "real rate of return" describes the value of your investment return after taking into account the effects of inflation. Thus, if you earn 10 percent annually on your investment, and the annual rate of inflation is 2 percent, your real rate of return is 8 percent.

8. **Stock Market Terms.**
   a. Bear market
   b. Bull market
   c. "Blue chips"—investors refer to both "blue chip companies" and "blue chip stocks"
   d. The year of the Crash, also known as the Great Crash, the 1929 Crash, and "Black Monday," was 1929.
   e. Dividends

9. **The Dow.**   The answer is *b*, the Dow Jones Industrial Average.

   The Dow Jones Industrial Average (DJIA) is a weighted average of thirty blue chip stocks selected by the editors of the *Wall Street Journal*. Originally (1896) a group of twelve handpicked stocks, the number was expanded to twenty in

1916 and to thirty in 1928. The companies included in the DJIA are reviewed and changed periodically. The last two changes were made in 1997 and 1999.

10. **Retirement Accounts.**   Correct answers include:
   - 401(k);
   - Individual Retirement Account (IRA);
   - "Roth IRA"; and
   - Keogh plan.

See the answer to question 9 in section 8 of the Answer Section for more on retirement accounts.

More Where This Came From

Readable materials on saving and investing include the following:

The Wall Street Journal *Guide To Understanding Money and Investment.* New York: Lightbulb Press, 1992, by Kenneth Morris and Alan Siegel (an informative, readable, succinct reference).

The Motley Fool book, *You Have More than You Think.* New York: Fireside, 2001, by David and Tom Gardner.

The Millionaire Next Door. Pocket Books, 2000, by Thomas Stanley and William Danko.

The RAT's Mouse

More information with the click of your computer mouse . . .
   - **www.finance.yahoo.com/** A general site with lots of financial information
   - **www.fdic.gov/about/learn/learning/index.html** A Federal Deposit Insurance Corporation site; basic, easy-to-understand discussion of the history of the FDIC, how it works, the who, what, when, where, and why
   - **www.fool.com/** The site for Motley Fool, with information for individual investors; assumes some understanding of markets and investing
   - **www.kids.infoplease.lycos.com/spot/stockmarket.html** Stock market basics aimed at kids

- **www.finaid.org/calculators/compoundinterest.phtml** Student financial aid site, including the "compound interest calculator"; type in the beginning amount and the interest rate and . . . voila!

7.   SHOPPING—ANSWERS

1. **Sales Days.**   The answer is *c,* the first day of summer.

   There are undoubtedly sales on the first day of summer—there are most days—but the first day of summer does not compare with the day after Christmas, notorious for large crowds of shoppers and reduced prices, or with Washington's birthday or the Fourth of July, both of which are traditional occasions for major sales.

2. **Online Shopping.**

   Online shopping has numerous advantages. Among them:
   - convenience—shop from home;
   - speed—if you know what you're after, you can shop for an item very quickly;
   - cheaper—buying products on-line often can be cheaper than buying them in stores because on-line retailers often have lower overhead;
   - comments by other customers may be available; and
   - 'round-the-clock shopping is available.

   Disadvantages:
   - no opportunity to feel the merchandise;
   - browsing can be time-consuming;
   - returns can be a hassle; and
   - you're unlikely to run into a friend or pass by a place to have coffee.

   You may think of a number of other factors, pro or con.

3. **Secondhand Stores.**   The answer is *a,* consignment shops.

   In consignment shops, the owner of the item entrusts, or "consigns," the item to the store owner, who agrees to try to sell it. Consignment stores usually agree to keep items for a specific period of time—three months, for example. If the item has not sold by then, the owner may retrieve it or simply

SHOPPING

give it to the store. If the item has sold, the shop keeps a percentage—50 percent, for example—and the owner gets the remainder of the sales price.

Pawnshops are stores to which you can sell merchandise, which is then offered for sale. If you wish to buy the item back later and it has not been sold, you pay the pawnbroker's price, which is higher than the price you were paid. If you are able to repurchase the pawned item, you will have effectively borrowed money from the pawnbroker, and for that privilege, will have paid the difference in the two prices.

Thrift shops typically sell clothing and merchandise that people have donated as charitable gifts. Goodwill Industries, the Salvation Army, and other charities operate thrift shops.

Outlets, or factory outlets, don't deal in used merchandise at all. Typically they sell products delivered directly from the factory (without the additional cost of a middleman). Sometimes outlets sell "seconds," products that have minor defects or imperfections.

4. **Returns.**   The right answer is *a*.

It is not common practice for a store to charge a customer a penalty or fee for returning merchandise. However, stores may refuse to accept a return or to give you a full refund for other reasons. First, the store may have a return policy. During sales, a store may post an "All Sales Final" policy. That means no returns. Or its policy may be that returns will be accepted only for store credit, which means that you cannot get your money back; instead, you can just buy other merchandise up to the amount of your original purchase. Whenever you make a purchase, particularly if you think you might want to return it, *ask* what the store's return policy is. If it's just for store credit, you may want to say thanks and keep looking.

In addition to checking on the return policy, make sure you keep your receipt. Also keep the tags (preferably keep them on the garment until you are sure you want to keep it) and the box or container. You may even want to keep the store bag. If you return armed with all of these, you'll be in good shape.

Generally, the financial mechanics of a return are simplest if the original purchase was by credit card because the card can simply be credited when you return the merchandise. Refunds for products paid for by check can be more complicated, and sometimes stores won't refund cash for a returned product that you paid for with cash.

Merely Informative Receipts

Keeping all of your receipts in the same place for three months can be a good idea. Also, some shoppers are careful not to keep receipts in the bags in which their new purchases are carried; if the bag with your new merchandise is stolen, the thief also has a copy of your receipt on which your credit card number might appear.

---

5. **Cars.**   The answer is *c*. It is usually most cost effective to purchase a late model used car.

A new car, for which you pay a hefty retail price, depreciates, or loses value, rapidly. Thus, the resale value of a car that is only a year or so old usually has dropped considerably from its original value. Leasing a new car can cost nearly as much as a car loan might cost, but at the end of the lease you're left with nothing. In addition, leases usually have an annual mileage limit, and if you exceed that limit, you must pay a premium. A car that needs repairs is a risk. Although its problems might depress its sales price, it may have more problems and need more repairs than you think, or than the seller suggests. Thus, an older car in need of repair is a gamble, and it could be one that costs you lots of money.

A used car that is not too old and has been well maintained is usually the best value. Its value has already depreciated from when it was new, but it may still be new enough that it may not need significant repairs for a while.

6. **Electronics.**   The answer is *a*, large stores or chains may be able to sell *electronic equipment for less because they buy in large quantities.*

The other statements are all false. "Manufacturer's Suggested Retail Price" is simply that. It is quite common for stores to sell products for less than "Suggested Retail," because doing so suggests that they are giving customers a discount.

Extended warranties or service contracts are not unprofitable acts of consideration for customers. To the contrary, service contracts are highly profitable, sometimes more profitable than the products for which they are bought.

Although it is unlawful in many states for sales clerks to "bait and switch"—advertise one product, but tell customers who come to buy it that the store is sold out and that another (more expensive) alternative is available—it is not unlawful for sales clerks to try to persuade customers to buy a more expensive product. This technique, sometimes called "bump" or "step up," is a tried-and-true sales technique in which salespeople emphasize the features, accessories, or benefits of higher-priced models.

Merely Informative Extended Warranties

According to Janice Lieberman, author of *Tricks of the Trade* (see More Where This Came From), extended warranties, or service plans, have been called "the consumer electronics equivalent to 'Do you want fries with that?'" She offers the following facts about extended warranties:

- Extended warranties are really service contracts, on top of the product warranties that are included in the price of the product.
- "In buying an extended warranty, you are gambling. If you bought a plan and the product breaks, great. But like any casino, the odds are with the house."
- "Of all of the consumers who buy warranties, only 15 percent ever use them."
- Because of low profit margins, extended warranties have become, for some stores, "their new cash cow."
- Estimates are that for every dollar of revenue that stores take in from sales of extended warranties, they spend "only 4 cents to 15 cents on service and repair." That's an enormous profit margin.

---

7. **Sales Tax.**   *False.* If you return an item for a refund, you are, in effect, rescinding the sales transaction. As a result, the tax you paid and the purchase price are returned to you.

8. **Efficient Grocery Shopping.**   The answer is *d,* use a shopping list.

Shopping with a shopping list will make your grocery shopping less costly and more efficient. (Experts say you can save up to 15 percent off your total grocery bill by planning your shopping trip in advance.)

All of the other practices have the opposite effect. In comparison shopping, comparing the unit prices (the cost for a common unit of food), not the total prices, is the way to compare apples to apples. *Never* shop when you're hungry. The effect is not to narrow your focus on just those things you need to eat; instead, everything looks good, and you are inclined to buy more than if you had just eaten. Store brands are typically less expensive, not more expensive, than national brands. Although the taste or quality may or may not be the same as with national brands, a comparison of the unit prices shows that store brands are frequently cheaper.

9. **Unbranded Medicines.**   The answer is *generics*.

Generic medications are analogous to store brands in grocery stores. They do not have the recognizable brand names of certain well-known products. Typically, however, they are chemically identical to the branded products and sometimes far cheaper.

10. **Grocery Store Techniques.**   The answer is *b*.

Grocery stores do not sell products identified as "lite" that have only slightly less fat than nonlite products. The reason is that the U.S. Food and Drug Administration (FDA) now regulates the use of such terms as "lite," "healthy," "low fat," and "no fat" by food manufacturers and grocers. Before these terms were regulated, they often were used purely as marketing hype.

All the rest are standard "tricks of the trade" in marketing, according to consumer expert Janice Lieberman. Consider the last time you were in a grocery store in which milk was near the front, and the checkout lines didn't have candy.

More Where This Came From

The Consumer Bible: 1001 Ways To Shop Smart, by Mark Green. Workman Publishing, 1995.
Tricks of the Trade: A Consumer Survival Guide, by Janice Lieberman. Dell Books, 1998.
Consumer Reports Buying Guide, 2001, by the Editors of the Consumer Reports. 2000.
Get Clark Smart—The Ultimate Guide for the Savvy Consumer, by Clark Howard, Mark Meltzer. Laystreet Press, 2000.

The RAT's Mouse

For a wealth of consumer information at the touch of a computer mouse, see

- **www.consumerreports.com**

8.   EMPLOYMENT—ANSWERS

1. **Job Information.**   Information about jobs is available from various sources, including:

- *The classifieds*—One of the most readily accessible sources of information about job openings is the newspaper. Most newspapers have classified ad sections with listings of job openings. Many newspapers in large cities have separate classifieds sections on the weekends, when there tend to be more listings than during the week.
- *Placement offices*—If you are at a school that has a placement office, it will have information, including information provided by employers, about career opportunities and job openings.
- *Individual companies and employers*—Employers themselves are obviously in the best position to advise about their job openings. Checking with individual companies or other employers requires you to contact them one at a time, but you can get up-to-date, company-specific information, and, if there is an opening that interests you, you can follow up immediately.
- *Job fairs*—Certain industries and certain communities hold job fairs, where employers come to interview prospective employees. Job fairs can be an efficient way to get acquainted with a number of prospective employers at a single location.
- *On-campus interviewing*—If you're in school, you can find out whether employers interview on campus for permanent employment or summer jobs. Usually coordinated by college placement offices, on-campus interviewing has the advantage of employers coming to you rather than the opposite. Treat it as a great luxury.
- *Employment agencies*—Some companies are in the business of matching up people and jobs. Upscale versions are known as executive search firms or "headhunters." For a fee (usually paid by the employer),

search firms look for qualified candidates to fill vacancies, sometimes conducting nationwide searches.

- *Word-of-mouth*—Talking to friends and learning about job possibilities through the grapevine ("networking") can be one of the best ways to learn about possible employment. If you hear from a friend that his or her company is hiring, for example, you already have one important piece of information, plus you know one person who works there. This person can tell you more about the company and may be able to help arrange for you to talk to the people or the office responsible for hiring.

More Where This Came From

To do some of this electronically, you may wish to consult:

Job Searching Online for Dummies. New York: Hungry Minds Inc., 2000, by Pam Dixon;

Job Hunting on the Internet. Berkeley: Ten Speed Press, 1999, by Richard Nelson Bolles (author of *What Color Is Your Parachute?*)

2. **Resumes.**

Resumes (also sometimes referred to as bios, curriculum vitae, or CVs) provide employers a summary of your education, experience, qualifications, and any other bits of information that may be relevant to their decision to offer you a job. A resume can arrive before you do, help determine whether you get a face-to-face interview, and remain after you leave as a part of the file that may be used later in making hiring decisions.

Some elements of a resume are essential to tell an employer how to contact you. Other elements cover the types of background information that most employers want to see. There may be additional elements that provide other information an employer considers relevant or informative.

The following are all correct answers to this question:

- your telephone number;
- your e-mail address;
- your educational background (where you went to school, when, degrees, honors, etc.);

- extracurricular activities (organizations or other activities in which you were involved at school);
- your work experience, if any (include full-time, part-time, and summer jobs, military experience, volunteer or unpaid jobs); or
- specific skills or accomplishments (keyboard, computer, or language skills, started an organization, published an article, etc.).

Other resume entries, also correct answers for this purpose, include information that is not necessarily essential for a resume but, depending on the circumstances or the type of job you are seeking, may be helpful. These include:

- *References* (the names of individuals whom an employer can call to get personal comments about their experience with you, whether in school, through a previous job, or through some activity)—People who are not related to you are more credible references than people who are.
- *Special interests*—Although some interests or hobbies may be of little interest to an employer, some reference to what interests you outside of school and work can provide a more complete picture of you, your initiative, your curiosity, and your range of abilities.
- *Goals*—If you have a particular job or career interest, you may want to state it. If your passion in life is computer programming or commercial real estate or cooking, and your passion relates to the job you're interviewing for, say so. Your resume is a snapshot of you.

More Where This Came From

There are scads of books on resume writing. Most large bookstores offer a dizzying selection. Here are a couple worth considering:

Resumes That Knock 'Em Dead. Holbrook, Massachusetts: Adams Media Corporation, 2000, by Martin Yate;

You're Hired! New York: NTC Contemporary Publishing, 1991, by Sharon McDonnell.

3. **Interviews.**   Your objective in an interview is to help the interviewer reach the conclusion that he or she wants to offer you a job. Some experts describe this as a process of selling yourself, of salesmanship. You may do so in a variety of ways and by being yourself. However, the process is one in which the

interviewer evaluates how you and your skills, experience, talents, and attitude match with the employer's needs.

In identifying what helps create a favorable impression in an interview, experts tend to mention the following:

a. *Enthusiasm*—If you appear to be flat and indifferent, the interviewer may reasonably assume that you would be flat and indifferent on the job. Enthusiasm, by contrast, tends to be at the top of the list of traits that make for a good interview.

b. *Sincerity*—If you are not genuine, it's likely to be obvious to an experienced interviewer. Insincerity is generally not an asset, and may be viewed as a form of dishonesty. Thus, you should be yourself; don't try phony enthusiasm or exaggerate your experience; be honest in your conversation.

c. *Preparation*—Do some homework. Learn something in advance about the company or employer with which you are interviewing. Think about what you're looking for in a job. Consider beforehand what questions you have about the company or the available jobs, and ask them.

d. *Courtesy*—Obvious, perhaps, but if you're rude, unresponsive, disrespectful, late, unprepared, sleepy, or daydreaming, most interviewers will react negatively.

e. *Answer questions fully*—Avoid simple yes or no answers that don't lead to further conversation. Elaborate on your answer, explain why your answer is what it is, or ask a follow-up question. Keep it going, and make it interesting. (See the Dealing with People section.)

f. *Ask questions*—Information gathering in an interview is a two-way street. Not only is it acceptable for you to ask questions, it also may help keep the interview moving and lively. You may want to have some questions in mind before you start, or you may just want to play off the interviewers' questions and comments. Example: "When would you be available to start work." "I could actually begin on October 1, but I was wondering if it might be possible for me to meet some of the people I would be working with before then. And what would be the best way for me to get some information on what the company's goals are for the next year?"

g. *Learn the interviewer's name and use it in the interview.* Example: "Mr. Hull, that's a really hard question. I'm not sure I have an answer, but I think I would think about that question by asking . . . ."

Merely Informative
Interviewing Basics

Here are a few basic rules of thumb about the mechanics of an interview:

- Double-check the time and place of the interview.
- Dress appropriately for the impression you wish to create.
- Get to the general location early so you can appear for the interview on time or a little early.
- Bring a pad and pen.
- Find out the interviewer's name in advance and remember it.
- Let the interviewer initiate the handshake; when you do shake hands, look the interviewer in the eye.
- Don't chew gum.
- Use good body language and good spoken language—don't slouch, look out the window, or stare at you own shoes.
- Focus outwardly: on the interview and the interviewer, not on yourself.
- If you enjoyed the interview, tell the interviewer so and thank him or her.

A useful reference on the subject of interviews is Anthony Medley's *Sweaty Palms,* Berkeley, California: Ten Speed Press, 1993, which discusses interview topics ranging from the use of silence to the misuse of sex.

In *You're Hired!,* Sharon McDonnell describes the 5 Ps of a successful interview:

- preparation,
- practice,
- positive thinking,
- punctuality, and
- politeness.

4.   **Minimum Wage.**   The answer is *b,* $5.15 an hour.

This is the federal minimum wage rate; most states also have minimum wage laws. For many, the state minimum wage is the same as the federal. As of January 1, 2000, a few states have a minimum wage rate that is higher than the federal rate (Alaska, California, Connecticut, Delaware, Hawaii, Massachusetts, Oregon, Rhode Island, Vermont and Washington); a few have a lower minimum wage rate (Georgia, Kansas, New Mexico, Ohio, Texas, and

Wyoming); and several have no state minimum wage law at all (Alabama, Arizona, Florida, Louisiana, Mississippi, South Carolina, and Tennessee).

5. **Overtime.**   *False.* The opposite is the case.

    As a general rule, salaried employees do not get paid overtime. The working hours of salaried employees are commonly less fixed, and working longer than normal business hours is sometimes expected of salaried employees. By contrast, employees who are paid at an hourly rate generally are paid extra for overtime work that is in excess of the hours they are normally expected to work. The hourly rate for overtime work is usually higher than the regular hourly wage. It can be, for example, time-and-a-half (150 percent of the regular hourly wage) or double time (200 percent).

6. **Workplace Terms.**   The correct terms are

    a. *Equal opportunity employment.* Employers who subscribe to this principle are known as "equal opportunity employers." The federal agency specifically charged with issues of equal employment is the Equal Employment Opportunity Commission (EEOC).

    b. *Unemployment compensation* (sometimes referred to simply as "unemployment" or as "worker's compensation").

7. **Benefits.**   Employers may provide employees with benefits, which may include:

    - paid vacations;
    - all or a portion of the cost of health insurance;
    - all or a portion of the cost of dental insurance;
    - contributions that match employee contributions to 401(k) retirement plans;
    - a separate pension plan;
    - life insurance coverage;
    - day care facilities;
    - employer matching of certain charitable gifts by employees;
    - counseling;
    - reimbursement of the cost of parking or mass transit; and
    - training or educational subsidies.

8. **Paycheck Deductions.**   *True.*

Employers typically withhold funds from employee paychecks to cover the employee's tax obligations. Typically withheld are funds for federal, state, and, where applicable, city income taxes. These funds are paid to the appropriate tax authorities and are credited against your income tax obligation. If your withholding exceeds the total amount of tax due, you will receive a refund. If it is less than your total tax obligation, you will have to pay the unpaid balance when you file your tax returns.

9. **Retirement Plans.**   Both government and private retirement options are available to most employees.

   a. *Social Security*—Under the Social Security program, which is administered by the federal government, all private sector employees are required to pay Social Security taxes on all earnings up to a designated income level. These funds are used to pay Social Security benefits to retirees who themselves paid Social Security taxes when they worked and are thus entitled to receive Social Security benefits.

   b. Three common private retirement plans are *Individual Retirement Accounts (IRAs), 401(k) plans,* and *Keough plans.* Each enjoys special tax advantages that allow money put in these plans to grow, or be withdrawn, without having to pay the same taxes that would have to be paid on an individual savings account.

Merely Informative
IRAs

There is now more than one type of IRA. Employees can make contributions to traditional IRAs without paying any tax on those contributed amounts. In addition, IRAs are exempt from tax on the interest or other increases in value that they achieve up until the point of retirement. Proceeds are taxed only when they are withdrawn and at the current tax rate of the IRA holder.

Roth IRAs are funded with money on which the employee has already paid taxes. From then on, however, these funds enjoy tax-free growth and accumulation. More important, when money is withdrawn from a Roth IRA, it is not taxable, regardless of how much the account has grown!

continued on next page

There are annual limits on how much an individual may contribute to an IRA, income limits for individuals and couples participating in Roth IRAs, and detailed rules about the terms and conditions of withdrawing IRA funds. Both types of IRAs enjoy substantial tax advantages, and financial planners typically advise those who have IRA or 401(k) accounts to take full advantage of the tax benefits by contributing generously to them.

10. **Tips.** *True.*

Tips, like most forms of income, are taxable. Because tips generally are paid in cash, and because employers keep no records of how much individual employees earn through tips, tax authorities make a special effort to advise taxpayers that tips are taxable to reduce underreporting of income.

More Where This Came From

The wonderful classic about finding the right career path is *What Color Is Your Parachute?* 2000, Berkeley: Ten Speed Press, 2000, by Richard Nelson Bolles.

The first eight chapters of *Welcome to the Real World.* New York: W.W. Norton & Company, 1997, by Stacy Kravetz, are devoted to Getting a Job, from the job search to alternatives to paid work.

You're Hired! New York: NTC/Contemporary Publishing, 2000, by Sharon McDonnell is a comprehensive, readable discussion of the entire process.

The RAT's Mouse

Among the web sites on employment that you can find with your computer mouse. . .

- **www.careers.yahoo.com/** Info on building your resume, finding a job, career building
- **www.careercity.com/content/cvlttr/index.cfm** A site on writing cover letters, with examples, suggested language, and tips

- **www.careerbuilder.com/gh_int_htg.html** Preparing for a job interview, making a good impression, common mistakes, and more
- **www.collegegrad.com/resumes/** The College Grad Job Hunter has lots of resume tips, cover letters, job search suggestions, etc.
- **content.monster.com/jobinfo/interview/questions/** More on job interviews, common questions, personality; many links
- **www.dol.gov/dol/esa/public/minwage/main.htm** Facts and history about the minimum wage

B. THINGS WORTH KNOWING

9. AUTOMOBILES—ANSWERS

1. **Parts of a Car.**

    a. *Spark plugs.*

    Each cylinder has a spark plug. A V-8 engine has eight cylinders and thus eight spark plugs. Spark plugs, which need to be replaced periodically, don't work if they get too heavily coated with residues or if the gap across which the spark jumps is not the correct length.

    b. *The transmission.*

    Transmissions are either automatic (the driver does not need to shift gears) or manual (the driver must physically shift gears whenever changing to a higher or lower gear). Stick shifts are cars with manual transmissions.

2. **Basic Operations.**   The answers are

    a. *False.*

    Generally, a car with front-wheel drive has better traction than a car with rear-wheel drive because the weight of the engine is over the drive wheels. The weight of the engine improves traction, and, as a result, cars with front-wheel drive generally do better in snow or mud.

    If a rear-wheel-drive car has its engine in the rear rather than in the front (an example is the classic Volkswagen Beetle), then it, too, has superior traction. Likewise, a heavy or heavily loaded car generally will have better traction than an otherwise identical but lighter car. This is why some drivers with rear-wheel-drive cars put bags of sand or cement in the trunk to improve traction (or why drivers stuck in snow or mud sometimes ask passengers to sit on the trunk to help them get unstuck).

b. *False.*

Antifreeze goes into your radiator, not your gas tank or gas line. It is designed to keep your radiator, which is filled with water, from freezing in cold weather. Because of its chemical properties, gasoline has a much lower freezing point than water and is not at risk of freezing unless temperatures are extremely low.

3.   **Basic Maintenance.**   The correct answer is *a.* This statement is *not* true. Statements *b, c,* and *d* are all true.

- The *octane rating of a gasoline* relates to its antiknock properties. High-performance engines generally require higher-octane gasoline, which is more expensive than regular gasoline, whose octane rating is slightly lower. The mileage you get depends on characteristics of your car and its engine, not on the gasoline used.
- *Air pressure in your tires*—If the pressure in your tires is too low, the ride may be squishy, your gas mileage may be reduced, and the tires will wear out faster than they would otherwise. If the pressure is too high, the ride may be unnecessarily rough and wear may be excessive.
- *Windshield washer fluid*—Most windshield washer fluid is a mild solution that helps clean your windshield and has a lower freezing point than water.
- *Engine oil*—Automobile manufacturers specify that engine oil, the lubricant for the internal parts of your engine, should be changed periodically. The reason is that, as the car is driven, engine oil gets dirty and accumulates particles of dirt and debris from operating the engine. Oil drained from an engine during an oil change is typically darker and thicker than the new oil that replaces it. If the oil is not changed, it can become so dirty that it ceases to serve its lubricating function well and can cause damage or unnecessary wear on engine parts.

AUTOMOBILES

Merely Informative
How to Perform Basic Maintenance

Tire pressure—Your owner's manual or a sticker on the door or door frame of the car should tell you the pressure to which your tires should be inflated (it may not be the same for the front and rear tires). You can check pressure with a hand pressure gauge. Air is added to tires through a valve on each tire. Find the valve, unscrew the valve cap, and add air from the air hose. (Air hoses are commonly found at gas stations or car washes.)

Two helpful things to remember:

- When adding air to your tire, make sure the air is going into the tire. To get the air into the tire, make sure that the pin in the center of the air hose is depressing the pin in the center of the tire valve. If it isn't, the air will escape, usually making a distinctive hissing sound that people at a gas station will recognize.
- Don't overinflate the tire. To avoid overinflating, add just a little air at a time and, unless the air pump has a pressure gauge that tells you as the pressure changes, check the pressure with a hand pressure gauge (the gas station will have one). If you put too much air in the tire, you can bleed off some by using the pin on the pressure gauge to depress the pin in the center of the tire valve and let some of the air hiss out.

If you're inflating a bicycle tire, it's relatively easy to overinflate the tire quickly, and even to burst the tube in the tire. This will amuse the gas station attendants.

Windshield washer fluid—To replenish your windshield washer fluid, you need to locate the reservoir that holds the fluid, which is usually under the hood. Either at or near the reservoir, you will find a spout or opening into which you should pour the windshield washer fluid. Some windshield washer fluid reservoirs are ingeniously located in hard-to-reach places and require a funnel, an abnormally long forearm, or the ability to pour accurately from a gallon jug into a small opening from a height of about three feet.

Checking the oil—Once you learn how, you can check to see if your engine oil is low yourself. Protruding somewhere from your engine is the handle of a device commonly known as a dipstick. A dipstick is a round or flat metal rod (picture it as a miniature, 12- to 18-inch sword). It allows you to check the level of engine oil, an essential fluid for your car.

continued on next page

To check your oil, remove the dipstick, wipe the oil off, reinsert the dipstick all the way, remove the dipstick again, and look to see how far up the stick you see oil. If oil is at or near the top line on the dipstick, you don't need to add oil. If it is at or below the second line, you need oil. If in doubt, ask. Remember: if you've been driving, the engine block may be very hot.

Changing your oil as frequently as, or more frequently than, the owner's manual recommends will prolong the life of your car. Driving with low or no oil can seriously damage your car. If your red oil indicator light comes on, stop.

4. **Flat Tires.** The answer is *b*.

Do not jack up the car before loosening the lugs because, if the car has been jacked up and the wheel is off the ground, you may not be able to loosen lugs that are very tight. If you turn the lug wrench hard, the tire may simply spin because it is off the ground and you can get no traction.

Instead, loosen each of the lugs a turn or two before jacking up the car. At that point, the flat tire will be flat on the ground, held there by the full weight of the car. Loosen each lug at that point so that when you jack up the car, you can loosen the lugs the rest of the way with your fingers.

Merely Informative
More on Changing a Flat

Here are a few of the things you want to be sure to do, including items *a*, *c*, and *d*:

- If you're driving when the tire goes flat, pull well off the road. If your flat is on the left side of the car, you want to pull the car even farther off the road so that while you're working on the tire, you and the car will be away from passing cars. A parking lot is ideal.
- Park on a flat spot, not an incline.
- Put the car in gear and apply the emergency brake to ensure that the car doesn't begin to roll once you've jacked up the car. If it rolls, it could fall off the jack and possibly crush anything (including fingers and hands) between the wheel and the ground.
- Locate the jack, lug wrench, and spare tire.

continued on next page

- Remove the hubcap and loosen the lugs (the nuts that hold the tire in place) before you jack up the car.
- Jack up the car, remove the flat, and replace it with the spare. You want to jack the car up higher than is needed to remove the flat tire—you'll need greater clearance to put on the spare, which is inflated and therefore bigger than the flat tire you have removed.
- Put the lugs on and tighten them by hand. (If you lower the car without doing this first, the weight of the car may push the wheel out of position and make it harder to tighten all the lugs completely.)
- Gently let the car down and remove the jack.
- Tighten the lugs with the lug wrench.
- Put the flat, jack, and lug wrench in the trunk. Replace the hubcap if it fits the spare.
- Take the flat to be repaired.

Common mistakes:

- Misplacing the lugs (put them in the upside-down hubcap)
- Jacking the car up enough to get the flat off but not enough to get the fully inflated spare tire on (the consequences are not serious: you just have to jack the car up a little higher)
- Jacking the car up before loosening the lugs
- Driving off and leaving the flat, jack, lug wrench, hubcap, or whatever you took out of the trunk to get to the jack

More Where This Game From

Your owner's manual almost certainly contains instructions for using the jack. See also, Bob Scher, *The Little Know-How Book*, New York: Harmony Books, 1993, pp. 196–99 ("Unscrew something, replace it with something else, screw it back on. Millions upon millions of people have changed tires without mishap and so can you."); S. Tompkins, *I Can Fix That,* New York: Harlequin Books, 1996, pp. 152–55 ("Learning to change a tire was one of the most liberating events of my Fix-It life."); Sheree Byofsky and Paul Fargis, *The Big Book of Life's Instructions,* New York: Stonesong Press, 1995, pp. 35–38 ("The most important thing is to recognize a flat immediately and get off the road.").

5. **Emergencies.**

    a. *Signaling for help.* Three signals of distress:
       - raise the hood of your car;
       - tie a white handkerchief or cloth to the top of the radio aerial, the side mirror, or the driver's door handle or;
       - turn on your flashers.

       Wait for help.

    b. *Overheating.* In case of overheating, immediately pull off the road and turn the ignition off. Driving with an overheated engine can seriously damage your car. Let the car cool down and try to get help. Don't try to check the radiator or add water until the car has cooled.

       There are at least two signs that a car is overheating:
       - a warning indicator light comes on or the needle of your temperature gauge is pointing at an "H" or is in a red zone, or
       - you—or other motorists who are glad they are not you—see steam coming out from under your hood.

       When your engine overheats, it must be allowed to cool down, and water must be added to the radiator. (*Note:* There are other reasons that cars overheat besides a radiator leak or low water—a malfunctioning fan belt or a blocked hose, for example.)

       Warning: Opening the radiator cap on an overheated car can be dangerous. First, the radiator and the radiator cap are likely to be very hot. You can easily burn yourself by touching a hot radiator. Second, and more important, if you do open the cap, you can be scalded by escaping steam. This is known as adding insult to injury. Safest plan: Let the car cool and have someone who opens radiators every day open your radiator cap.

    c. *Jumper Cables.* Jumper cables may be used to jump-start a car that has a dead battery. Through jumper cables, power is passed from the car with electrical power to the car that has none. Once the car with the dead battery starts, it will keep running. If you turn off the engine soon after it has been jump-started, it may not start again under its own power. *Follow the instructions for jumper cables exactly.* Doing it wrong can damage one or both batteries. Among the things to remember:

- Both cars should be turned off and in neutral or park, not in gear. They should be parked so that the jumper cables can reach from one car's battery to the other.
- One end of one jumper cable should be attached to the positive (+) terminal of one battery; the other end of the same cable should be attached to the positive (+) terminal of the other battery. A jumper cable should *never* connect a positive terminal to a negative terminal.
- One end of the other jumper cable should be attached to the negative (-) terminal of the good battery; the other end of that cable should be attached to a ground—that is, to some metal part of the body of the car with the dead battery.
- Start the car with the good battery, and let it idle for a minute. Then start the car with the dead battery. Once both engines are running normally, let them idle for another couple of minutes.
- Disconnect the cables in reverse order from how they were connected. First remove the connection to the ground, then the other end of the same cable. Then disconnect the second cable.

6. **Safety Tips.**

a. *Tailgating*

One rule of thumb is that you should *be far enough away from the car in front of you that it takes you at least two seconds to reach the spot where that car is.* For example, if the car ahead of you passes a road sign, you should be able to count, "one-thousand-one, one-thousand-two," before you pass that same sign.

Another rule of thumb is that you should allow one car length of distance between you and the car ahead of you for every 10 miles per hour (mph) that you are moving. At 30 mph, you should be 3 car lengths away; at 50 mph, 5 car lengths away.

b. *Combating Drowsiness*

If you get sleepy when driving, the safe solution is to stop driving. The first three remedies listed below achieve that objective:

- If another person is with you, pull over, switch drivers, and let that person drive.
- Pull in to a rest stop, get out of the car, and do some stretching or exercise to get your blood moving.

- Pull in to a rest stop or pull safely off the road, lock the car, and take a nap.

  Sometimes you can fend off drowsiness and invigorate yourself before you get sleepy using some of the following techniques:

- Open the windows and get a blast of fresh air. Lower the temperature: if it's winter, turn the heat down; if it's summer, turn the air conditioning up.
- Wiggle your toes vigorously.
- Sing out loud—loudly. The national anthem, camp songs, musicals, nursery rhymes—anything will do.
- Think about something that makes you mad, is funny, is stimulating, or makes you jealous.
- Bite the insides of your cheeks, suck in your stomach, or flex your pectoral muscles.
- Eat or drink.

7. **Stick-Shift Cars.**

   a. *False.* When you downshift into a lower gear while driving, your engine's RPMs *increase.* Because your maximum speed in a lower gear is lower than in a higher gear, the high RPMs in the lower gear have the natural effect of braking or slowing your car. (Don't downshift too quickly or you risk abruptly increasing the RPMs to a level that is too high.)

   b. *False.* Depressing the clutch disengages the gears and allows you to shift to a different gear. Thus, in shifting from first to second gear, for example, you depress the clutch, shift into the next gear, and then slowly release the clutch. Shifting without fully depressing the clutch can result in gears grinding and causing damage to your transmission.

Merely Informative   Stick Shifts

In a car with a manual transmission, or a "stick shift," the driver must change gears manually as the speed of the car increases or decreases. When starting from a stop, the driver begins in first gear and, as the speed of the car increases,

continued on next page

shifts into second gear, then third, then fourth. Most cars have four or five forward gears.

By contrast, cars with automatic transmissions change gears—as the term suggests—automatically. As the speed of the car increases, the transmission changes gears without the driver having to do anything. If you listen for it, you can hear or feel the change when the transmission shifts to a higher gear.

You can always tell if a car has a stick shift by looking to see if the car has a clutch. Every car with a manual transmission has a clutch pedal next to the brake pedal. You must depress the clutch whenever you shift gears.

The gearshift for most cars with standard transmissions is on the floor. (That is also the case with many automatic transmissions.) The pattern of the forward gears, usually depicted on the gearshift housing, is normally an "H," with first gear it upper left, second gear at lower left, third gear at upper right, and fourth gear at lower right. In a car with a stick shift, the gearshift indicator shows all of these gears, including first. It does not show a "D" for drive, which is a telltale sign of an automatic transmission.

Being able to drive a stick shift well requires you to shift smoothly from one gear to the next as the car accelerates without grinding the gears or causing the car to lurch. You also should be able to downshift into a lower gear as the car decelerates. And you should be able to start smoothly from a stop in both first gear and reverse. Last, you must be able to start in first gear from a stop while parked on an uphill incline.

8. **Cars and the Law.**

    a. *Title.* Your title to a car is your official certificate of ownership and the most authoritative proof of ownership. It is like a deed to a piece of property or title to a house. Unlike your registration and insurance information, your title need not be carried with you in your car. It should be kept in a safe place, however. If you sell your car, you transfer title to the person who buys it.

    It is a good idea to keep information about your automobile insurance in your car (in some states it is required), including your policy number and a telephone number you can call in case of an emergency.

If you belong to an emergency road service, such as the American Automobile Association (AAA), you should also keep your membership card with you or in the car. Otherwise, you need not have bothered to join.

b. *Points.* Unlike all the other "points" you have encountered elsewhere in life (basketball, diving, history essay tests, etc.), in driving you don't want points. A moving violation, such as speeding, usually results in your receiving "points" on your driver's license. If you accumulate a specified number of points within a designated period, you can lose your driver's license.

c. *The Denver Boot.* The Denver Boot, or simply "the Boot," is a dreaded device that police sometimes use to immobilize a car that has been ticketed and/or has unpaid traffic or parking tickets. Attached to the wheel, the Denver Boot cannot be removed without risking serious damage to the wheel, and when it's on a wheel, the car cannot be driven.

Merely Informative
Maintaining the Right-of-Way

There are those whose driving decisions appear to be dictated solely by a determination of who has the "right-of-way." That may not always be the most important factor, however. Consider the following verse.

Maintaining the Right of Way

Here lies the driver we're mourning today,
He died maintaining the right-of-way,
He was right, dead right, as he sped along,
But he's dead, just as dead, as if he'd been dead wrong.

---

9. **Engines—The Basics.** The correct answers are

a. The essential elements are

- *fuel* (gasoline, petrol),
- *air* (oxygen), and
- *a spark* (fire).

The fundamental concepts are not as complicated. Cars today operate in many of the same basic ways that Model A Fords operated in 1930. For both, the source of power is the internal combustion engine.

Three basic ingredients are essential for combustion to occur. If your car won't start, it's probably because one of the three—*fuel* (gasoline), *air* (oxygen), or a *spark* to ignite the other two—is missing.

Combustion occurs when fuel burns, and combustion in a confined space can produce a controlled explosion. In automobile engines, combustion occurs through small, controlled explosions inside chambers in the engine—hence, the term, "internal combustion engine."

Except for London taxis and other vehicles powered by diesel engines, the fuel for most cars is gasoline.

b. Essential engine parts are
   (1) *fuel pump,*
   (2) *cylinders,*
   (3) *piston,*
   (4) *drive train* (also correct if you named any of its components, including the crankshaft, the drive shaft, the transmission, the axle, or the differential)
   (5) *exhaust system* (exhaust manifold, muffler, tailpipe).

In your automobile engine, a *fuel pump* moves gasoline from the gas tank through the fuel line and through a gasoline filter to the engine.

Gasoline, which is mixed with air in a carburetor or through a fuel injection system, is then injected into combustion chambers called *cylinders.* Inside the cylinders, the fuel mixture is compressed by the up-and-down motion of snug-fitting plungers called *pistons.* The car's electrical system then provides a spark to the compressed air and gasoline mixture. The resulting combustion forcefully pushes the piston back to the other end of the cylinder.

Most cars have four, six, or eight cylinders. Each cylinder has a piston. The combustion "explosions" that occur in each cylinder are numerous—thousands a minute—and are carefully sequenced. The sound that results is the familiar hum of an automobile engine.

The force of the pistons being driven back to the end of the cylinders is the source of power in a car engine. Through a series of mechanical connections, that power is translated from the motion of the pistons ultimately to the wheels that power the car. That power is transmitted through a series of rapidly rotating gears and shafts. The parts through which that motion and power are transmitted include the *crankshaft,* the gears of the *transmission,* the *drive shaft,* and the *power axle.* Together, the shafts and gears are sometimes referred to as the *drive train.*

The gases that remain after combustion in the engine are removed from the engine through the *exhaust system.* Components of the exhaust system include the *exhaust manifold,* the *muffler,* and the *tailpipe.*

When the wheels turn, the car moves. To make it move faster, you press the accelerator, which increases the flow of gasoline to the engine, the rate of combustion in the engine, and the power transmitted ultimately to the wheels. Let up on the accelerator, and the car moves more slowly.

Merely Informative
A Car's Systems

Just as the human body has various systems—skeletal, muscular, nervous, circulatory, respiratory, digestive, etc.—so, too, does a car have separate systems. It may be helpful to think about each of those systems separately.

a. *Electrical system*—A car stores and generates electricity, which in turn operates many devices in the car. Electricity is stored in the battery, which is the source of electricity when you first start the car. When a car is being driven, it generates electricity through a generator or alternator. Although gasoline is the primary fuel for the car, electricity is also an essential source of power.

b. *Cooling system*—With its fast-moving metal parts, an automobile engine gets hot. If It Is not cooled properly, it can overheat and stop working. Although some engines are air-cooled, most car engines are water-cooled. The water, stored in the radiator, is circulated around the engine block and then cooled by the force of air against the radiator.

c. *Oil system*—With metal moving against metal, it is essential that metal parts be lubricated. Motor oil is the lubricant; it is added to the engine and lubricates its moving parts. As the car is driven, the oil gets dirty and must be changed periodically—drained out and replaced with new oil.

continued on next page

d. *Braking system*—Brakes stop the car by rubbing against the wheels and slowing them down. The self-contained system that applies the brakes when you press the brake pedal is the braking system. This system includes a second set of brakes, the emergency or hand brake.

e. *Suspension system*—Cars ride more smoothly than wagons because they have suspension systems to cushion bumps in the road. Suspension systems can include various types of springs, shock absorbers, air cushions, and inflated tires to help absorb bumps and make the ride smooth.

10. **Insurance.**

a. *Liability insurance.* Auto liability insurance provides insurance protection in case you injure another person or damage another person's property when you are driving. It is the most important type of insurance to have and is mandatory in most states.

The limits of your liability insurance, which can be increased by paying a higher premium, establish a maximum amount that the insurance company must pay to any one person or for any one accident. For example, $50,000/$100,000 coverage means that, in the case of an accident in which you are at fault, the insurance company pays for your legal liability up to $50,000 to each individual injured and up to a total of $100,000 for any single accident.

b. *Collision Coverage.* Collision coverage pays for damage to the vehicle caused by a collision—a mashed fender, for example. In many states collision coverage is not mandatory. If you do not have this coverage and you are involved in an accident in which you were at fault, your insurance coverage will pay none of the cost of repairs to your car. It is also common for collision coverage to be subject to a deductible (see below), in which event you share the cost of repairing damage to a vehicle you caused, even if you have collision coverage.

c. *Deductible.* A policy deductible is the amount you must pay before your insurance coverage kicks in. For example, if you do $800 worth of damage to your car in a collision, and your have a $250 deductible, you pay the first $250, and the insurance company pays the remaining $550. The higher a deductible you're willing to accept, the lower your premium.

More Where This Came From

The Car Book. J. Gillis, Hammersmith, UK: Harper Collins, 2001, *How to Make Your Car Last Almost Forever,* New York: Perigee Books, 1987.

 *The RAT's Mouse*

If you want to find out more by using a computer to check some informative web sites, you might use your mouse to check the following:

- **www.cartalk.cars.com** Access to the website of NPR's *Car Talk,* a weekly radio show with a devoted following that provides humor to real world automotive advice and reports on particular car models
- **www.madd.org** Mothers Against Drunk Driving
- **www.autos.yahoo.com** Information on buying and selling cars, car maintenance, news stories, and more
- **www.aol.com/webcenters/autos** Check the maintenance link—how to change a tire, change the oil, jump-start a car; also get a tour under the hood

10. COMPUTERS—ANSWERS

1. **Computer Functions.**   The correct answers are

   a. *Modem*

   b. *Software*

   c. *Word processing*

   a. A *modem* allows you to connect your computer to other computers or other destinations outside your immediate system, such as Internet sites or e-mail connections. The faster the modem, the more quickly it can transfer information. A fast modem will reduce the amount of time you spend online. In a modem, you want speed.

COMPUTERS

**Merely Informative
Modems, and Better**

The term *modem* comes from the two words: "modulation" and "demodulation." Modulation is the process of converting digital signals (the form of computer signals) to analog signals (the signals used in most telephone systems); demodulation is the opposite. Modems operate through existing telephone lines.

A faster alternative to a modem is a Digital Subscriber Line (DSL). DSL lines, marketed by telephone companies and Internet Service Providers (ISPs), are separate cables that provide faster Internet access than is available through a modem (often 10 times faster than a 56K modem).

Cable modems, marketed through cable companies, are another fast alternative to modems. Cable modems can be less expensive because a single coaxial cable can be shared among several users; the increased traffic can slow access.

T1 lines are considerably faster than either DSLs or cable modems, but because they are so expensive, they typically are used only in commercial applications.

---

b. *Software* is the intelligence in a computer. Without it, computer hardware will not operate. Once installed on a computer, software—which comes stored on a disk or CD—tells the hardware what to do and when, where, and how to do it. Certain software is built into the computer (operating system software); other software may be bought or downloaded and added to the computer system to allow the computer to perform a particular function (application software). Examples of popular software are word processing software, games, and spreadsheets.

c. *Word processing* is used to draft documents, write letters, and create fliers, newsletters, invitations, and great novels. It is electronic typing but with such advantages as ease of correction, ease of editing, multiple versions, convenient storing of drafts, etc. Compared to the dinosaurs that preceded it—carbon paper, correction fluid, self-correcting typewriters, etc.—it is enormously efficient. One potential horror of word processing is losing a document. (See question 6.) Examples of word processing software are WordPerfect and Microsoft Word.

2. **Hardware.**   Each of the following is an example of computer hardware (as distinguished from software, which is found on disks or CDs):
   - Monitor (the computer screen)
   - Computer, or central processing unit (CPU)
   - Keyboard
   - Printer
   - Mouse
   - Speakers
   - Cables, connectors

3. **Laptops.**   The answer is *b*.

   LCD screens are more space efficient, but they also use considerably *less* electricity than do conventional desktop monitors. As a result, they draw less battery power.

   A laptop, designed to be more compact and lighter but equally powerful, is generally more expensive than a similarly equipped desktop version. Because laptops are portable, battery life is important; the more expensive, newer lithium-ion batteries give longer battery life. Also because they are portable and compact, laptops typically do not have a mouse, which is an external feature on most desktops. Instead, laptops use a touchpad, pointing stick, or trackball as pointing devices.

4. **Units of Data.**   The correct order, from smallest to largest, is

Byte	One byte is one character (letter, number, etc.), and a byte of data consists of eight bits of data
Kilobyte (K)	1,024 characters (about one double-spaced page of text)
Megabyte (M)	1,048,576 characters (about a novel)
Gigabyte (GB)	1,073,741,824 (about a thousand novels, or what you'll be expected to read in college [just kidding])

5. **Complex Programs.**   The correct answer is *b*, memory.

   Memory, or random access memory (RAM), determines how much data a computer can access selectively. Random access allows a computer to retrieve particular data (like accessing a particular song on a CD) without searching or sifting through all the data (without listening to each song in order). Certain programs require substantial memory to function effectively. If a computer does not have adequate memory, it will not be able to run Windows 95, for example. You can enhance a computer's performance by adding memory.

6. **Data.**   There are several correct answers to how to save or how to lose data on a computer.

Saving Data. Ways that you can save data on a computer include:

a. Use the "Save" command—On most computers a document can be saved by using a keyboard command or clicking on an icon that saves the document.

b. Name the document—Naming a document does not, in and of itself, save a document. However, if you name a document, you will be asked whether you want to save it. Click on "Save" and resume work on the document.

c. Exit the document—Again, this doesn't save the document automatically, but the process of exiting will cue you to save the document, which you must do to preserve it.

d. Make an extra copy—You can do this by giving a document two different names, by copying the document to both your hard drive and a floppy disk, or by printing a hard copy. The hard copy solution is a bit antiquated, but it is a copy.

Losing Data. You can lose a document in the following ways:

a. Drafting a document on a laptop, not saving it, and allowing your battery to run out.

b. Exiting the document or exiting word processing without saving, or naming and saving, the document first.

c. Deleting the document inadvertently.

d. Losing the floppy disk the document is on. (This is not a technology-based risk. It's also possible to lose your entire computer.)

e. Being infected by a virus—Computer viruses can wreak all types of havoc, including destruction of data.

7. **Floppy Disks.**   *True.*

Floppy disks store data through the use of magnetic impulses. As a result, new magnetic impulses over information on a disk can destroy or scramble that data. Magnetic culprits can include refrigerator magnets, photocopiers, audio speakers, phone handsets, etc. (Now you have one more correct answer for the preceding question.)

Storing floppy disks in very cold or very hot place, or spilling beverages on them can also cause problems with the data. While we're on the subject, spilling a soft drink or coffee onto your computer or your keyboard can be worse, as well you might guess. While working at your computer, chewing gum is generally safer than drinking from plastic cups.

8. **Computer Acronyms and Symbols.**   The correct answers are

   a. *Read Only Memory.* This term, a part of the familiar term CD-ROM, refers to a memory chip that can be accessed but not manipulated. Thus, the data on a CD-ROM can be read, but they cannot be edited, changed, or modified.

   b. *Central Processing Unit.* The central processing unit is the heart of the computer. It specifically refers to the main microprocessor or "chip." The capacity of the CPU determines how fast the computer will operate. Speed is measured in millions of cycles per second, or megahertz (MHz). Recent generations of CPUs include the Pentium (586) and the Pentium Pro (686). The MMX (multimedia extension) may be added to either chip to improve multimedia tasks dramatically.

Merely Informative "Clean Rooms"

Microprocessors are manufactured in facilities that must be spotless and dust-free. Such "clean rooms" are found in all semiconductor manufacturing plants. Computer manufacturers' clean rooms are usually far cleaner than hospital operating rooms: according to one book, "tens of thousands of times cleaner than hospital operating rooms."

Intel, Motorola, AMD, and Cyrix are some of the companies with rooms like that.

---

   c. *A:.* "A:" is the symbol that refers to the computer's first drive. It is usually assigned to the floppy disk or 3.5" disk drive of the computer. By contrast, the hard disk drive, embedded in the computer, is usually signified by the symbol "C:."

d. *Graphic User Interface.* This term (pronounced "gooey") refers to a computer environment that is based more on pictures or images than on text. Through a GUI, you can give commands or make choices by clicking on icons or images rather than by typing in commands.

9. **Computer Terms.**

a. *Right-click.* This term, as you would guess, refers to clicking on the button on the right side of the mouse. The left-click is the signal normally used to make a simple selection or give a simple command. A double-click is often required to open a program or a document. "Drag and Drop" is another mouse function that allows you to move an item on the screen to a different location or a different file.

b. *Mac.* Macs, or Macintosh computers, were introduced in 1984 and were the first successful computers to have a mouse, icons, windows, and other types of graphical interface. Although they have a smaller share of the market than PCs, Macs have a devoted following that proudly cites the various advantages that Macs are widely regarded as having, including their desktop layout and design capabilities.

c. *Reboot.* When you reboot by holding down the Ctrl and Alt keys and then hitting the Delete key, you instruct your computer to erase data currently in memory and reload the operating system. This process is sometimes necessary if your computer appears to be stuck and does not respond to commands. By rebooting, however, you may lose the data in the document on which you are working if it has not been saved.

d. *DVD-ROM.* DVDs arc Digital Video Disc-ROMs, a medium that has capacity and versatility beyond that of CDs. Movies are increasingly available in DVD format. A DVD-ROM drive can also read CD-ROM discs.

e. *Scanner.* A scanner is a piece of equipment (a flatbed scanner looks like a flat copying machine) into which text or graphic documents can be inserted. The scanner reads the document and then enters it into your computer database.

10. **The Internet.**   The correct answer is *e*. None of the first four statements is true.

> The Internet is essentially unregulated. Who establishes a web site and what it says are not subject to government control or regulation, and there are no controls over the accuracy of the information.
>
> Information transmitted by e-mail over the Internet is not secure from interception by unauthorized persons. Using the Internet for e-mail is more like using a cell phone, conversations may be intercepted or overheard, than it is like using a telephone whose signals are transmitted over hard wire.
>
> The rules governing electronic commerce are still being debated and developed, and consumer protections have not yet been established in the same manner as they have for other, more conventional means of commerce.
>
> Certain web sites may be accessed only for a fee. This is often the case with sites containing pornographic information or information that is essentially being offered for sale.

More Where This Came From

A wonderfully readable and understandable book on computers is *Computers Simplified* (3rd edition). Foster City, California: IDG Books Worldwide, 1996. (one of the IDG 3-D Visual Series)

See also:

PCs for Dummies. Foster City, California: IDG Books Worldwide, 1996. by Dan Gookin;

How To Use Your Computer. Emeryville, California: Ziff Davis Press, 1996. by Lisa Biow.

 *The RAT's Mouse*

Web sites you can reach using a computer and a mouse:

- **www.homepages.enterprise.net/jenko/Glossary/G.htm** A glossary of PC and Internet terminology, arranged alphabetically

- **www.sc.edu/beaufort/library/bones.html** Basics about how to use a search engine, search tips, etc.
- **www.cnet.com/** Includes everything from games to tech news to downloads to financial reviews to web building
- **www.magicpub.com/netprimer/acronyms.html** Acronyms (like "gtg" for "got to go") that are popularly used in e-mails and over the internet

11. THE BIBLE—ANSWERS

1. **The First Five Books of the Bible.** The correct answer is *c.*

The *Torah,* the holy book of Judaism, consists of the first five books of the Bible, authorship of which Jews ascribe to Moses.

The Old Testament, including the first five books of the Bible, does not deal with Jesus Christ. Rather, the life and teachings of Jesus are subjects of the New Testament.

The holy book of Islam, the *Koran,* discusses some of the same people and events as the Bible (Moses, Joseph and his brothers, Abraham, Noah, Sodom and Gomorrah), but it does not directly incorporate portions of the Bible. In Islam, the *Koran* contains the collected revelations received by Mohammed and treats Jesus as one in a series of God's prophets.

The Old Testament was written primarily in Hebrew (some Aramaic) and later translated into Greek.

2. **Books of the Old Testament.** The books of the Old Testament, which are sometimes grouped as noted below, are the following:

The Pentateuch (Creation through the death of Moses, just before the Israelites entered the Promised Land, is covered chronologically in the Pentateuch, which also sets forth guidance for the moral behavior of the Israelites)

Genesis   Numbers
Exodus   Deuteronomy
Leviticus

The Historical Books (from the death of Moses to the conquest of Canaan through the postexile period of 400 B.C.:

Joshua	1 Chronicles
Judges	2 Chronicles
Ruth	Ezra
1 Samuel	Nehemiah
2 Samuel	Esther
1 Kings	
2 Kings	

The Wisdom Books (poetry and philosophical maxims expressing the faith of the Israelites; widely reflected in Western literature):

Job	Ecclesiastes
Psalms	Song of Solomon
Proverbs	

The Prophets

Isaiah	Jonah
Jeremiah	Micah
Lamentations	Nahum
Ezekiel	Habakkuk
Daniel	Zephaniah
Hosea	Haggai
Joel	Zechariah
Amos	Malachi
Obadiah	

3. **Prophets.**

Isaiah, Jeremiah, and Ezekiel are often regarded as the three great prophets. Daniel, who rose from captivity to become prime minister of Babylon, and Hosea, who married an adulteress to show that God was faithful even when Israel was not faithful to him, are also prominent figures. In addition, each of the other authors of books of the last section of the Old Testament, set forth above, are correct answers.

4. **The Exodus.**

   a. The ten plagues visited on the Egyptians in the book of Exodus were

   - turning the water of the Nile to blood,
   - frogs,
   - lice,
   - flies,
   - death of livestock,
   - boils and sores,
   - hail, which destroyed the crops,
   - locusts,
   - darkness for three days, and
   - death of all firstborn sons.

   b. *Passover Seder.* Passover celebrates the angel of death's passing over the homes of the Israelites whose doorways were marked with lamb's blood as a sign of obedience to God. The Last Supper in the New Testament was Jesus's celebration of Passover the night before he was crucified.

   c. *The Covenant and the Ark.* (Both featured in the celebrated film, *Raiders of the Lost Ark.*) The Ten Commandments, the laws of the covenant, were engraved on two stone tablets and deposited in the ark. The ark was described as a wooden chest made of acacia wood, overlaid with gold, with a solid gold lid and two golden rings on each side through which poles could be inserted for carrying the ark.

5. **The Ten Commandments.**   According to the books of Exodus (chapter 20) and Deuteronomy (chapter 5), the Ten Commandments given by God to Moses were

   - You shall have no other gods before me.
   - You shall not make unto thee any graven image. . .
   - You shall not take the name of the Lord thy God in vain.
   - Remember the Sabbath day, to keep it holy.
   - Honor your father and your mother.
   - You shall not kill.
   - You shall not commit adultery.
   - You shall not steal.
   - You shall not bear false witness against your neighbor.
   - You shall not covet . . . anything that is your neighbor's.

6. **Biblical Pairs.**

 a. *David and Bathsheba* (2 Samuel: 11). David had an affair with Bathsheba, the wife of Uriah the Hittite. When David learned that Bathsheba had become pregnant, David arranged for Uriah to be killed in battle. As punishment from God for their sin, David and Bathsheba's baby died; however, their next son, Solomon, succeeded David as king.

 b. *Cain killed Abel* (Genesis 4:1–16). According to the book of Genesis, Cain, a son of Adam and Eve, killed his brother, Abel, out of jealousy. After the murder, God asked Cain where Abel was, and Cain gave his famous reply, "I do not know; am I my brother's keeper?" After Abel was killed, Adam and Eve had another son, Seth.

 c. *Samson and Delilah* (Judges 16:4–22). Bribed by the Philistines, Delilah (after three unsuccessful attempts) persuaded Samson to tell her the source of his strength—his long hair. Delilah then shaved his head as he slept; Samson lost his strength; and the Philistines gouged out his eyes. When Samson was brought out later to be ridiculed, his hair had grown back, and he pulled down two pillars, killing all of the lords of the Philistines, as well as himself.

 d. *Sodom and Gomorrah* (Genesis 19:1–29). Sodom and Gomorrah, two evil cities, were destroyed by God with "brimstone and fire." Before the destruction, two angels warned Lot and his family to flee the city and not look back. They did, but Lot's wife did look back and was turned into a pillar of salt.

 e. *Sinai* (Exodus 20:20–25) *and Ararat* (Genesis 8:4). Speculation about the exact location of these two biblical landmarks has focused, for Sinai, on Jebel Musa in the mountain range on the Sinai peninsula in modern day Egypt and, in the case of Ararat, on a mountainous area of Turkey, near Armenia.

7. **The Languages of the Bible.** The answer is *c*, the Old Testament was written primarily in Hebrew, the New Testament in Greek.

 Although some small portions of the Old Testament were written in Aramaic (parts of Ezra, Daniel, and Jeremiah), most of the original language was Hebrew. The New Testament was written in *koine*, or common, Greek, the language of the people, in contrast to classical Greek, in which earlier Greek literature was written.

Merely Informative
Origins of Biblical Text

There has been much scholarship on both the origins and the translations of the books of the Bible. The books of the Old Testament, which present special translation problems from the original Hebrew and Aramaic, were accumulated over several hundred years. Parts of the Book of Deuteronomy have been traced to a document dated as older than 600 years B.C.E. (B.C.). Other books were compiled and edited at about the same time. Various books were disputed (the books of "the Apocrypha" are excluded from most versions of the Old Testament), and the current Old Testament is largely based on an edited Hebrew text done by Jewish scholars, the Masoretes, between 600 C.E. (A.D.). and the 10th century.

The books of the New Testament, by contrast, are believed to have been written within a period of less than 100 years. The notes to the *New Oxford Annotated Bible* attribute the first written gospels to John Mark, a disciple of the apostle Peter. According to the New Oxford Bible, existing primary sources of New Testament text are "Greek manuscripts, early translations into other languages (primarily Syriac, Latin, and Coptic), and quotations from the New Testament made by early ecclesiastical writers."

8. **The New Testament.**   The answer is *c*, which is the only statement about the New Testament that is *false*.

Most of the books of the New Testament that are letters, or "epistles," are believed to have been written not by Jesus, but by the apostle Paul. The New Testament comprises nearly 30 books, 23 of which are letters. Paul's letters were to, among others, the people of Rome, Corinth, Galatia, Ephesia, Colossae, and Thessalonica and to Timothy and Titus.

Each of the other statements is true.

- Jesus was born of a Jewish mother, Mary. The New Testament traces Jesus's lineage to King David.
- At that time, the Roman empire stretched from northwestern Europe to Egypt, and Augustus was the emperor.
- The disciples of Jesus were Simon Peter, James, John, Andrew, Philip, Bartholomew, Matthew, Thomas, James the son of Alphaeus, Thaddeus, Simon the Zealot, and Judas Iscariot.
- When crucified, Jesus was in his 30s.

9. **The Teachings of Jesus.**

   a. *The Gospels.* The word "gospel" means good news, specifically the good news of salvation as described in the New Testament.

   b. *Parables.* Another example of a parable—a story with a religious message—is the story of the prodigal son.

   c. *Eternal life, or salvation.*

10. **The Letters of Paul.**   The answers are *f* and *g*, Turkey and Greece.

   Ephesus and Galatia were in Asia Minor, which is now Turkey. Corinth, Thessalonika, and Philippi are in modern day Greece. At the time of Paul's journeys, however, Thessalonika and Philippi were part of what was then Macedonia. Like most countries that existed 2,000 years ago, Macedonia's boundaries have changed, and current day Macedonia, which only recently became an independent country again, is considerably smaller than it once was.

   In addition to Asia Minor, Greece, and Macedonia, Paul's journeys also took him to cities that are in current day Lebanon, Syria, Cyprus, Crete, Malta, Sicily, and Italy (Rome).

Merely Informative
More Geography of the Bible

Other tidbits of modern geography . . . In what modern countries would you have found Mount Ararat? Sheba (as in Queen of . . .)? Babylon (and its king, Nebuchadnezzar)? Sodom and Gommorah?

   The answers are, in order, Turkey (now Agn Dagi, in northeastern Turkey near the border of Armenia and Iran); Yemen (southwestern Arabia, near the southern end of the Desert Quarter of Saudi Arabia); Iraq (on the banks of the Euphrates River and the site of a grand capital during the 6th century B.C.); Israel or Jordan (believed possibly to have been in a valley now covered by shallow waters of the Dead Sea).

More Where This Came From

See "Introduction to the New Testament," The New Oxford Annotated Bible, Revised Standard Version. New York: Oxford University Press, 1973.

Two of the large number of reference books on the Bible are

The Oxford Companion to the Bible, edited by Bruce Metzger and Michael Coogan, New York: Oxford University Press, 1993;

Linda Grenz, *Doubleday Pocket Bible Guide.* New York: Doubleday, 1997.

And, yes, there is *The Complete Idiot's Guide to the Bible,* UK: Macmillan Distribution, 1999, by Jim Bell and Stan Campbell, as well as *That's in the Bible?* New York: Dell Publishing, 1994, a Bible quiz book by Wick Allison.

12.   GEOGRAPHY—ANSWERS

1. **Time Zones.**   The answer is *b*, 9 hours later. Because the sun moves from east to west, California is 9 hours *earlier* than Paris. Paris and London are not in the same time zone; Paris is an hour later.

2. **Populous Countries.**

    The World Almanac and Book of Facts, citing the Bureau of the Census, identifies the 1999 populations of the four most populous countries to be

    1. People's Republic of China—comfortably over 1 billion (1,246,872,000)
    2. India—just over a billion (1,000,849,000)
    3. United States—less than a quarter of China's population (272,640,000)
    4. Indonesia (216,108,000)

Merely Informative
More on Populous Countries

Before its dissolution, the Soviet Union was 3d, just ahead of the U.S. Russia alone is now 6th, behind Brazil, the 5th most populous. Pakistan and Bangladesh, numbers 7 and 8, respectively, have passed Japan, now number 9. Nigeria and Mexico, numbers 10 and 11, both have populations in excess of 100 million.

   Projections for the year 2025 show India catching China, and Russia falling to 9th.

Source: *The World Almanac and Book of Facts* (2000). Mahwah, New York: World Almanac Books, 1999.

3. **Earth.**   The answer is *b*.

      The opposite is true: There is water under the Arctic ice cap, but at the South Pole, Antarctica is under the ice. This explains why you may have heard of submarines passing under the northern polar ice cap, but not of their passing under the South Pole.
      Statements a, c, and d are all true.

   a. More than two-thirds of Earth's surface is water, nearly 71 percent. The Pacific Ocean is more than twice as large as either the Atlantic Ocean or the Indian Ocean, and more than 10 times the size of the Arctic Ocean.

   c. The circumference of Earth is, in fact, about 25,000 miles. If you are flying from one city to another in the Northern Hemisphere, it is often shorter to fly in a circular route arcing north toward the North Pole than to fly on a route parallel to the equator, which may seem more logical, but is often longer.

   d. Italy and South Africa have opposite seasons because in any country south of the equator, the season is the opposite of the season in countries north of the equator. The closer you get to the equator, of course, the less of a contrast there is in the seasons.

4. **Africa, Asia, and Europe.**

      Not every country that is a correct answer is listed below. Principalities and many island countries, for example, are not included. If you happen to know correct answers that are not listed, give yourself credit for them.

GEOGRAPHY

If you happen to know the capital of Seychelles, an island country in the middle of the Indian Ocean, add one correct answer to any continent where you need it.

Countries and Capitals of Europe. We have defined Europe to include, in addition to Western and Central Europe, the former Soviet republics west of the Ural Mountains. For Europe, correct answers include:

Countries	*Capitals*
In the British Isles:	
United Kingdom	London
Ireland	Dublin

Continental Europe, generally from west to east:

Portugal	Lisbon
Spain	Madrid
Italy	Rome
Greece	Athens
France	Paris
Switzerland	Bern
Austria	Vienna
Belgium	Brussels
The Netherlands	Amsterdam (or The Hague)
Luxembourg	Luxembourg
Germany	Berlin (or Bonn)

Scandinavia:

Denmark	Copenhagen
Norway	Oslo
Sweden	Stockholm
Finland	Helsinki

Central and Eastern Europe:

Albania	Tirana
Bulgaria	Sophia
Romania	Bucharest
Hungary	Budapest
Czech Republic	Prague
Slovakia	Bratislava
Poland	Warsaw

Former republics of Yugoslavia:

Slovenia	Ljubljana
Bosnia and Herzegovina	Sarajevo
Croatia	Zagreb
Macedonia	Skopje
Yugoslavia (Serbia and Montenegro)	Belgrade

Former republics of the Soviet Union (in Europe):

Estonia	Tallinn
Latvia	Riga
Lithuania	Vilnius
Russia	Moscow
Belarus	Minsk
Ukraine	Kiev
Moldova	Chisinau

Merely Informative Others

Scotland, Northern Ireland, and Wales are part of the United Kingdom; they are not independent countries. Greenland is part of Denmark. Crete is part of Greece, Sicily part of Italy, and Corsica part of France. Monaco, on the southern coast of France, is an independent monarchy.

There have been numerous recent changes in the array of European countries and capitals. When East and West Germany were reunified in 1993, Berlin became the capital of the new Germany. The capital of West Germany had been Bonn; the capital of East Germany, Berlin. Conversely, when republics of the former Soviet Union and the former Yugoslavia declared their independence, numerous new countries and capitals came on the scene. And when Czechoslovakia divided to become the Czech Republic and Slovakia, Bratislava became a new capital.

Countries and Capitals of Africa. Geographically, the boundaries of Africa are more natural and clearer than those of Europe and Asia. Here we include Madagascar, a large island off the southeastern coast of Africa. We also count Pacific island countries as part of Asia.

Countries	Capitals
Northern and northeastern Africa:	
Morocco	Rabat
Algeria	Algiers
Tunisia	Tunis
Libya	Tripoli
Egypt	Cairo
Sudan	Khartoum
Eritrea	Asmara
Ethiopia	Addis Ababa
Somalia	Mogadishu
West Africa:	
Mauritania	Nouakchott
Senegal	Dakar
Guinea Bissau	Bissau
Guinea	Conakry
Sierra Leone	Freetown
Liberia	Monrovia
Mali	Bamako
Côte d' Ivoire (Ivory Coast)	Abidjan (de facto)
	Yamoussoukro (official)
Ghana	Accra
Burkina Faso	Ouagadougou
Togo	Lomé
Benin	Cotonou (de facto)
	Porto-Novo (official)
Niger	Niamey
Nigeria	Abuja
Central Africa:	
Chad	N'Djamena
Cameroon	Yaoundé
Central African Republic	Bangui
Congo (formerly Zaire)	Kinshasa
Gabon	Libreville
Congo Republic	Brazzaville

East Africa:

Kenya	Nairobi
Tanzania	Dar es Salaam
Uganda	Kampala
Rwanda	Kigali
Burundi	Bujumbura

Southern Africa:

Angola	Luanda
Zambia	Lusaka
Malawi	Lilongwe
Mozambique	Maputo
Namibia	Windhoek
Botswana	Gaborone
Zimbabwe	Harare
South Africa	Pretoria (administrative)
	Cape Town (legislative)
Madagascar	Antananarivo

The capital of the Seychelles is Victoria.

Countries and Capitals of Asia. For our purposes, Asia is defined to include—to the southeast—the major island countries off Southeast Asia and—to the southwest—all of the Middle East. Russia is included in Asia and in Europe.

Countries	*Capitals*
China	Beijing
Mongolia	Ulan Bator
Russia	Moscow
North Korea	Pyongyang
South Korea	Seoul
Japan	Tokyo
Taiwan	Taipei

Southeast Asia:

Vietnam	Hanoi
Laos	Vientiane
Myanmar (formerly Burma)	Rangoon
Thailand	Bangkok

Cambodia	Phnom Penh
Malaysia	Kuala Lumpur
Brunei	Bandar Seri Begawan
Indonesia	Jakarta
Philippines	Manila

The subcontinent:

Pakistan	Islamabad
Nepal	Kathmandu
Bhutan	Thimphu
Bangladesh	Dhaka
India	Delhi
Sri Lanka	Colombo

Former republics (Asian) of the Soviet Union:

Kazakhstan	Astana
Kyrgyzstan	Bishkek
Uzbekistan	Taskent
Turkmenistan	Ashgabat
Tajikistan	Dushanbe
Georgia	Tbilisi
Armenia	Yerevan
Azerbaijan	Baku

South Central Asia:

Afghanistan	Kabul
Iran	Teheran
Turkey	Ankara

Middle East:

Syria	Damascus
Jordan	Amman
Lebanon	Beirut
Israel	Jerusalem
Iraq	Baghdad
Kuwait	Kuwait
Saudi Arabia	Riyadh
Bahrain	Manama
United Arab Emirates	Abu Dhabi

Qatar	Doha
Oman	Muscat
Yemen	Sana

Merely Informative Independents

Tibet is a part of China. Siberia is part of Russia. Hong Kong, until recently a territory under British administration, became a part of China in 1997. Singapore, at the tip of Malaysia, is an independent city-state.

---

5. **Cities, Rivers, and Islands.**

   a. *World's Ten Largest Metropolitan Areas*

   Time Almanac 2001 (2000) lists estimated 2000 metropolitan populations as follows:

City	Population
1. Tokyo, Japan	34,750,000
2. New York City, U.S.	20,250,000
3. Seoul, South Korea	19,850,000
4. Mexico City, Mexico	19,750,000
5. São Paulo, Brazil	17,900,000
6. Bombay (Mumbai), India	17,850,000
7. Los Angeles, U.S.	16,150,000
8. Buenos Aires, Argentina	13,250,000
9. Calcutta, India	12,900,000
10. Shanghai, China	11,800,000

Merely Informative

Number 11 is Beijing, China. Lagos, Nigeria, the largest city in Africa, is number 14.

b. *World's Five Longest Rivers*

River	Square miles
1. Nile (Africa)	4,180 miles
2. Amazon (South America)	3,912 miles
3. Mississippi-Missouri-Red Rock (U.S.)	3,710 miles
4. Yangtze Kiang (China)	3,602 miles
5. Huang H. (China)	3,459 miles
6. Ob (Russia)	2,900 miles

Since some authorities list the Ob as 5th, count it as correct if it was one of your answers.

c. *World's Ten Largest Islands* (don't count Australia)

Island	Square miles
1. Greenland (Danish)	839,999
2. New Guinea (SW Pacific)	316,615
3. Borneo (West mid-Pacific)	286,914
4. Madagascar (Indian Ocean)	226,657
5. Baffin (Canada)	183,810
6. Sumatra (Indonesia)	182,859
7. Honshu (Japan)	88,925
8. Great Britain (England, Scotland, and Wales)	88,758
9. Ellesmere (Canada)	82,119
10. Victoria (Canada)	81,930

Merely Informative
Other Islands

New Zealand's South Island and North Island are number 12 and 14. Celebes and Java, two more islands of Indonesia, are number 11 and 13. Cuba, number 15, is a hair larger than Newfoundland (Canada).

6.   **Canada and the Former Soviet Union.**

The Ten Provinces of Canada

From west to east along the U.S. border, they are

British Columbia	Manitoba
Alberta	Ontario
Saskatchewan	Quebec

The eastern provinces ("the Maritimes") are

Newfoundland	Nova Scotia
New Brunswick	Prince Edward Island

Merely Informative
More about Canada

Canada also has three territories: Northwest Territories, Yukon, and Nunavut. In the province of Quebec, French is an official language. Behind Russia, Canada is the second largest country in the world in land mass.

The Fifteen Republics of the Former Soviet Union

Armenia	Azerbaijan	Belarus	Estonia	Georgia
Kazakhstan	Kyrgyzstan	Latvia	Lithuania	Moldova
Russia	Tajikistan	Turkmenistan	Ukraine	Uzbekistan

Merely Informative
The Former Soviet Union—as of 2000

As of 1994, all fifteen republics are now independent countries. Latvia, Lithuania, and Estonia have reacquired their status as independent Baltic states. Russia alone is still the largest country in the world in land mass. Nearly twice the size of the United States, China, or Canada, it spans ten time zones.

Source: *The World Almanac and Book of Facts* 2000. Mahwah, New Jersey: World Almanac Books, 1999.

7. **The Continental United States.**

   a. The northernmost state is neither Maine nor Washington. It is Minnesota. Look for International Falls, Minnesota, on the map.

   b. The easternmost state, by a comfortable margin, is Maine. Look at the meridians on a map or globe.

   c. The westernmost state in the continental United States is not California, but Washington state.

   d. The southernmost is Florida, whose southernmost city, Key West, is farther south than the southern tip of Texas.

   If you include Hawaii and Alaska, not just the continental United States, Hawaii is farther south than Key West, and the southernmost part of Alaska is north of Minnesota. Which is farther west? You may be surprised.

8. **The Globe.**   The answer is *c*. This statement is *not* correct.

   You cross the international date line and it becomes the next day when you travel *west* from Hawaii to Japan, not the opposite.
   Statements a, b, and d are correct.

   a. Latitudes do measure degrees north or south from the equator. Longitude measures east-west location on a map. Longitude and latitude are measured in degrees. Hawaii, for example, is located at 20 degrees north latitude, which is expressed as 20.00N, and 157.45 degrees west longitude. If you know the longitude and latitude of any location, you should be able to locate it on a map or globe.

   b. The "tropics" is defined by the Tropic of Cancer and the Tropic of Capricorn, both of which run parallel to the equator. The Tropic of Cancer runs north of the equator, passing through such countries as Mexico, India, and Saudi Arabia. The Tropic of Capricorn, running south of the equator, passes through Brazil, Botswana, and Australia.

   d. The Prime Meridian of longitude runs through Greenwich (pronounced "gren-itch"), England. On a globe, all of the vertical lines that connect the north and south poles are called meridians. The Prime Meridian is the starting point for time zones and is the meridian from which longitude is measured. The International Date Line is on the opposite side of Earth from the Prime Meridian.

9. **Mountains and Deserts.**

    a. The correct answer is *iii*, Mount Kilimanjaro.

        At more than 19,000 feet, Kilimanjaro is the highest mountain in Africa. Mt. McKinley, more than 20,000 feet, is higher, but is in Alaska, not Africa. Likewise, Mt. Everest, the tallest mountain on earth at 29,029 feet, is in Asia, not Africa.

    b. The correct answer is *i*, the Sahara.

        The Sahara Desert is by far the world's largest, stretching all the way across northern Africa. Although most of Saudi Arabia is desert, its land mass is considerably smaller.

10. **The Americas.**

    If you're short of right answers and want to use Caribbean island countries, you may add them to either North or South America, wherever you need more help.

    South America. Generally from north to south, the countries and capitals of South America are as follows:

Countries	*Capitals*
Colombia	Bogotá
Venezuela	Caracas
Guyana	Georgetown
Suriname	Paramaribo
French Guiana	Cayenne
Ecuador	Quito
Peru	Lima
Bolivia	La Paz
Paraguay	Asunción
Brazil	Brasilia
Chile	Santiago
Argentina	Buenos Aires
Uruguay	Montevideo

Merely Informative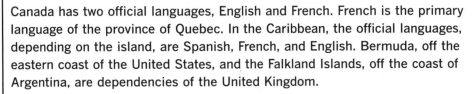
South American Languages

The primary language of every country in South America, except one, is Spanish. The exception is the biggest country, Brazil. Its official language is Portugese.

Central and North America. Included below are only a few of the island countries of the Caribbean. The actual number is larger.

Countries	*Capitals*
Panama	Panama City
Costa Rica	San José
Nicaragua	Managua
Honduras	Tegucigalpa
El Salvador	San Salvador
Guatemala	Guatemala City
Mexico	Mexico City
United States of America	Washington, D.C.
Canada	Ottawa

The Caribbean:

Cuba	Havana
Jamaica	Kingston
Haiti	Port-au-Prince
Dominican Republic	Santo Domingo
Puerto Rico	San Juan
Trinidad and Tobago	Port-of-Spain

Merely Informative
Official Languages

Canada has two official languages, English and French. French is the primary language of the province of Quebec. In the Caribbean, the official languages, depending on the island, are Spanish, French, and English. Bermuda, off the eastern coast of the United States, and the Falkland Islands, off the coast of Argentina, are dependencies of the United Kingdom.

EXTRA CREDIT: A good geography trivia question.

Here are three:

1. If you travel due south from Miami, Florida, what is the first non-island country that you run into?
2. What two states in the United States have contiguous borders with eight other states?
3. Of the following four cities—New York, Rome, Tokyo, or Johannesburg, South Africa—which is the closest to the equator and which is the farthest from the equator?

For the answers, see below and the next page.

The RAT's Mouse

If you want to find out more by using a computer to check some informative web sites, you might use your mouse to check the following:

- **www.nationalgeographic.org** But you would have thought of this yourself
- **www.geography.about.com** Lots of information—population, weather, cultural geography, historical maps, longitude and latitude; easy links
- **www.mapquiz.com** Fun; quizzes, colors, maps
- **www.randmcnally.com** Good travel site; maps, road trip information, a link to randmcnally world site
- **www.tycho.usno.navy.mil/tzones.html** A Navy site with lots on time zones—map, laws, explanations; search by country

Trivia Answers:

1. The correct answer is—believe it or not—Panama.

   If you go due south from Miami, you will first hit Cuba, which is of course an island. The first non-island country you come to is Panama.

   This answer will give you some sense of the extent to which South America is southeast, rather than due south, of the United States. No South American country is due south of New Orleans; all are to the southeast.

2. The correct answers are Missouri and Tennessee.

Missouri, in addition to having long borders with Arkansas, Kansas, Iowa, and Illinois, also has short borders with Nebraska, Oklahoma, Tennessee, and Kentucky.

Tennessee has common borders to the west not only with Missouri but also with Arkansas, with Mississippi, Alabama, and Georgia to the south, with North Carolina to the east, and with Kentucky and Virginia to the north.

3. (Almost no one gets this right.) A very common answer to this question is that Rome is the closest and Johannesburg is the farthest.

In fact, the correct answer is the opposite. By a wide margin, Johannesburg is the closest to the equator, even though it is a long way from Europe. And by just a small margin, sunny Rome is farther north than either New York or Tokyo.

If you don't believe these answers—and you may not—check a map or globe.

13.   ELECTRICITY—ANSWERS

1.   **Sources of Electricity.**   The answer is f, all of the above.

Electric power, or electricity, is usually produced in power plants in which steam is used to power turbines, which drive generators, which convert mechanical power into electricity.

The steam that turns the turbines can be produced by a variety of fuels. Coal, oil, or natural gas (fossil fuels) can be used as the fuel to heat water to produce steam. More than two-thirds of the electric power in the United States is produced in steam electric plants powered by fossil fuels.

Nuclear power plants work similarly, with the heat produced through nuclear fission producing steam from water. The steam drives the turbine, which powers the generator. About 15 percent of the electricity produced in the United States is produced in nuclear power plants.

About the same amount of electrical power is produced in the United States in hydroelectric power plants. These plants do not rely on steam; instead, the power comes from the force of falling water. The water is usually contained in a reservoir created by a dam. The force of the water turns hydraulic turbines that run generators.

Wind can turn windmills, which, in turn, can power electrical generators. Historically a source of power in The Netherlands and other locations, windmills with huge, propeller-shaped blades can be found in California and other locations with prevailing winds.

The energy of the sun, or solar energy, can also be converted into electricity by solar cells. This very clean way of producing energy remains relatively expensive, so it has not become a common source of producing electrical power.

2. **Household Current.**   The answer is c, alternating current.

Almost all electrical household current in the United States is alternating current. The current is alternating because the source of the electricity produces alternating current. Car batteries produce direct current. Alternating current is easier to transmit over distances than direct current, and certain appliances, such as radios and televisions, require alternating current. Analog and digital are terms typically used to describe different ways in which electronic signals or data flows are transmitted, not to describe household current.

3. **Defective Wiring.**   The answer is a short circuit, or a short.

A short circuit occurs when frayed wires allow a connection between two wires that are normally insulated from one another. It is called a "short circuit" because the two wires are part of a circuit that includes the appliance or appliances connected to that wire. Because the appliance (light bulb, radio, etc.) offers some resistance to the flow of electricity, an unintended connection across the wires allows the electrical current, which always follows the path of least resistance, to take a shortcut and bypass the appliance. The result is typically a surge of electricity that blows a fuse or trips a circuit breaker and leaves scorch marks around the point of the short.

4. **Circuitry Safety Devices.**   The answer is circuit breakers or fuses.

Circuit breakers and fuses are safety devices designed to keep wiring from overheating and causing a fire. If an electrical circuit does overheat—for example, from a short circuit or a strong power surge—the circuit breaker trips or the fuse blows and stops the flow of electricity through the overloaded circuit. For the current to resume, the circuit breaker must be reset or the fuse replaced.

ELECTRICITY

Circuit breakers are now much more common than fuses. Unlike fuses, which screw into sockets in fuse boxes and must be replaced once blown, circuit breakers merely need to be reset.

5. **Light Bulbs.**   *False.*

A fluorescent bulb uses about one-fifth the amount of electricity of an incandescent bulb of similar brightness uses.

Fluorescent bulbs also generate about one-fifth the amount of heat of incandescent bulbs thus they sometimes are known as "cool" lights. The reason for the difference is that the light of incandescent bulbs is generated by electricity heating a filament in the bulb until it shines brightly. In a fluorescent bulb, by contrast, electrodes at each end of the tube establish an electric arc that travels through a gas mixture (most commonly mercury vapor and argon) in the tube. When exposed to the electrical particles of the electric arc, these gases give off light.

Merely Informative
More Light

Which of the following statements are true?

- Electric lights did not become common until the early 1900s.
- Fluorescent bulbs last much longer than incandescent bulbs.
- Fluorescent bulbs outsell incandescent bulbs.
- High-wattage bulbs give off more light but cost more to burn.

Answers: All are true. Although invention of the incandescent bulb by Thomas Alva Edison occurred in 1879, which was two years after arc lights had been demonstrated in Paris, the use of electric light bulbs did not become common until the early 1900s. Fluorescents have been the better sellers since the 1950s.

---

6. **Old Wives' Tales.**   The untrue "old wives' tale" is *a.*

Lightning does often strike the same spot more than once. That is why lightning rods sell. Lightning rods—which are designed to divert the electricity of a lightning strike into the ground rather than into the structure on which the lightning rod is mounted—are commonly used on high structures (chimneys, barns, tall buildings) that are likely to be struck by lightning repeatedly.

The other three statements are true. Dry rubber boots may help prevent electrical shock because rubber acts as an insulator, not as a conductor of electricity. The insides of fluorescent bulbs are lined with phosphors, which are toxic, so it is prudent to wear gloves when dealing with a broken fluorescent bulb. Copper wiring is superior to aluminum wiring, and is now standard in most residential construction.

7. **Currents and Plugs.**   The answer that is false is *c*.

The third, round prong on many appliance plugs is a ground, not something that allows more current to flow through the plug.

European and American wall plugs are not compatible. European plugs typically have round pins and, sometimes, three pins set at different angles. Standard American plugs—either standard two-prong plugs or two prongs plus a round ground pin—can operate in European sockets or receptacles with the aid of an adapter.

Car batteries generate direct current, which powers all of a car's electrical equipment.

Voltage in the United States and Canada—110 to 120 volts—is different from that in most European countries, which commonly have voltage of 220 in wall circuits.

8. **Electrical Hazards.**   The correct answer is *d*, changing a broken bulb with the power on but the wall switch off.

Changing a broken light bulb can result in electrical shock unless there is no power running to the fixture. Power can be cut off by turning off the entire circuit at the circuit breaker or unscrewing the fuse for the corresponding circuit. Alternatively, the wall switch that controls a particular light fixture can be used to turn off the power to that fixture. The risk with the wall switch approach, however, is that wall switches generally are not marked, and not all light switches in the down position are off. This is why electricians typically cut off all of the power to the circuit to make certain that the wires to that fixture are not "hot." The same approach is prudent when changing a broken bulb.

The others are all common electrical hazards. Continuing to play any outdoor sport—particularly activities in open spaces such as golf courses or soccer and football fields—during an electrical storm is highly dangerous. Lightning continues to cause death and injury in such circumstances.

Operating any electrical appliance—hairdryer, radio, TV, etc.—near a bath tub or sink full of water risks severe electrical shock or electrocution if you are touching or are in the water.

The first rule of safety in doing any electrical repair is to turn the power off. In the case of a lamp, unplug it. In the case of a light switch or wall socket, turn off the circuit by turning off the circuit breaker controlling that fixture or by removing the fuse for that circuit.

9. **Electrical Safety.**

   a. A first step in the case of an electrical fire is to turn off the electric power. A small electrical fire can be extinguished by a fire extinguisher that uses liquefied gas or dry chemicals. It may be possible to extinguish a small electrical fire by suffocating the fire with a blanket or beating out the flame. Water or water-based foam should not be used on an electrical fire because water is a conductor of electricity.

   b. For an electrical shock or lightning victim who is not breathing, first aid should include an immediate call to 911 for emergency medical assistance and mouth-to-mouth resuscitation.

10. **Electrical Terms.**   The correct match-ups are the following:

    Tungsten   b. It is the commonly used filament because it is so resistant to melting or burning when electricity is passed through it. Combustion is further retarded by putting gases such as nitrogen in the bulb rather than air.

    Voltage   d. Voltage represents the amount of electromotive force at the source of the circuit and, therefore, the potential flow of current through the circuit. A sign warning "High Voltage" signals a powerful source of electricity and, therefore, a potentially fatal electrical shock.

    Rheostat: e. A rheostat is a device that adjusts the amount of resistance in a circuit and, therefore, the amount of current flowing. As wall switches, rheostats are commonly referred to as "dimmer switches."

    Solder   a. A metal alloy that can be heated easily, and cooled quickly, to form a hard connection between two wires or a wire and another electrical component.

Amperes   c. Amperes, or amps, measure the flow of current through a circuit. Thus, fuses for circuits that are intended to carry only a certain amount of current will be identified as, for example, 30 amp fuses.

More Where This Game From

For a useful reference on electricity and electrical wiring, see the Black and Decker book, *The Complete Guide to Home Wiring*. Minnetonka, Minnesota: Creative Publishing International 1998. Also, see *The Complete Idiot's Guide to Electrical Repair,* by Terry Meany Alpha Books, 2000.

The RAT's Mouse

For a good online glossary of terms on electricity, try:

• **www.curriculumvisions.com/electricity/electricityGlossary.html**

14.   SPORTS—ANSWERS

1. **Championships.**

   a. *The Grand Slam of Tennis.* The four Grand Slam tournaments of professional tennis are

      1. *The Australian Open*—Played in January at the Australian Tennis Center in Melbourne on a hard surface, this tournament originated in 1969.
      2. *The French Open*— Played for more than 100 years, this tournament is played on red clay at the Stade Roland Garros, near Paris.
      3. *Wimbledon*—The Lawn Tennis Championships of the All England Club is played each July in Wimbledon, England. Dating back to the 1870s, Wimbledon is the one Grand Slam championship still played on grass courts.

SPORTS

4. *The U.S. Open*—Played each year at the end of the summer, the U.S. Open is played on hard surface courts in Flushing Meadow, just outside of New York City.

b. *The Triple Crown of Horse Racing.* The three races that comprise the Triple Crown of horse racing are run during May and June. The races, run by three-year-old thoroughbreds, are

1. *The Kentucky Derby*—The first of the Triple Crown races each year, the Derby is a 1¼-mile race run at Churchill Downs in Kentucky.
2. *The Preakness Stakes*—The Preakness is a 1³⁄₁₆-mile race run at Pimlico, outside of Baltimore, Maryland.
3. *The Belmont Stakes*—The longest of the three, the Belmont is a 1½-mile race at Belmont, in New York State.

c. *The Majors of the Men's PGA Golf Tour.* No golfer has ever won all four of the majors in the same calendar year, although Ben Hogan won three of the four in 1953. Only five golfers have won all four over the course of their careers. In 2000-01 Tiger Woods won four consecutive majors within 12 months, a spectacular and historic achievement. The majors are:

1. *The Masters*—The Masters is always played in the spring at the Augusta National Golf Club in Augusta, Georgia.
2. *The U.S. Open*—Won four times by Bobbie (Robert Tyre) Jones and four times by Jack Nicklaus, the U.S. Open dates back to 1895.
3. *The British Open*—The oldest of the majors, the British Open was first played in 1860.
4. *The PGA*—The Professional Golfers' Association championship, like the U.S. and British Opens, is played at different locations in different years.

2. **Individual Sports.**

a. *Bogie* is one stroke more than par. Thus, a score of five strokes on a par four hole is a bogie. A score of three, one under par, is a "birdie."

b. *Deuce* is the same as a 40–40 score. From deuce, a player must win by two points. The player who wins the next point wins "advantage," or "ad." If that player loses the next point, the game is at deuce again.

c. *Port*—As you face forward in a boat or ship, the left side of the vessel is the "port" side. The right side is "starboard"; the front, the "bow"; and the rear, the "stern."

d. *Marathon*—An open road race of 26 miles, 385 yards, the marathon is named after the legendary Greek runner who ran from Marathon to Athens to tell of the Greeks' victory over the Persians in 490 B.C.E. (B.C.) The marathon is usually the last event in the Summer Olympics.

3. **Team Sports.**

    a. *A 3-pointer*—Any basket scored from that distance or more is worth 3 points. Field goals scored inside the 3-point line are worth 2 points. Free throws count 1 point each.

    b. *A safety*—Two-point safeties, the least common type of scoring in football, usually occur when a quarterback is sacked or a runner is tackled in his own end zone. If a punt or kickoff is intentionally downed in the end zone, with no attempted runback, that is a "touchback," not a safety.

    c. *The shortstop*—The shortstop plays on the third base side of second base, across the infield from the first and second basemen.

    d. *Offside*—The same infraction can occur in hockey, for essentially the same type of violation. In football, offside involves lining up or encroaching onto the opposing team's side of the line of scrimmage. In soccer, an offside violation can result in stopping play and giving the ball to the opposing team.

4. **Professional Sports Teams.**

    A good way to learn the names and nicknames of professional sports teams is to start with the teams in or near your hometown. Listed below (as of the year 2000) are the names and locations of major professional football, basketball, baseball, and hockey teams. There are others, and if you know any of them, they also count as correct answers. A correct answer requires knowing four teams in any one category.

    a. *Football*

    The National Football League is divided into two conferences, the American Football Conference (AFC) and the National Football Conference (NFC). As realigned in 2001, each has four divisions: East, North, South, and West. Each division has four or five teams, the locations of which usually—but not always—correspond to the geographical region suggested by their conference designation.

National Football League
American Conference

East:

Buffalo Bills   Miami Dolphins
New England Patriots   New York Jets

North:

Baltimore Ravens   Cincinnati Bengals
Cleveland Browns   Pittsburgh Steelers

West:

Denver Broncos   Kansas City Chiefs
Oakland Raiders   San Diego Chargers

South:

Houston Texans   Indianapolis Colts
Jacksonville Jaguars   Tennessee Titans

National Conference

East:

Dallas Cowboys   New York Giants
Philadelphia Eagles   Washington Redskins

North:

Chicago Bears   Detroit Lions
Green Bay Packers   Minnesota Vikings

West:

Arizona Cardinals   San Francisco '49ers
St. Louis Rams   Seattle Seahawks

South:

Atlanta Falcons   Carolina Panthers
New Orleans Saints   Tampa Bay Buccaneers

b. *Basketball*

The National Basketball Association (NBA) has a Western Conference and an Eastern Conference. Each has two divisions. The Western Conference includes the Pacific Division and the Midwest Division; the Eastern Conference includes the Central Division and the Atlantic Division. Each division has six or seven teams.

National Basketball Association
Western Conference

Pacific Division:

Golden State Warriors	Los Angeles Clippers	Los Angeles Lakers
Phoenix Suns	Portland Trail Blazers	Sacramento Kings
Seattle SuperSonics		

Midwest Division:

Dallas Mavericks	Denver Nuggets	Houston Rockets
Minnesota Timberwolves	San Antonio Spurs	Utah Jazz
Vancouver Grizzlies		

Eastern Conference

Central Division:

Atlanta Hawks	Charlotte Hornets	Chicago Bulls
Cleveland Cavaliers	Detroit Pistons	Indiana Pacers
Milwaukee Bucks	Toronto Raptors	

Atlantic Division:

Boston Celtics	Miami Heat	New Jersey Nets
New York Knicks	Orlando Magic	Philadelphia '76ers
Washington Wizards		

c. *Baseball*

Major league baseball, the national pastime, consists of the American League and the National League. Each has an Eastern Division, Central Division, and Western Division. Each division has 4 or 5 teams.

Major League Baseball
American League

American League East:

Baltimore Orioles	Boston Red Sox	New York Yankees
Tampa Bay Devil Rays	Toronto Blue Jays	

American League Central:

Chicago White Sox	Cleveland Indians	Detroit Tigers
Kansas City Royals	Minnesota Twins	

American League West:

Anaheim Angels	Oakland Athletics	Seattle Mariners
Texas Rangers		

National League

National League East:

Atlanta Braves	Florida Marlins	Montreal Expos
New York Mets	Philadelphia Phillies	

National League Central:

Chicago Cubs	Cincinnati Reds	Houston Astros
Milwaukee Brewers	Pittsburgh Pirates	St. Louis Cardinals

National League West:

Arizona Diamondbacks	Los Angeles Dodgers	Colorado Rockies
San Diego Padres	San Francisco Giants	

d. *Hockey*

The National Hockey League has a Western Conference, which includes a Pacific Division, a Central Division, and a Northwest Division, and an Eastern Conference, which includes a Northeast Division, an Atlantic Division, and a Southwest Division. Each division has four or five teams.

This organization, adopted in 1993, replaced the more colorful structure of the Campbell Conference, which included the Smythe and Norris divisions, and the Wales Conference, which included the Adams and Patrick divisions.

National Hockey League
Western Conference

Central Division:

Chicago Blackhawks	Columbus Blue Jackets	Detroit Red Wings
St. Louis Blues	Nashville Predators	

Northwest Division:

| Calgary Flames | Colorado Avalanche | Edmonton Oilers |
| Vancouver Canucks | | |

Pacific Division:

| Anaheim Mighty Ducks | Dallas Stars | Los Angeles Kings |
| Phoenix Coyotes | San Jose Sharks | |

Eastern Conference

Atlantic Division:

| New Jersey Devils | New York Islanders | New York Rangers |
| Philadelphia Flyers | Pittsburgh Penguins | |

Northeast Division:

| Boston Bruins | Buffalo Sabres | Montreal Canadiens |
| Ottawa Senators | Toronto Maple Leafs | |

Southeast Division:

| Atlanta Thrashers | Carolina Hurricanes | Florida Panthers |
| Tampa Bay Lightning | Washington Capitals | |

5. **Sports Common outside the United States.**

   a. *Cricket*—A venerable British tradition in which, in the year before publication of this book, the Australians gained a dominant position.

   b. *Soccer*—The world's most popular sport, and one of the oldest, is widely known as "football" in countries other than Canada and the United States.

   c. *Curling*—Now a sport in the Winter Olympics, it isn't the Winter Olympics' fastest-moving event.

   d. *Rugby*—This bruising sport was first played at Rugby School in England. Its players typically wear jerseys with broad, brightly colored stripes and white collars and plackets. It is the precursor of American football.

6. **The National Pastime.**

   a. Among the New York Yankees in the Hall of Fame (about 30 members played for the Yankees, although the principal teams of several of them were not the Yankees) are

Babe Ruth, right fielder
Lou Gehrig, first baseman
Joe DiMaggio, center fielder
Mickey Mantle, center fielder
Yogi Berra, catcher
Phil Rizzuto, shortstop

Leroy Satchel Paige, pitcher
Whitey Ford, pitcher
Casey Stengel, manager

The top five players of the post-1900 era, who were picked in 1936, the year the Hall of Fame was established, were:

Ty Cobb	Babe Ruth
Walter Johnson	Honus Wagner
Christy Matthewson	

b. Ways to make a double play, other than by a ground ball double play, include:
 • Strike out the batter and pick off a runner.
 • Strike out the batter and throw out a base runner attempting to steal.
 • Retire the batter by catching a fly ball or line drive and double up a base runner who has left his base.
 • Throw out two base runners, as, for example, a runner attempting to steal second from first and a base runner attempting to come home from third on the steal.

c. Jackie Robinson. In his first year with the Brooklyn Dodgers, Jackie Robinson was Rookie of the Year. Two years later, he won the batting title and was the league's MVP.

7. **Women Athletes.**   The correct answers are
      f. gymnastics   (Mary Lou Retton and Nadia Comaneci)
      c. tennis   (Billie Jean King and Serena Williams)
      a. track   (Wilma Rudolph and Marion Jones)
      d. ice skating   (Sonja Henie and Kristi Yamaguchi)

More Where This Came From

Who's Who of Sports Champions. Boston: Houghton Mifflin, 1995, by Ralph Hickok.

8. **The Olympics.**   The Winter and Summer Olympics that have been held since 1990 were in the following locations:

	Winter	*Summer*
1992	Albertville, France	Barcelona, Spain
1994	Lillehammer, Norway	
1996		Atlanta, U.S.A.
1998	Nagano, Japan	
2000		Sydney, Australia

The 2002 Winter Olympics will take place in Salt Lake City, Utah, U.S.A. The 2004 Summer Olympics are scheduled for Athens, Greece.

9. **The World Cup.**   The winners in the 1990s were

1990	West Germany
1991	United States (women)
1994	Brazil
1995	Norway (women)
1998	France
1999	United States (women)

10. **Cardiovascular Endurance.**   The answer is *b*, weight lifting.

Sports that enhance your cardiovascular endurance, or aerobic capacity, are long-duration, low-intensity, large-muscle activities.

Bicycling, swimming, and brisk walking—as well as jogging, rollerblading, rowing, aerobics, jumping rope, and cross-country skiing—all elevate your pulse on a sustained basis and are good for cardiovascular endurance.

Weight lifting, one of the most important forms of exercise for adults age 50 and older, improves muscle strength and enhances anaerobic capacity. Aerobic capacity, anaerobic capacity, and strength are three of several different aspects of fitness.

More Where This Came From

For lots of sports data, try *The 2001 ESPN Information Please Sports Almanac*, New York: Hyperion, 2000, edited by Gary Brown and Mike Morrison.

For information on sports from auto racing to extreme sports, see *The Handy Sports Answer Book*, Visible Ink Press, 1999, by Kevin Hillstrom, Laurie Hillstrom, and Roger Matuz.

For sports stories, see *The Best American Sports Writing of the Century*, Boston: Houghton Mifflin, 1999, edited by David Halberstam.

All are available in paperback.

The RAT's Mouse

If you want more sports information, some interesting web sites you can access with your computer mouse include:

- **www.olympic.org** An impressive site with links to the 2002 Winter Olympics in Salt Lake City, the 2004 Summer Olympics in Athens, the Olympic Museum, and more
- There are sites for many individual sports, such as **www.baseball.com, www.football.com,** etc; in addition, sites for newspapers such as the *Los Angeles Times* and the *Washington Post* have good sports sections
- **www.hickoksports.com/history.shtml** Lots of sports history, particularly for North American sports; champions, record holders, trivia
- **www.goaskalice.Columbia.edu** Columbia University health site; see "fitness"
- **www.discoveryhealth.com** A fascinating site with lots of information, articles; check out the stretching exercises
- **www.espn.com** Of course
- **http://baseballguru.com**

15.   IMPROVISING—ANSWERS

1. **Measuring.**   For measuring a short distance accurately, you need a readily available standard. Although you may know approximately how many inches long *your foot* is, or how many inches your fingers span, if you are measuring just a few feet, your handiest yardstick may be *a dollar bill.* Use a new bill if possible. A dollar (or any other denomination) is precisely $6\frac{1}{8}''$ long. If the distance you are measuring is shorter, *a penny* is precisely $\frac{3}{4}''$ in diameter.

    If you have other standardized, readily accessible frames of reference, count them as a correct answer.

2. **A Missing Button.**   From the inside of the garment (so it won't show), use a *safety pin,* a *straight pin,* or even a *paper clip* to hold the two pieces of fabric together. *Double-sided adhesive* tape may work, as may *a loop of masking tape.* *Silly Putty* might work as well, but it may not come off as cleanly as you hope.

3. **Jar Lids.**

    If the lid on a jar is stuck and you are unable to twist it off, run *hot water* over the metal lid for 30–60 seconds. The heat may expand the lid slightly and make it easier to twist off.

    As with all things, the right tools also solve the problem. For jar lids, one is a thin, *round rubber pad* that will keep your hand from slipping. It works magically.

    When all else fails, give the jar to someone else to try. One of the unexplained laws of the universe is that *the second person* always has an easier time, whether or not he or she has a stronger grip.

4. **Screwing in a Screw.**

    The universal aid is *a dime. Nail clippers* sometimes work. A knife blade or tip of a letter opener may not work and may end up bent.

5. **Shining Shoes.**

    If you are desperate and no Kiwi polish, brush, or buff cloth is to be found, polish your leather shoes with the inside of a *fresh banana peel.* Wipe off any residual banana.

IMPROVISING

A damp cloth will remove dust but do little to improve the shine or texture. Some oil-based fluids may help, but they are risky.

A faster fix for dusty shoes is to rub the top of each shoe on *the back of your opposite trouser leg*. This moves the dust from the top of your shoe to the back of your pants, which in some circumstances may be an improvement.

Don't use both a banana peel and the back of your pants leg.

6. **Polishing Silver.**

Need to polish a silver ring or bracelet but have no silver polish? Use *toothpaste* and rinse with warm water, then cold. An alternative? Two *Alka-Seltzer* tablets in water; immerse jewelry for two minutes.

Toothpaste also cleans ivory piano keys. (Don't use too much toothpaste or too much water.)

7. **Getting Wrinkles Out.**

Hang a wrinkled dress or suit in the bathroom when you take a shower. If the bathroom fills with *steam,* many of the wrinkles will disappear.

Merely Informative Packing

In packing a suit or dress, you can reduce wrinkling if you:

- fold it around other garments so that you avoid sharp folds and creases;
- wrap it around a rigid frame or luggage divider in such a way that the fabric remains stretched flat and doesn't crumple; and
- insert tissue paper or a dry cleaning bag between different layers of garments.

---

8. **Collar Stays and Panty Hose.**

Although this question is designed to give every test taker a gender-friendly alternative, feel free to answer either one.

If you find yourself without collar stays, take a piece of *cardboard* (like the kind used to pack most shirts that have been laundered; a stiff magazine cover may also work), and cut or tear small strips that will slide into your shirt collar where stays normally go.

A run in panty hose may be stopped by applying *clear nail polish* and letting it dry. The larger the run, the less effective this technique.

Merely Informative
Bounce

More on panty hose. To eliminate static electricity that panty hose sometimes generate, rub a damp, used sheet of Bounce over the hose. I'm not making this up.

And on the subject of Bounce, it reportedly can be used as an air freshener (put a piece under the front seat of your car); to repel mosquitoes (pull a strip through your belt loops); and to remove food that has been baked onto a pan (put a sheet in the pan, fill it with water, and sponge the pan clean the next morning).

---

9. **Spots.**

Food can be the source of greasy or nongreasy stains. The procedures for each are a little different, and could each be the subject of a small book. In general, however, good ways to improvise are the following:

Greasy food stains—butter, mayonnaise, oily foods—are generally best dealt with by, first, removing or *gently scraping* away any residue food. Then, dampen the fabric slightly, rub the spot with a little *detergent*—preferably a powder detergent—or *dry cleaning fluid.* An alternative is to use an absorbent powder, such as *cornstarch,* which will absorb any grease left on the stain.

Nongreasy food stains—juice, coffee, tea—should be sponged off and then soak the article of clothing in *cool water.* If needed, these stains can be rubbed gently with a *liquid detergent.*

Merely Informative
Stain Removal Techniques

Some general guidelines for stains, according to *The Stain and Spot Remover Handbook* by Jean Cooper (Storey Communications, Inc., 1995) include the following:

- Always treat stains quickly, while they are still fresh.
- Always remove as much of the spill as possible before beginning to treat the stain.
- Start at the outer edges of a stain and work in toward the center.
- Try the simplest approach first: use clean, cold water.

A universal first treatment for spots of food or beverages is club soda, applied as soon as possible.

Merely Informative
Carbonated Beverages

Club soda also cleans grease from your windshield. Both club soda and cola can be used to loosen rusty nuts and bolts. Cola also can be used to clean a toilet bowl by dumping a can in the bowl overnight and flushing the next morning. Together with crumpled aluminum foil, cola can be used to remove rust spots from chrome automobile bumpers.

If you have a spot or stain on a piece of white clothing, you can often camouflage it by sprinkling *baby powder* on the spot.

10. **Starting a Fire.**
   a. Should you have a *magnifying glass* (or *reading glasses* or a *clear bottle partly filled with water*) and it happens to be a sunny day, it may be possible to start a fire by concentrating the sunlight into a fine point on dry leaves or shreds of paper.
   b. With a similar small pile of dry leaves or twigs, find *two stones*, flinty if possible. Repeatedly strike one with the other in a sweeping motion until a spark from the stones ignites the leaves.
   c. Using *two dry sticks*, dig out a depression or groove in one and put it flat on the ground. Stand the other up vertically, placing its point in the depression or groove of the other. Roll the vertical stick back and forth between the palms of your hand so that its point moves back and forth in the flat stick, causing friction and, ultimately, heat. You need the same little mound of dry leaves, grass, or shredded paper around the stick on the ground to catch fire when the sticks start to smolder. (This is not easy.)
   d. If your car is nearby, you can hold in the *cigarette lighter* to override the "pop-out" function, and it will get hot enough to light paper.

More Where This Came From

See *The Big Book of Life's Instructions* by Sheree Bykofsky and Paul Fargis, New York: Harper Collins, 1995, 434.

11. **Staying Dry in a Sudden Rain Shower.**

Garbage bags can be converted into makeshift panchos. Smaller *trash bags* or *plastic shirt bags* can cover the top of your head. Holding *newspapers* over your head works for a while, at least until the paper becomes soaked.

If you really like the garbage bag idea, you can make a "vest" by punching three holes in the bag; a slit in the bottom of a second garbage bag will let you make a "skirt" out of it. Should you happen to have a *latex glove,* you can stretch it to become a hat; of course, if you've used white trash bags, you may create something of a bleached rooster look.

12. **Drying a Just-Washed Item of Clothing.**   Each of these steps can help:
    * *Wring out* excess water.
    * *Roll* the item snugly in a dry towel, squeeze the rolled-up towel, unroll and repeat with a dry towel.
    * Dry with an electric *hair dryer.*
    * Repeatedly *iron* the garment, but without scorching it.

13. **Windshield Ice.**

If you have none of the right tools or implements, try a *credit card,* making sure not to scratch the magnetic strip across the back of the card (use the edge farthest from the magnetic strip).

A sure, but often not fast, way is to start your car, let it warm up, turn on the *defroster,* and wait for it to melt the ice or frost.

14. **Bad Breath.**

Eat several sprigs of *parsley.*

Merely Informative
Baking Soda

While you're at it, if you need deodorant, but don't have any, you can improvise by sprinkling *baking soda* into your hand and applying it to your underarms.

More Where This Came From

Two books, which suggest a variety of improvised uses for brand-name products, are relevant to this general topic: *Polish Your Furniture with Panty Hose,* New York: Hyperion, 1996, and *Clean Your Clothes with Cheese Whiz,* Los Angeles: Renaissance, 2000, both by Joey Green.

The RAT's Mouse

For a host of secret tips, have your computer mouse lead you to this web site:

*   **www.chefnoah.com/secret_tips!.htm**

Alternatively, go to chef noah's homepage: **www.chefnoah.com/** Click first on "Nonfood Areas," then on "Secret Tips."

C. THINGS IT IS RISKY NOT TO KNOW

16.   SEX—ANSWERS

1. **Conception.**   The best answer is *c*, 11 days.

> The problem with relying on this answer is that 11 days is an average; it assumes a regular, average-length menstrual cycle, and you can never be entirely certain about which 11 days.
>
> Any attempt to determine when the risk of conception is low must take into account a number of variables. First, the length of most women's menstrual cycles can vary from cycle to cycle. The length of the cycle, the exact time an egg is released, how rapidly the egg travels from the ovaries to the uterus, and the length of time sperm live are all variables. As a result, there are a number of unavoidable uncertainties in attempting to calculate when the risk of pregnancy is low.
>
> One theoretical approach to avoiding pregnancy is to abstain from sex during those days when conception might occur. Sometimes called the "rhythm" method, this unreliable system seeks to identify a "safe" period by counting calendar days or by other methods. This is one means of calculating the number of days during a menstrual cycle during which conception is unlikely.
>
> In their book, *Heterosexuality*, Masters, Johnson, and Kolodny, after describing the uncertainties and assumptions on which this method depends, state that after measuring the length of six consecutive menstrual periods, the "calendar method" is arrived at by estimating the beginning of the unsafe period by subtracting 18 from the number of days in the shortest menstrual period, and then estimating the end of the unsafe period by subtracting 11 from the number of days in the longest of the six cycles. Applying this system to the example in question 1 yields a theoretically "safe" period of approximately 11 of the 26–30 days of a woman's menstrual cycle.
>
> Masters, Johnson, and Kolodny describe the calendar method as "one of the least effective forms of birth control available, with a failure rate of approximately 40 percent." In short, unprotected sexual intercourse always presents a significant risk of pregnancy.

SEX

Merely Informative
Statistics on Getting Pregnant

Masters, Johnson, and Kolodny give the following statistics on the risks of conception from engaging in sexual intercourse without contraception. Of women who engage in unprotected sexual intercourse for one month, 25 percent conceive. Of those who engage in unprotected intercourse for six months, 63 percent conceive. Unprotected intercourse over the period of a year results in 80 percent of the women becoming pregnant.

---

2. **Masturbation.**   *False.*

Most experts believe that masturbation causes no physical or psychological harm. Beliefs of a few generations ago that masturbation could cause blindness or insanity have been discredited as old wives' tales. Surveys suggest that between 60 and 80 percent of American women have masturbated.

3. **Sex Terms.**

a. *Incest.*

Sexual intercourse between individuals who are related is generally considered to be incest if the two individuals are so closely related that they could not lawfully marry one another. The term is also associated with sexual molestation of a young person by an adult relative.

b. *Sodomy.*

The etymology of the word "sodomy," for which the precise definitions sometimes vary, derives from the city of Sodom, mentioned in the Old Testament. The book of Genesis describes Sodom and Gomorrah as wicked cities that were destroyed by God. According to Genesis 19, it was for looking back at Sodom during her escape that Lot's wife was turned into a pillar of salt.

c. *Testosterone.*

Testosterone ($C_{18}H_{28}O_2$) is the male, steroid sex hormone produced in the male's testicles. It controls secondary sex characteristics and increases a male's sex drive, or libido.

d. *Cramps.*

Women sometimes experience moderate menstrual cramps, technically known as dysmenorrhea, during the menstrual cycle, particularly at the beginning of the cycle. Attributed to hormonal changes, this discomfort is usually treatable with over-the-counter pain medications.

4. **Birth Control.**   The answer is *b*, birth control pills.

Birth control pills, or contraceptive pills, are generally regarded as the most effective means of birth control. Taken by the woman, these pills inhibit ovulation and create a hostile environment for sperm in the uterus. Birth control pills normally are prescribed by a physician.

The effectiveness of birth control pills depends on their being taken correctly, however. They generally must be taken every day for three weeks, stopped for one week, then resumed for three weeks, etc. (With 21-day packs, no pills are taken for a week; with 28-day packs, a sugar pill or placebo is taken for the fourth week to maintain the pattern of taking a pill every day.)

If birth control pills are taken correctly, their failure rate is less than 1 percent. If the routine is not maintained strictly, however, the pills may fail. Note also that some women suffer adverse health effects from taking pills. Check with a doctor.

Merely Informative
Birth Control Measures

There are various means of birth control or contraception.

Abstinence is the surest way to avoid pregnancy. Since conception typically occurs through sexual intercourse, refraining from sexual intercourse altogether is a virtually foolproof way to avoid becoming pregnant.

Sterilization—a procedure that is most commonly considered after a couple has had children—is likewise a highly reliable means of preventing pregnancies. Men are most commonly sterilized through a vasectomy, a process that cuts the tube that carries semen from the testicles to the penis. Women are most commonly sterilized by sealing off or cutting the fallopian tubes through which eggs travel from the ovaries to the uterus. Both are routine surgical procedures. Most, but not all, stories of pregnancies occurring after sterilization are apocryphal.

continued on next page

Birth control pills—discussed above, an oral contraceptive that inhibits ovulation and creates a hostile environment in the uterus for sperm. If pills are taken correctly, the failure rate is less than 1 percent; however, studies show that the actual failure rate in the first year is 7.3 percent. Birth control pills are prescribed by a physician.

IUD—or intrauterine device—is a tiny device inserted into the uterus by a physician and usually replaced annually. Its contraceptive action is achieved by preventing sperm from fertilizing an egg and by creating a hostile environment for implantation. New IUDs are 98 percent effective.

Condoms—a condom is a tight-fitting elastic sheath designed to fit over an erect penis, providing a barrier that prevents sperm from entering the vagina. For maximum effectiveness, condoms should be used with a spermicidal lubricant containing nonoxynol-9 (not an oil-based lubricant such as Vaseline, which can quickly deteriorate latex). When used in this fashion, latex condoms effectively block the HIV virus as well. However, condoms can be defective, break, or come off. The failure rate for condoms used for birth control is nearly 15 percent.

Diaphragms—a rubber cup that fits inside the vagina over the cervix (the opening to the uterus). It is used with a spermicidal jelly or cream containing nonoxynol-9, and can be inserted up to 2 hours before intercourse. It must remain in place 6 to 8 hours after intercourse to be effective. A proper fit is critical, so a diaphragm must be fitted by a physician. Diaphragms have a 6–10 percent failure rate.

5. **Unwelcome Sex.**   The answer is *d*. The statement is *not* correct.

A female supervisor who insists on sex with a male subordinate is unlikely to be found guilty of rape. Rape is generally regarded (or sometimes specifically defined) as a crime involving sex forced on a woman by a man. Although there have been some attempts to use rape laws in the case of forced sex by an older female with a boy, they generally have not succeeded. Such conduct, however, may constitute a variety of other crimes.

All of the other statements are correct.

a. A rape victim may indeed be someone who has agreed to go out with you on a date. Neither the fact that she is your date nor the fact that you may have had sex with her before is a defense of rape if sex has been forced on her. Hence the term, "date rape."

b. Sexual harassment is generally defined broadly enough that it can occur even without physical touching. Repeated suggestions or comments about sex to a subordinate who objects to them may constitute sexual harassment.

c. "Statutory rape" is the crime of having sex with someone below the age of consent, which is defined by law. Thus, the fact that someone below that age may be mature for her age and may have made the decision to have sex voluntarily (or even instigated the sex) is not a legal defense to a charge of statutory rape.

6. **Pregnancy.**   The answer is *d*, pregnancy cannot occur while a female is menstruating.

When a female is menstruating, or having her period, her body is discharging the unfertilized egg and the endometrium, or the lining of the uterus that has developed during the course of the menstrual cycle in anticipation of possible fertilization of the egg. Pregnancy can occur during ovulation—that is, the period following release of the egg into the fallopian tubes. Menstruation, or the shedding of the endometrium, is a sign that conception has not occurred.

7. **AIDS.**   You may count the following as correct answers:

- Abstinence from sexual activity
- Limiting contact to hugging, touching, massaging, stroking
- Having sexual contact only with a person uninfected with HIV
- Using a condom when having intercourse (low risk, not 100 percent safe)

But Keep Reading . . .

A person may not know whether he or she is infected with the AIDS virus. The use of condoms during intercourse may help reduce the risk of infiltration of HIV. However, using certain petroleum-based lubricants—petroleum jelly, Vaseline Intensive Care, baby oil, and Nivea, for example—can cause microscopic holes in condoms or diaphragms large enough for HIV to pass through. Moreover, using condoms to prevent the spread of HIV has the same risks as when they are used as birth control devices. If they didn't, they would be foolproof, which they aren't.

Merely Informative
AIDS

AIDS—acquired immune deficiency syndrome—is the deadliest of all of the sexually transmitted diseases (STDs). AIDS is a viral infection caused by the introduction of HIV (human immunodeficiency virus) into the bloodstream. The resulting disease breaks down the immune system, which protects the body from infection. AIDS generally develops seven to ten years after the initial HIV infection. The virus can lie dormant in the body for years with no apparent symptoms (nonsymptomatic HIV). Five to seven years later, symptoms may begin to occur (symptomatic HIV), such as swollen lymph glands, diarrhea, weight loss, and fatigue.

Although substantial medical and scientific research on AIDS continues, Masters, Johnson, and Kolodny make the following points:

"In more than 78 percent of all AIDS cases the virus has been sexually transmitted."

Although the risk of contracting HIV from a single act of heterosexual intercourse is low, "there have been numerous instances documented in which infection occurred with a single episode of heterosexual intercourse."

"Oral-genital sex . . . has now been shown conclusively to be a means of transmitting HIV."

"Substantial evidence has accumulated showing that having another STD is an important risk factor for becoming infected with HIV via sexual contacts."

"There is no evidence at all that the AIDS virus is transmitted by casual contact" such as shaking hands with an infected person, contact with the virus on doorknobs, toilet seats or water fountains.

Heterosexuality (1994), pp. 395–400.

8. **STDs.**   Other sexually transmitted diseases include
   - Chlamydia;
   - genital herpes;
   - genital, or venereal, warts;
   - gonorrhea ("clap");
   - pubic lice ("crabs");
   - syphilis;
   - viral hepatitis; and
   - vaginal infections.

Chlamydia—The most common bacterial STD in the United States can be transmitted through any sexual contact. It is more common in women than men, but both are at risk if they come in contact with an infected partner. Symptoms in women, often mild or unnoticeable, are difficult to detect, although symptoms may include infection of the urethra, abdominal pain, or inflammation of the cervix or fallopian tubes. In men, symptoms may include urethritis, causing painful urination, swelling of the penis, and/or a discharge from the penis; if left untreated, it can lead to infertility. Chlamydia can be treated successfully with antibiotics. Both partners must be treated to prevent reinfection.

Genital herpes—This STD is caused by the virus known as HSV 2 (herpes simplex virus type 2). It cannot be cured. Characterized by painful blisters or sores on or near the genitals, genital herpes is a chronic disease that is highly infectious and is transmitted by any means of sexual contact when lesions are present. While this is the highest time for transmission, "there is no time when it is safe to believe that there is absolutely no risk of transmission," according to Masters, Johnson, and Kolodny. There is no cure, but early treatment with an antiviral medication can reduce the severity of the recurring attacks. HSV 1 (herpes simplex virus type 1), which infects almost all adults in the United States, is not an STD. Symptoms include most commonly cold sores and conjunctivitis.

Genital warts—Accepted as an STD only in the second half of the twentieth century, genital warts are painless warts growing on or around the genitals or the anus. Genital warts can be treated chemically, by laser surgery, by freezing with liquid nitrogen, or by protein injections.

Gonorrhea ("clap")—A highly contagious, bacteria-caused STD, it is found most commonly in teenagers and young adults, and the risk of transmission is higher for women than for men. Treatable with antibiotics, it can coexist with other STDs such as chlamydia. Symptoms for both males and females include painful burning with urination and a milky discharge, although women have no symptoms in the early stages. If left untreated, it can cause infertility in both sexes. Gonorrhea is one of the most common infectious diseases in the world.

Pubic lice ("crabs")—Parasitic insects, which live in the pubic hair of infected people, bite, suck blood, lay eggs, and are easily transferred from one person to another. Crabs are treated with a specially formulated preparation, available in pharmacies, that kills them and their eggs.

All bedding and clothes should be washed in water hotter than 140 degrees before reuse.

Syphilis—Five centuries ago, a deadly epidemic of syphilis swept across Europe. Caused by a bacterium, syphilis was also a major public health problem in the United States in this century until the advent of penicillin. Characterized by skin sores, syphilis in later stages can cause heart failure, mental disorders, and cardiovascular damage. Treatable by penicillin, syphilis is relatively rare today.

Viral hepatitis—A viral infection of the liver, hepatitis can be one of a series of viruses. Hepatitis A can be transmitted by homosexual conduct, but the risk of heterosexual transmission is limited. Hepatitis B can be transmitted through a variety of sexual activities. Although most common among homosexual males, Hepatitis B can be transmitted sexually by heterosexuals. The principal preventive for hepatitis is vaccine.

Vaginal infections—Vaginal infections (or "vaginitis"), common among women, are of various types. *Trichomonas vaginalis,* for example, is highly infectious, commonly transmitted sexually, and characterized by unpleasant symptoms. It is typically treated with a drug. *Candida albicans,* also common, has a variety of causes and is transmitted sexually in only about a third of cases. It can be treated locally or orally. Although most vaginal infections can be cured easily, some can be chronic and recurring.

9. **Abortion.**   The answer is *c*, the first three months.

In 1973, the U.S. Supreme Court decided by a 7–2 vote in *Roe v. Wade* that a woman's constitutional right to privacy protects her right, in consultation with her doctor, to an abortion during the first trimester of her pregnancy. The court ruling struck down a Texas law that prohibited abortions except when the life of the mother was in danger.

Between 1973 and 2000, the Supreme Court and other U.S. courts decided a variety of abortion cases. Most of the issues raised have involved constitutional challenges to laws that regulate or impose procedural restrictions on a woman's right to decide whether to have an abortion. These cases have dealt with whether husbands were entitled to prior notification, whether husbands have a veto power over their wives' decisions, whether states may require a pregnant unwed minor to get consent from her parents, mandatory 24-hour waiting periods, record-keeping requirements, and the extent to which the federal government can impose abortion restrictions on public facilities, public employees, and federally funded clinics.

In 1992, however, the Supreme Court reaffirmed the central tenet of *Roe v. Wade,* while upholding a state's authority to regulate abortion as long as such regulations do not impose an "undue burden" on a woman's right to decide to end her pregnancy.

10. **Responsibilities of an Unmarried Father.** The answer is *e*, the unmarried father of a child is generally required to provide financial support to the child.

Under the Welfare Reform Act of 1996, states are required to enforce child support laws that require unmarried fathers to pay child support.

More Where This Came From

Heterosexuality by Masters, Johnson, and Kolodny, New York: Gramercy Books, 1994, covers a wide variety of subjects related to sex, from physiology to sexual diseases to sexual dysfunction to contraception.

J. Reinisch and R. Beasley, *The Kinsey Institute New Report on Sex: What You Must Know to Be Sexually Literate.* St. Martin's Press, 1991.

V. Rutter and P. Schwartz, *The Love Test* (1998); see the quiz in Chapter 11.

The RAT's Mouse

Use your computer mouse to check some of these informative web sites:

- **www.iwannaknow.org** Good site with lots of information—STDs 101, quizzes, FAQ
- **www.epigee.org/guide/** "A woman's guide to contraception and responsible sex"; excellent site; describes different types of contraception; diagram of female reproductive anatomy; section on reproductive health
- **www.reproline.jhu.edu/** Reproductive health online; covers family planning, STDs, lots of health topic
- **www.avert.org/young.htm** Site about AIDS, focused on young people

17.   DRUGS—ANSWERS

1.   **Acetylsalicylic Acid.**   The answer is *a*, aspirin.

2.   **Analgesics.**   The answer is *b*, Percocet, an analgesic that contains oxycodone, a narcotic analgesic, and requires a prescription.
    Ibuprofen, the active ingredient in Advil, is also an anti-inflammatory. Aspirin, a common analgesic for generations, is also the active ingredient in Bufferin. Acetaminophen is the active ingredient in Tylenol.

3.   **Generic Drugs.**   *True.*
    The names of generic drugs are the official names adopted and approved for particular drugs. Brand names are names that individual pharmaceutical companies have chosen for a particular drug that they manufacture.

4.   **Drugs and Their Uses.**   The correct pairings are

Valium	c. muscle relaxant (also an anti-anxiety drug)
Ritalin	f. hyperactivity (a stimulant used to treat hyperactivity)
Viagra	e. sexual function (the heralded miracle for seniors)
Amoxicillin	a. antibiotic (along with penicillin and others)
Benadryl	g. allergies (the standard for bee stings, other reactions)
Retin-A	d. acne
Steroids	b. muscle strength and bulk (anabolic steroids build protein)

5.   **Steroids.**   The answer is *d*, which is *not* correct.
    Cortial and estrogenic (female) steroids are not as subject to the same sorts of abuses and are commonly used for various medical purposes.
    Anabolic steroids are closely related to the male hormone, testosterone, and have a protein-building effect similar to that caused by the male sex hormone. As a result, by speeding recovery of fatigued muscles and thus permitting more rigorous training schedules, they can improve athletic performance. Thus, they are banned in most intercollegiate and Olympic competition. In addition to providing an unfair advantage, steroids have a variety of side effects, and long-term abuse can cause a variety of health risks,

including liver and adrenal gland damage, impotence and infertility, heart disease, cancer, or death.

6. **Addictive Drugs.** The answer is *c*, Dramamine, a medication often used to prevent motion sickness.

Nicotine, found in cigarettes; caffeine, found in coffee, tea, and sodas; and codeine, a mild painkiller, are all addictive.

Merely Informative
Dependencies

American Medical Association publications indicate that several million people in the United States are dependent on nicotine, caffeine, or alcohol. Fewer people are dependent on tranquilizers.

Drug addiction can take the form of psychological dependence or physical dependence. Psychological dependence is characterized by craving or emotional distress when the drug is withdrawn. Withdrawal in the case of a physical dependence can cause physical distress, including vomiting, trembling, cramps, and even seizures or coma.

The most addictive drugs are narcotics such as heroin and morphine. Severe addiction is generally not treatable through self-help methods. The National Drug Information and Treatment Hotline is 1-800-622-HELP; another help line is 1-800-HELP-4-ME.

DRUGS

7. **Illicit Drug Use.** The answer is *d*, which is *not* correct. Illicit drug use among whites is similar to that of Hispanics and only slightly below that of blacks. Asian Americans use less than half of each of the other groups mentioned.

Illicit drug use by ethnic groups is as follows: Asian Americans (3.2 percent), whites (6.6 percent), Hispanics (6.8 percent), blacks (7.7 percent) Native Americans (10.6), and multiple race (11.2).

The other answers are all correct. Between 1979 and 1999, the number of Americans engaged in illicit drug use dropped from about 25 million to 14.8 million.

Not only are youth between ages 18 and 25 who smoke cigarettes four times more likely to engage in illicit drug use than those who do not smoke, but in the 12–17 age range those who smoke are more than seven times more likely to be using illicit drugs.

According to the Substance Abuse and Mental Health Services Administration of the U.S. Department of Health and Human Services, a survey by the Office of Applied Studies showed that in 1999 approximately 45 million Americans engaged in binge drinking, as defined by the survey. This is approximately 16 percent of the population.

Merely Informative
Binge Drinking

The age of peak prevalence of binge drinking and heavy alcohol abuse is 21.

---

8. **Marijuana.**   The answer is *c*, which is *not* true.

As a general rule, the duration of the effects of ingesting marijuana is 2–4 hours.

The other statements are correct. Marijuana is the illicit drug of choice among teenagers and young adults. The effects listed are all effects that accompany the initial euphoria and relaxation produced by marijuana. In addition, use of marijuana by pregnant women can cause birth defects in their children.

9. **Drug Facts.**   The answer is *d*, which is *inaccurate*. Neither heroin nor cocaine is made from cannabis.

Merely Informative
Sources of Drugs

Heroin, like morphine and codeine, is a derivative of opium, which is produced from the seeds of opium poppies. It is strongly addictive, and its manufacture and importation into the United States is prohibited. Cocaine, also a crystalline, white powdery substance, is derived from coca plants.

Cannabis is a tall Asiatic herb, also known as hemp. The tough fiber of the cannabis stem is used to produce rope or sailcloth. Marijuana is made from the dried leaves and flowers of the plant. The resin of the plant is known as hashish. The active ingredient of marijuana, tetrahydrocannabinol, or THC, is intoxicating and causes a mix of physical effects.

---

10. **Hallucinogens.** The answer is *b*, which is *not* true.

Notwithstanding their other effects and risks, there are no known withdrawal symptoms from using hallucinogens, although they may have recurring effects, such as unpleasant flashbacks.

The other statements are correct. Each of the drugs mentioned, as well as the "designer drugs," Ecstasy and PCE, are hallucinogens. (A combination of PCP and cocaine is sometimes called "Beam Me Up, Scottie.") Designer drugs may be stronger than the originals and can cause the serious, irreversible health effects listed, and large doses of other hallucinogens can cause severe damage to the heart, lungs, or brain.

More Where This Came From

General information can be found in the American Medical Association's Charles B. Clayman, *Home Medical Encyclopedia*. New York: Random House, 1989, or Jeffrey R. Kunz, Asher J. Finkel, *Family Medical Guide*, New York: Random House, 1987.

The RAT's Mouse

Your computer mouse can lead you to the following websites on drugs.

- **//www.nlm.nih.gov/medlineplus/substanceabuse.html** A National Institute of Health site on substance abuse, with a directory containing a wide range of topics, from alcohol to hallucinogens
- **www.nida.nih.gov/MarijBroch/Marijintro.html** A good website on marijuana, put out by the National Institute on Drug Abuse
- **www.dancesafe.org/ecstasy.html** A site on the drug, Ecstasy, promoting safety in the raving nightclub community; see the "slide show" that shows how Ecstasy affects the brain and how it ultimately causes a "low"
- **www.thetruth.com** An antismoking site focusing on young people
- **www.nida.nih.gov/ResearchReports/Steroids/AnabolicSteroids.html** A site on anabolic steroids
- **www.nida.nih.gov/NIDAHome1.html** A large site on drugs
- **www.health.org** An extensive site with detailed profiles of a number of illicit drugs, including street names, definitions, and possible effects

18.   ALCOHOL ABUSE—ANSWERS

A. Generally

1. **Alcohol Content.**   The answer is *d;* they all have approximately the same amount of alcohol.

      This is a trick question. Although the percentage of alcohol in beer, wine, and liquor is different, a bottle of beer, a glass of wine, and one mixed drink each contain approximately equal amounts of alcohol. The arithmetic is as follows:

Amount of Alcohol in Standard Drinks

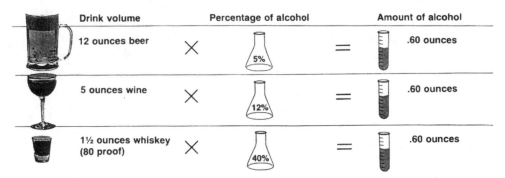

From *Drive Right* by Margaret Johnson, Owen Crabb, Richard Kaywood, Arthur Opfer, and Ronald Budig. © 1991 by Addison-Wesley. Published by Prentice Hall, Inc. Used by permission.

2. **The Effects of 1 Drink.**   The answer is *b*, on average, an hour and a half.

Merely Informative
Dealing with Effects

After three drinks, the average time required is more than 4 hours. Black coffee, a shower, or vigorous exercise will not sober anyone up.

From *Drive Right* by Margaret Johnson, Owen Crabb, Richard Kaywood, Arthur Opfer, and Ronald Budig. © 1991 by Addison-Wesley. Published by Prentice Hall, Inc. Used by permission.

3. **Treacherous Drinks.**

Certain types of drinks present an above-average risk of intoxication because their flavor obscures the taste of the alcohol, or because they are smooth or tasty and go down easily. For this reason, people who are trying to get friends or dates drunk may push such drinks. They include:

- *Fruit drinks*—Fruit drinks tend to disguise the taste of liquor. As a result, it is easier to overlook or discount the liquor content, or to drink fruit drinks faster than drinks that taste more like liquor. Examples are Planter's Punch, Fog Cutters, and Rum Punch (all three are mixes of fruit juices, rum, and other liquors); likewise, Screwdrivers (orange juice and vodka), Margaritas (lime juice and tequila), Piña Coladas (coconut); Brandy Alexanders (brandy, milk), and Sangria (wine with fruit juices).
- *Vodka drinks*—Because vodka has little flavor or aroma, its taste is not prominent in drinks. Vodka drinks therefore tend to be a bit more treacherous. Examples: vodka and tonic; Bloody Mary (vodka with spicy tomato juice); Screwdrivers; Gimlets; Vodka Martinis (or the standard gin martini, for that matter).
- *Cocktails containing more than one type of liquor*—Unlike highballs, which tend to have one jigger of liquor plus mixer, some mixed drinks include two or more types of liquor. The result is—you guessed it—a higher alcohol content per drink. Many mixed rum drinks—Planter's Punch, Singapore Sling, Fog Cutter—are examples. There is also a new generation of lethal drinks, including Nuts and Berries, B-52s, and Sex on the Beach. And there are others, some with even more provocative names. Perhaps most dangerous of all is Long Island Iced Tea, a concoction of vodka, gin, rum, tequila, triple sec, sour mix, and Coke.
- *Shots and shooters*—By definition, a shot (a jigger of liquor drunk by itself, often in one gulp) is potent because in one swallow you consume the same amount of alcohol in one mixed drink, which you might sip over 20 or 30 minutes. Cowboys in old Westerns drink shots of warm whiskey; patrons of Mexican restaurants are sometimes given the opportunity to consume a shot of tequila. Sweet tarts, melons, and lemon drops are examples of shooters, although some are small, sweet mixed drinks.
- *Drinks that include a sweet mixer (a soft drink)*—Wine coolers are an example, as are rum or bourbon (or anything else) and Coke, and Seven and Seven (Seagrams 7 mixed with Seven-Up). Although tonic (quinine

water) is not quite a sweet soft drink, gin and tonics also have a slightly sweet taste.

- *Cold drinks on a hot day*—Obvious reason: on a hot day you're more likely to be thirsty and to drink more. Hot days and cold beer can lead to higher than usual consumption.

Tip: Don't start drinking any alcoholic beverage when you're thirsty. Have a soft drink or water first to quench your thirst.

Merely Informative
Proof

"Proof" is the measure of alcoholic content that appears on most bottles of hard liquor. The scale used for proof is 0 to 200 and reflects alcohol content from 0 to 100 percent. Thus, "proof" is precisely twice the percentage of alcoholic content. Liquor that is 90 proof is 45 percent alcohol.

Most hard liquor (whiskey, rum, vodka, gin, etc.) is 80 proof, or 40 percent alcohol. Some rums, whiskeys, and other liquors are sold at 100 proof and are obviously more potent than standard 80 proof liquor. After-dinner drinks (brandies, liqueurs) typically are 60 to 70 proof. All bottles of liquor state the proof on the label.

The alcoholic content of wine and beer is not described in terms of proof. Instead, wine and beer labels state the percentage of alcohol. Wine is generally 10 to 14 percent alcohol. Most beer is 5 percent alcohol. Beer called "3.2 beer" contains 3.2 percent alcohol. "Nonalcoholic beer" contains none. If measured in terms of "proof," most wine would be 20 to 28 proof, and beer would be 10 proof.

---

4. **Nonalcoholic Drinks.**

Nonalcoholic Beer: O'Doul's is a nonalcoholic beer. So are Coors Cutter, Buckler, King's, Sharp's, and Clausthauer. If you order one of these, most people won't know it's not a regular beer, even if they hear you place your order.

Nonalcoholic Bar Drinks: A Shirley Temple and a Roy Rogers are both nonalcoholic drinks familiar to most bartenders and waiters. Since they are bright pink (lots of grenadine) and popular with 8-year-olds, however, they aren't very surreptitious. You may prefer a Virgin Mary (a Bloody Mary without the vodka). In fact, you can order a "virgin" version of many drinks (dacquiri, margarita, piña colada) and get an alcohol-free drink. Perrier,

Saratoga, or seltzer is just carbonated water. With a slice of lime, carbonated water looks like a gin and tonic.

5. **Saying No.** Whatever works best for you is best. In the meantime, here are some possibilities:
   - No, thanks.
   - No, thanks; it makes me fall asleep.
   - No, thanks; I'm already at my limit.
   - Oh, yuck!!
   - Thanks, but I'm the designated driver.
   - No, thanks. The stuff makes me cross-eyed (or grumpy/start speaking my first language/violent).
   - I'd love to, but I have to get up a 6 A.M. (to run in a race/for my first date/to go to karate class/to get the free early-bird concert tickets).
   - Can you believe it? I actually can't stand the taste.
   - I can't have a drink right now because of the medicine I'm taking.
   - It kind of reminds me of cough syrup (lima beans/moldy cheese/what I used to clean my motorcycle with).
   - Sorry, I can't—third-generation alcoholic.

6. **Reducing the Effects of Drinking.** Although nothing will prevent alcoholic beverages from affecting you, other than the first option listed below, the effects may be marginally reduced by the following:
   - Don't drink at all. Have a soft drink or mineral water with a slice of lime.
   - Don't drink when you're thirsty. If you are thirsty, start with a Coke or bottled water until your thirst is quenched.
   - Sip. If you nurse a drink, you can make it last for 30 minutes, maybe an hour. When your ice melts, ask for more ice and nurse it more. Don't finish your drink completely; an empty glass invites a refill.
   - Munch food while you drink. Snacks or other food slow the absorption of alcohol into your bloodstream.
   - Eat before you drink—bread, salad dressing, pasta, pizza, milk. All help slow the absorption of alcohol. Eating any of them first is preferable to drinking on an empty stomach.

- If you order a mixed drink from a bartender, ask for a "light" drink, for example, a "light gin and tonic." If your drink is too strong, tell the bartender and ask for more mixer.

7. **Long- and Short-term Effects of Drinking.**

   a. Here are some possible short-term effects of excessive drinking:

   - Intoxication or drunkenness—In most states, intoxication is defined as a blood-alcohol concentration of 0.10 percent.
   - Vomiting
   - Impaired reasoning ability—The part of the brain first affected by alcohol is the part that controls judgment and reasoning. Physical impairment follows.
   - Impaired vision—Night vision, peripheral vision, color vision, and depth perception all deteriorate.
   - Impaired muscular coordination
   - Loss of consciousness
   - Hangover—This usually includes the attendant headache and bad breath.

   b. Possible long-term effects of excessive drinking:

   - Alcohol dependence (alcoholism)
   - Cirrhosis of the liver
   - Flushing or redness in the face
   - Alcoholic hepatitis or other liver diseases
   - Hypertension, heart failure
   - Impotence
   - Heavy drinking during pregnancy can cause fetal alcohol syndrome, which entails various birth defects.

   Source: *Home Medical Encyclopedia,* Random House, 1989, 81–85.

8. **Alcohol Content.**   The answers are

   - The lowest alcohol concentration is in *a*, beer.
   - The highest alcohol concentration is in *b*, grain alcohol.

   In order from lowest to highest level of alcohol content: beer, wine, whiskey, and grain alcohol.

So-called 3.2 beer is a maximum of 3.2 percent alcohol, so it is less strong than regular beer, which is 5 percent alcohol, as is so-called lite beer. Wine is 12 percent alcohol, most distilled spirits (whiskey, bourbon, scotch, gin, vodka, rum) are 40 percent alcohol, and 100 proof liquor is 50 percent alcohol. Grain alcohol can be up to 190 proof and dangerous.

B. Drinking and Driving

9. **Alcohol and Traffic Deaths.**

   a. The answer is *iii;* 50 percent of all traffic deaths are alcohol-related.

Merely Informative
More Statistics

The statistics are even worse for young people 16 to 20. Approximately 30 percent of all traffic deaths—or 60 percent of all alcohol-related traffic deaths—involve young people.

Between 10 P.M. and 3 A.M. on Friday and Saturday nights, the statistics are even more amazing. During those hours, approximately one in ten drivers is legally drunk. Of fatal collisions involving only one vehicle, two-thirds of the drivers are legally drunk.

Source: *Drive Right,* Glenview, Illinois: Scott Foresman and Company, 1991.

---

   b. The answer is *iii;* 90 percent of all single-car traffic deaths after midnight are alcohol-related.

10. **Getting a Drinking Driver to Stop and Let You Out.**   Here are four possibilities:
    - "Better pull over. I think I'm about to throw up."
    - "I really have to go to the bathroom. Stop right now. Just for a minute."
    - "Stop! I just dropped my wallet out the window."
    - When the car stops at a traffic light, just get out. Once out, don't get back in unless you are allowed to drive.

 *The RAT's Mouse*

A few web sites accessible with your computer mouse:

- **www.AA.org** A link to "a message to teenagers"
- **www.niaaa.nih.gov** See "frequently asked questions"; facts about alcoholism, treatment, signs of a problem, how to get help, safe levels of drinking, drinking during pregnancy
- **www.library.thinkquest.org/23713** A site on driving under the influence; lots of information in various chapters—alcohol, long- and short-term effects of drinking, driving—with a quiz at the end of each chapter (*The RAT's* kind of web site)
- **www.beeresponsible.com** From Anheuser-Busch, a good site that you must be 21 to enter (honor system)

19. **CARDS AND GAMBLING—ANSWERS**

1. **A Deck of Cards.**   The answer is *a.*

    In bridge, poker, and other games in which suits are ranked, the correct ranking, from highest to lowest, is spades, hearts, diamonds, and clubs.

    The three face cards in decks of cards are kings, queens, and jacks. Jokers are wild cards; they typically come two to a deck and are not used in many games. The ace is the highest card, but the 2 is the lowest. There is no "1" other than the ace. In some card games, the ace can be counted as high, low, or either. The dealer deals *left,* proceeding clockwise, dealing to himself or herself last. Cards are shuffled to mix the sequence of cards, and they typically are cut just before the deal to change the top and bottom cards—not the opposite.

2. **Classic Card Games.**

    a. *Social Card Games*
        Dozens of card games are played socially (as opposed to professional competitions) by two or more players. The following are among the classics, together with the object of the game and a few of the most important features of each:

i. *Gin Rummy*—Typically, this is a game for two people. Each player is dealt ten cards; one card is then turned face up, and the remainder of the deck becomes the draw pile. The object is to form matched sets of three or four of a kind or sequences of three or four of the same suit of all the cards you hold in your hand, and to lay down your hand—saying "gin"—before your partner does. An alternative to declaring "gin" is "to knock," a gamble that your opponent will be stuck with unmatched cards with a higher total value than your unmatched cards. Gin Rummy, like the various Rummy games, comes in many variants.

ii. *Hearts*—Three to seven players can play Hearts. All cards are dealt. For each play, every player must discard one card, face up. The highest card played wins the play and takes the played cards ("the trick"). Hearts are "trump." The object is to avoid taking any hearts or the queen of spades. Because it involves both tricks and trump, learning how to play hearts is a big step towards learning how to play Bridge.

iii. *Blackjack*—A common casino game, the rules of Blackjack are relatively simple. Each player is dealt two cards, one face up, one face down. The numbered cards have their face value; all face cards are worth 10 points; an ace can be counted as either 1 or 11 points, at the option of the person holding the card. The object is to accumulate, by asking for additional cards one at a time, 21 points, or as close to 21 as possible without going over. Any player who goes over 21 "busts" (loses). The combination of an ace and a face card is blackjack and is automatically a winning hand.

iv. *Bridge*—Contract Bridge is a partnership game of cards played by four players. Highlights of the rules, which are complicated, include the following: After all 52 cards are dealt, players bid. The partner of the player who wins the bid lays down all of his or her cards and is the "dummy" for that hand. The object of the game is for the player with the winning bid to "make his bid," which means to take six tricks plus as many or more tricks as you bid in your winning bid (e.g., "three hearts"). The suit of the winning bid (hearts, for example) becomes the trump suit.

Bridge can be played casually or seriously. It is a game of great subtlety with many possible conventions and countless devotees. In

CARDS AND GAMBLING

addition, it has been the subject of countless books and other teaching mediums and the object of clubs, classes, and tournaments.

b. *Children's Card Games*

Among the card games that may appeal to children from age 5 or 6 are:

- Slapjack (players try to slap the first jack played)
- War (all players play a card simultaneously; highest card takes the pile)
- Go Fish (players ask one another if they have particular cards; if not, the asker is told to "go fish" in the "fish pile")
- Old Maid (the player left with the odd queen ["the Old Maid"] loses)

Detailed rules of each of these children's games, together with illustrations, can be found in *The Little Giant Encyclopedia of Card Games,* *Hoyle's Rules of Games,* and other similar books (see More Where This Came From).

3. **Solitaire.**   Although you may not know them by their names, there are three common varieties. Some books on card games list dozens of varieties of solitaire.

a. *Klondike*—Perhaps the best-known solitaire game is Klondike, although the name is not well known. It is played with one deck of 52 cards. Cards are arrayed in seven piles and may be played from one pile to another and from the deck to the piles. The object is to accumulate above the row of seven piles, four separate piles—one for each suit—beginning with the ace as the foundation and, ultimately, all other cards in order.

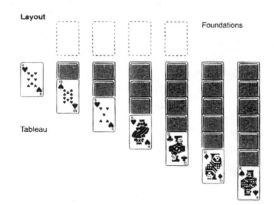

Used with permission of Sterling Publishing Co., Inc., N.Y., N.Y. from *The Little Giant Encyclopedia of Card Games* by The Diagram Group, © 1995 by Diagram Visual Information Ltd.

b. *Accordion*—Played with one deck, the cards are laid out, face up, in a row from left to right. In accordance with the rules, the object is to combine cards into piles and to end the game with just one pile. Also known as Tower of Babel, idle year, or Methuselah.

Detailed rules for Klondike, Accordion, and other solitaire games may be found in *The Little Giant Encyclopedia of Card Games*.

c. *Eight-card solitaire*—Deal eight cards, face up, in two rows of four. Cover any two cards of the same denomination—two jacks, for example—with two cards from the deck. Repeat so long as the eight cards contain two or three cards of the same denomination. The object is to continue until all cards in the deck have been played. If you reach a point where no two of the eight cards are the same denomination, the game is over.

4. **Poker.**   Sometimes called the national card game of the United States, poker is a betting game. The object is to win the pot, which goes to the player with the best hand.

Although there are numerous types of poker, the typical poker hand consists of five cards. The best poker hands are, in increasing rank:

- A pair (two nines, or two aces, for example)
- Two pairs
- Three of a kind
- A straight (five consecutive cards as, for example, 7, 8, 9, 10, jack)
- A flush (five cards of the same suit—for example, five spades)
- A full house (a pair and three of a kind—for example, three 6s and a pair of queens)
- Four of a kind
- A straight flush (five consecutive cards in the same suit—for example, 4, 5, 6, 7, and 8 of diamonds). The highest variant of a straight flush is a "royal flush": 10, jack, queen, king, and ace of the same suit.

Different poker games allow players to be dealt additional cards to replace the ones they discard. In many poker games, certain cards are designated as "wild cards."

5. **The Lottery.**   The answer is *c*, which is *false*. Slot machines pay a higher percentage of what is bet than do lotteries.

The amounts that slot machines return varies—from state to state, casino to casino, and slot machine to slot machine. However, most states require a minimum payback level by law, amounts that tend to range from about 75 percent to up to close to 90 percent. Certain casinos guarantee higher win percentages, sometimes more than 90 percent.

By contrast, the percentage of revenue from lotteries that goes to the winners is typically much smaller. For example, *The Absolute Beginner's Guide to Gambling* reports that of all of the money raised by ticket sales for the California Super Lotto, half goes to the state of California. Out of California's half, a portion (16 percent of the total) goes to operating expenses and commissions, while the remainder (34 percent of the total) goes to education. The other half of the proceeds is divided up among the lottery winners.

The other statements are all true. Although lotteries, after being common in the American colonies, were outlawed by all of the states by the end of the nineteenth century, beginning in the 1960s, states began legalizing lotteries again, and lotteries are now lawful in a majority of states.

One of the reasons states outlawed lotteries was that many were corrupt. One of the most celebrated of the scandals occurred in 1824 when British Treasury officials disappeared with the money from the national lottery. Most U.S. lotteries are now run by states or state entities and generally are perceived as being free from corruption.

Lottery winners who win, for example, $10 million paid out over twenty years actually win less than $10 million in terms of the current value of their winnings. This is because the amounts paid annually are typically paid without interest, so that the lottery, not the winner, gets the benefit of the "time value of the money" (the right to earn interest on the money). As a result, if the winner of a $10 million jackpot to be paid out over time wanted to sell her winnings for a single, immediate cash payment, she could sell it only for the "discounted present value," a sum considerably less than $10 million.

Merely Informative
Voluntary Taxation

Because substantial portions of the revenues collected from lotteries are used to pay for education, roads, and other state government activities, these portions serve the same functions as revenues from taxes. The amount of revenue that states now earn from state lotteries is well into the billions of dollars, and many states have come to depend on lotteries as a source of state revenue.

As a result, "national governments all over the world . . . recognize that lotteries are a form of voluntary taxation . . ." (*The Absolute Beginner's Guide to Gambling,* p. 28). Popularized by the lure of winning large sums of money with a bet of only a dollar or two, lotteries generate revenue that is dedicated, in part, to various public purposes. Viewed as a form of voluntary taxation, lotteries spark lively debate about whether they are regressive taxes (the burden of which falls proportionately more heavily on low-income earners than on the wealthy).

6. **The Odds of Winning the Lottery.** The answer is d, the odds are 1 in 18,009,460.

   The odds of matching five of six are 1 in 66,702; the odds of matching four of six are 1 in 1,213; the odds of matching three of six are 1 in 60.

Merely Informative
What the Odds Really Mean

Quoting statistician Mike Orkin, the *Absolute Beginner's Guide* states that "most people can't fathom what their real chances are like. 'To put these odds in perspective, if you buy fifty Lotto tickets a week, you'll win the jackpot about once every five thousand years.'"

7. **Casino Gambling.** The answers are
   a. *True.*
   b. *False.*
   c. *True.*
   d. *False.*

a. The odds always favor the house, which is why casinos make money.

b. Casinos' actual win percentage is *not* lower than their mathematical advantage. The opposite is the case, primarily because casinos benefit from unskilled players, who often make mistakes or don't know how to maximize their chances.

c. Casinos often provide free or discounted food or drinks, and sometimes elaborate stage shows or other entertainment, in an effort to attract customers, who they hope will gamble.

d. Time is *not* on your side, because the odds in most games favor the house. If, for example, you're winning, the longer you play, the greater the chances—purely as a statistical matter—that the odds will catch up with you and you'll lose.

Merely Informative
Gambling Addiction

Gambling can become compulsive, and it is possible to become addicted to gambling. A gambling addiction can ruin relationships, families, careers, and individual lives. Some of the circumstances that may contribute to gambling addictions are:

- borrowing money to gamble;
- going into debt by gambling, as by using credit cards;
- gambling when inebriated;
- gambling to make up for a loss; or
- gambling to relieve stress, grief, loneliness, anger, or depression.

Organizations that can provide help with gambling addictions include Gamblers Anonymous in Los Angeles, The National Council on Problem Gambling, Inc., in New York City, and Gam-Anon in Whitestone, New York.

---

8. **Blackjack.** *True.* Blackjack is both the most popular casino game and the game with the best chances of winning. For an educated player who follows sound strategies, the odds are close to even—some authorities give the house a .5 percent edge; others give the skilled player a slight edge.

Although the rules of Blackjack are relatively simple, to minimize the advantage of the house, a player must understand a few basic principles or strategies.

9. **Casino Games.**   *Craps.*

Craps is the most complicated of the casino games. Like most others, it is purely a game of chance. The skill involved is in the betting, in that the odds of particular combinations being rolled is higher than for other combinations, so some bets are smarter than others.

Merely Informative
A Few Helpful Principles

A few useful tidbits from *The Absolute Beginner's Guide to Gambling:*

- When gambling, "take only as much money with you, in cash, as you plan on losing. . . . Never bet money you're not prepared to lose" (pp. 21–22).
- "Gambling, because the odds are weighted against you, should be viewed as a form of entertainment and not as an investment" (p. 20).
- "The real object in Blackjack is not to get as close to 21 as possible but to beat the dealer" (p. 123).
- "The key to winning at slot machines . . . is to *quit when you're ahead!*" (p. 77).
- One of the "technological gimmicks to keep gamblers spending money [is] having slot machines emit a special scent, Odorant 1, developed by a Chicago neurologist, which allegedly keeps slot addicts at the machines longer" (p. 16).
- "Always keep in mind that if you play long enough, you *will* lose when gambling" (pp. 20–21).
- "Lotteries are a form of voluntary taxation" (p. 28). Corollary: If you want to lower your taxes, don't play lotto.

---

10. **Gambling Facts.**   The answer is *a.*

If you played the odds, you answered *b*, because there are six possible combinations of true/false answers that would make *b* the correct answer (TTF, TFT, TFF, FFT, FTF, FTT). However *a* would be the correct answer only with one combination of true/false answers (TTT), and likewise with *b* (FFF). In this case, however, if you played the odds and answered *b*, you were wrong.

The correct answer is *a.* Each of the three statements in question 10 is true.

More Where This Game From

Hoyle's Rules of Games, by Albert Morehead and Geoffrey Mott-Smith, is a classic reference on hundreds of indoor games, particularly card games, casino games, and other games of chance.

The Absolute Beginner's Guide to Gambling, New York: Pocket Books, 1996, by Robert J. Hutchinson, from Bingo to bridge, lotteries to race tracks.

The Everything Casino Gambling Book, Holbrook, Massachusetts: Adams Media Corporation, 1998, by George Mandos, is a readable reference on casino gambling, games and guidance.

The Little Giant Encyclopedia of Card Games, New York: Sterling Publishing Co., 1995, by the Diagram Group. Fat but pocket-sized, covering over 200 card games, with illustrations.

The RAT's Mouse

Your computer mouse can lead you to:

*   **www.conjelco.com/pokglossary.html**   A glossary of poker terms
*   **www.solitairecentral.com/**   A lively site on solitaire with a casino-like feel
*   **www.insidepreakness.com/**   A good site on horse racing, with a selection on "betting terminology" under "betting resources"

D. THINGS TO GIVE YOU AN EDGE

20. INTERNATIONAL FUNDAMENTALS—ANSWERS

1. **Crossing International Borders.**   The answer is *d*, a visa.

    Many countries, although not all, require that travelers have a visa to enter the country. Visas typically are in the form of a stamp that is put on one of the blank pages of your passport. They are usually obtained in your own country through the embassy or chancery of the country to which you are traveling. Visas are typically of limited duration—for example, six months or a year. Before traveling to a particular foreign country, find out if you need an entry visa.

Passports are issued by the country in which you reside. They are typically required for international travel and are inspected by border officials of your country when you return and of the countries you are visiting.

A tariff is a duty, or tax, imposed at the border on the value of newly purchased goods being brought into a country. A customs declaration is a form on which travelers are required to disclose the value of purchased products they are bringing into a country. Health certificates, or proof that you have had certain inoculations, are required to enter some countries where particular diseases are common.

2. **Centigrade and Fahrenheit.**   The answer is 68 degrees Fahrenheit.

Merely Informative
Converting from Centigrade

The centigrade scale, also known as the Celsius scale, is a part of the international metric system and is used in most of the world other than in the United States. In centigrade, the freezing point is 0 degrees, and the boiling point of water is 100 degrees.

To convert from centigrade to Fahrenheit, remember a simple formula: On the Fahrenheit scale, the difference between freezing (32 degrees) and boiling (212 degrees) is 180 degrees, so one degree centigrade equals 1.8 degrees Fahrenheit. And on the Fahrenheit scale, freezing is 32 degrees above 0.

Thus, to convert centigrade to Fahrenheit, multiply the number of centigrade degrees by 1.8, then add 32.

Hence: 0 degrees centigrade = 32 degrees Fahrenheit

    10 degrees centigrade = 50 degrees Fahrenheit
    20 degrees centigrade = 68 degrees Fahrenheit
    25 degrees centigrade = 77 degrees Fahrenheit
    30 degrees centigrade = 86 degrees Fahrenheit
    35 degrees centigrade = 95 degrees Fahrenheit
    40 degrees centigrade = 104 degrees Fahrenheit

INTERNATIONAL FUNDAMENTALS

3. **International Phrases.**   Here are, among others, a greeting, a farewell, and thank you in a few languages:

Spanish:

Buenos días; hola	Good day; hello
¿Cómo está?	How are you?
Gracias	Thank you
Adiós	Good-bye
Sí; no	Yes; no
Senor, senora, senorita	Mr., Mrs., Miss
Mañana	Tomorrow
Gringo	American

French:

Bonjour	Good day
Comment allez-vous?	How are you?
Merci	Thank you
Au revoir	Good-bye
Bon appétit	Enjoy your meal
Bonne chance	Good luck
Monsieur, madame	Mr., Mrs.
Mademoiselle	Miss
Allez-vous-en!	Get lost!; go away!

German:

Guten Tag	Good day
Wie geht's?	How are you?
Sehr gut	Very well
Auf Wiedersehen	Good-bye
Herr, Frau, Fraülein	Mr., Mrs., Miss
Sprechen sie deutch?	Do you speak German?
Danke schön	Thank you
Bitte	Please, you're welcome
Verboten	Forbidden
Dummkopf	Dumbhead

Russian (phonetic spellings):

DOH-bree-d'yen	Good day
da svee-DA-n'ya	Good-bye
spa-SEE-ba	Thank you

da; n'yet	Yes; no
iz-vee-NEE-t'yeh	Excuse me
pa-ZHAHL-sta	Please
met-RO	Subway
twa-LET	Toilet
DOH-bra	Welcome

Japanese (phonetic spellings):

ko-nee-chee-wa	Good day
kohn-ban-wa	Good evening
sa-yo-na-ra	Good-bye
doh-zo	Please
bahn-zai!	Hurrah!
Moyer-san	Mr., Mrs., or Miss Moyer
hai	yes
ah-ree-ga-toh	thank you
o-hi-o	good morning

More Where This Came From

One handy reference for key words and phrases in major languages other than English is *Passport to the World,* New York: Signet, 1995, by Charles Berlitz, from which many of the phonetic pronunciations above were taken.

4. **Driving Abroad.**

There are more than 50 countries in which automobiles are driven on the left side of the road. Biggies include England (the United Kingdom), Australia, India, and Japan. The full list, which includes large numbers of former British colonies, includes the following:

Antigua	Australia	Bahamas
Barbados	Bermuda	Bhutan
Botswana	Brunei	Cayman Islands
Channel Islands	Cyprus	Dominica
Fiji	Grenada	Guyana
Hong Kong	India	Indonesia
Ireland	Jamaica	Japan

Kenya	Lesotho	Macao
Malawi	Malaysia	Malta
Mauritius	Montserrat	Mozambique
Namibia	Nepal	New Zealand
Pakistan	Papua New Guinea	Seychelles
Singapore	South Africa	Sri Lanka
St. Christopher, Nevis	St. Lucia	St. Vincent
Suriname	Swaziland	Tanzania
Thailand	Trinidad and Tobago	Uganda
United Kingdom	Peninsular Malaysia	Zambia
Zimbabwe		

5. **Foreign Languages.**   The answers are

   a. Mandarin Chinese
   b. English
   c. French

   Mandarin Chinese is spoken by more people in the world than any other single language. The other top five include English, Hindi, Spanish, and Russian.

   English has become the language of international business and international air traffic control, and it is the second most commonly spoken language. It is also the official second language of more countries than any other.

   The traditional international language is French, the language of France and of many countries around the world that were once French colonies or protectorates. In Quebec, the Canadian province adjacent to northern New England, French is one of the two official languages. French is also the most common foreign language spoken in Louisiana (a state that has drawn on the French legal system), and Maine, New Hampshire, and Vermont (all of which border Quebec).

Merely Informative
Speaking a Second Language

Speaking one or more foreign languages unlocks many doors. As M. D. Berlitz put it, "'Speaking only one language is like living in a great mansion of many rooms,

continued on next page

each filled with fascinating treasures, but staying always in one room only'"
(*Passport to the World,* p. 13).

Census studies released in 1993 show that 14 percent of the U.S. population
age 5 or older—some 31.8 million Americans—speak a language other than
English. Spanish is the foreign language spoken by more U.S. residents than any
other. The most common foreign language in 39 states, Spanish is spoken by
more than 17 million Americans. In addition to Spain, Spanish is the official
language of almost all of the countries of Central and South America (except
Brazil, whose language is Portuguese).

The next most common foreign languages in the United States are German,
Italian, and Chinese. In Hawaii, Japanese is the most common foreign language;
in Rhode Island, it's Portuguese.

Apart from courses and language labs in school, other ways to master a
foreign language are summer language camps, language tapes, foreign language
television, and visiting a foreign country or where a language other than English
is spoken. *Tip:* One proven formula for learning conversational Spanish is to
conscientiously listen to foreign language instructional tapes in your car or on a
portable stereo every day for three months. Then rent three Spanish movies and
watch each one repeatedly until you are able to understand everything that is
said. Then, use it or lose it!

Sources: *The World Almanac, 1997* ed., Robert Famighetti (K-III Reference
Corporation 1996); *The Universal Almanac,* 1997 ed., John Wright, Andrews and
McMeel, 1996.

6. **Time differences.**

If you live in the Eastern Standard time zone (New York, Washington,
Boston, Atlanta, Miami, Cleveland), the time differences are

London:	5 hours later: at 12 noon in Boston, its 5 P.M. in London
Vancouver:	3 hours earlier, like California
Moscow:	8 hours later

If you live in the Pacific time zone (Los Angeles, San Francisco, Seattle),
the time differences are:

London:	8 hours later
New York:	3 hours later
Moscow:	11 hours later

Merely Informative
Time Zones

Note that some countries or regions observe Daylight Savings Time, but others don't. As a result, normal time differences may vary by an hour if one city is on Daylight Savings Time but the other is not, or if one of the two has gone onto or off of Daylight Savings Time and the other hasn't yet.

Time zones are often identified with reference to "Greenwich Mean Time," referring to Greenwich, England, through which the Prime Meridian passes. There are 24 time zones around the globe, although in Asia, some time zones are 30 minutes different from adjacent zones. When you cross the international date line, the day of the week and the hour change. The international date line runs through the Pacific Ocean and through the Bering Strait that separates Alaska from far eastern Russia (Siberia).

7. **International Travel.**

    a. *Tips for minimizing jet lag.*

    - Don't drink alcohol while traveling across time zones.
    - Drink lots of nonalcoholic liquids.
    - Eat lightly on a long flight.
    - Adjust your schedule before you leave to move closer to the time zone to which you are traveling.
    - Use hand lotion or moisturizer to minimize dehydration on a long flight.
    - When traveling east and arriving during the day, take a morning nap if you arrive early, but otherwise try to avoid a nap and stay awake until after dinner.
    - In your new time zone, get outside during the daylight hours.
    - When traveling west, try to sleep one-third the number of hours you gain by crossing time zones. For example, if traveling from Frankfurt to New York, and thereby gain six hours, try to sleep about two hours on the flight. (This technique maintains roughly the same ratio between waking hours and sleeping hours that you keep when you aren't traveling.)

    b. *Medications*

    The classic medication for travel or motion sickness is Dramamine. Other nonprescription medications are Marezine and Bonine. Prescription drugs include Phenergan and Transderm Scop. All should be taken before travel, and all induce drowsiness, so they should not be used by drivers).

The New England Journal of Medicine reports that ginger has a natural ingredient that relieves motion sickness. Available in capsule form in health food stores, ginger reduces nausea without inducing drowsiness.

For diarrhea, Pepto-Bismol, Lomotil, Kaopectate, and Imodium are commonly used medications. If you have diarrhea, it is also critical to rehydrate, which requires drinking lots of liquids. Some experts recommend water with sugar, salt, and baking soda added.

8. **Foreign Currencies.**

a. *False.*

When the U.S. dollar is strong, the exchange rate for changing U.S. dollars for a foreign currency is favorable and, as a consequence, purchases of foreign currency are relatively cheaper, not more expensive. Here's why: Many currencies have "floating exchange rates," which means that their value fluctuates. For example, the number of francs that one U.S. dollar will buy changes over time. Sometimes changes occur rapidly, such as between the time you enter a country and buy its currency and the time you leave and trade in your local currency for dollars or some other currency. (Some currencies have "fixed exchange rates," which means that they don't fluctuate. Thus, a currency that is fixed on the U.S. dollar maintains the same relative value to the dollar.)

When the U.S. dollar is "strong" relative to another currency, such as the British pound, one U.S. dollar will buy more pounds than when the dollar is weak. Thus, Americans traveling in other countries benefit from a strong dollar because it buys more. (Conversely, U.S. companies selling American products in foreign countries are disadvantaged by a strong dollar because a strong dollar makes U.S. products relatively more expensive to buy.)

b. *Units of Currency in some foreign countries.*

Russia	Ruble
Japan	Yen
Canada	Canadian dollar
Mexico	Peso
United Kingdom	Pound sterling
France	French franc and euro

Germany	Deutsche Mark and euro
Italy	Lira and euro
Austria	Schilling and euro
China	Yuan

Merely Informative
More Currencies

Less widely known:

| Brazil | Real | Vietnam | Dong | Sweden | Krona |
| Albania | Lek | Israel | Shekel | Bahrain | Dinar |

---

9. **Violating Local Laws.**   The answer is *c;* you may be prosecuted in accordance with local law.

If a U.S. citizen is facing a very severe penalty, particularly one not imposed in the United States, the U.S. embassy in the country may attempt to intervene on the American's behalf. However, the United States has no legal authority to prevent punishment according to local law and custom, and Americans who violate laws of the country they are visiting sometimes have been given harsh prison sentences or subjected to physical punishment, such as caning.

Many countries impose severe punishments for drug use, sex crimes, or other crimes considered by them to be reprehensible. This is just one of the reasons that travelers to any country should be aware of local customs and laws.

10. **Neighboring Countries.**

The prime minister of Canada is Jean Chretien, a native of Quebec who is a member of Canada's Liberal Party. He was elected in 1993 and reelected in 2000.

In December 2000, Vincente Fox Quesada was elected the new president of Mexico, representing the first shift in political power in Mexico in more than two generations. He succeeded Ernesto Zedillo, a member of the PRI party, which had controlled the government for more than 70 years. Zedillo was elected in 1994.

More Where This Came From

The Fearless Diner, San Francisco: Travelers' Tales Inc., 1998, by Richard Sterling, provides "travel tips and wisdom for eating around the world."

There's No Toilet Paper on the Road Less Traveled, San Francisco: Travelers' Tales Inc., 1998, edited by Doug Lansky, is a collection of humorous essays on international travel adventures.

Without a Guide, Toronto: MacFarlane Walter and Ross, 1994, edited by Katherine Govier, is a collection of "contemporary women's travel adventures."

The RAT's Mouse

International information at the touch of your computer mouse . . .

- **www.campustravel.com/resources/driving.htm** Select a country and learn about driving there, learn about the cars, review a map; also information on international driver's licenses

- **www.finance.yahoo.com/m3?u** An easy currency exchange rate site

- **www.weather.com/** Weather around the world

21. ETIQUETTE—ANSWERS

1. **Expressing Thanks for Having Been a Guest in Someone's Home.**

    a. *Thank your hosts when you leave.* Perhaps the most obvious way to express your appreciation is to say thanks in person to your host(s) as you leave. You should always do this, at a minimum.

       If your hosts are not nearby when you leave, find them. If they aren't at home when you depart, leave them a note. If you're staying at the family home of a friend, you must thank the parent(s) as well as your friend.

    b. *A gift for your hosts.* Giving your hosts a gift can be a thoughtful gesture of thanks. Such a gift need be neither elaborate nor expensive; the thought behind the gesture is more important than the gift itself. If it's something your hosts may need or especially enjoy, that is even more thoughtful.

It is also appropriate to give such a gift at the beginning of your visit, rather than at the end. Among the gift possibilities are a small book, a bottle of wine, flowers, a plant, nice soap, an unusual jam, nuts, mints, or candy. More exotic: wild rice, a picture calendar, wind chimes, a framed photo of your hosts from an earlier occasion. Use your imagination.

c. *Telephone the next day and express your thanks.* Calling back the next day is another thoughtful and appropriate way to thank your hosts. Although less formal than the next option, a follow-up call adds to the bare minimum of expressing your thanks as you leave.

d. *A thank-you note.* A note expressing your appreciation for your stay is perhaps the most gracious of the four options and may be appreciated the most.

Thank-you notes don't have to be lengthy nor gushing. They should be handwritten, not typed, and they should be sincere. Say something positive and appropriate about your visit—what an enjoyable time you had, how welcoming your hosts were, some particular moment that you especially appreciated, that you look forward to seeing them soon, that you hope they have a pleasant holiday, etc.

If you send a thank-you note, try to send it as soon as possible after your visit. If you buy a card that has "thank you" as its printed message (not recommended), add your own personal note.

Merely Informative
Thanks for Other Occasions

The same four alternatives generally apply to other occasions as well as a visit to someone's home. Any of the four are appropriate thanks, for example, for having been a dinner guest. Which of the four is appropriate may depend on the circumstances. A warm thank you to your hosts as you leave may be sufficient for certain parties; on the other hand, if you've stayed with someone for a week, a thank-you note or a small gift, or both, is advisable.

2. **Sneezing.**   Right answers include:

   a. Turn away from the table, which is where all of the food and your dinner companions are located.

   b. Head off the sneeze. Some people can do this, some can't. If you have some sneeze-avoidance technique that is not offensive (some people can avert a sneeze by pressing the back of their index finger against the bottom of the nose, or by pinching the outsides of the nostrils), try it.

   c. Cover your nose and mouth with your napkin, a tissue or handkerchief, or, as a third choice, your hand.

   d. If you do sneeze, say, "excuse me."

   Unnecessary: speculating about what nasal sensation or other stimulation brought on the sneeze. Likewise, not necessary to underscore the event by combining the sneeze with a loud, clever sound, such as AAAAH-CHOOO, or HAAA-CHA-MIGHTY!

Merely Informative
Yawns and Other Body Sounds

Although you don't risk showering your friends with a yawn, the same rules generally apply as with sneezes.

In American culture, many body noises are regarded as impolite and should be avoided in public. These include slurping your coffee or soup, loud sniffing, or expelling gas from either end of your alimentary canal. If some truly involuntary body sound occurs, such as a loud stomach growl, just say, "excuse me," and act as if it was the uncontrollable act of some third party.

---

3. **Formal Meals.**   The details of a formal place setting may vary, depending on how fancy the dinner is and how many pieces of silverware are used. The basics, which generally don't change, are:

   • Forks on the left of the plate
   • Knives and spoons on the right (the knife is next to the plate, sharp edge of the knife blade facing in toward the plate; spoons on the outside)
   • Salad plate and bread and butter plate are on the left, salad plate below, bread and butter above (if the salad is served as a separate course, it

usually is placed in the middle, on top of your dinner plate or where your dinner plate was)

- Beverages are on the right, at about one or two o'clock in relation to your dinner plate (if there is both a water glass and a wine glass, the wine glass is on the outside)
- Your napkin may be on top of your empty dinner plate, folded under your forks, or even folded and placed in your empty water glass; under the forks or in the center of the plate is a safe choice
- Even more silverware may appear in one or two other places; a butter knife may be on your bread and butter plate; sometimes a dessert fork or knife is placed horizontally above your plate; a small fork for an appetizer may also be placed above the plate

b. *Deciding Which Piece of Silverware to Use.* Two rules of thumb will get you through most moments of doubt or panic.

You generally start with the piece of silverware on the outside and work your way in toward the plate. If, for example, a salad is the first course that calls for a fork, the fork on the outside, farthest away from the plate, will normally be the one to use. If the next course is your entree, or main course, the fork for that course should be next in line.

There are always potential complications. The person who set the table may not have done it right, or may be a troublemaker. Should you end up with the wrong fork, it might not be entirely your fault. In any event, if using the wrong fork turns out to be your greatest mistake, you're doing very well and can skip the rest of the questions.

Traditional rule of thumb number two is simply to watch the hostess and do whatever she does. We all hope she knows what she's doing. If not, your mimicry will be flattering and will keep her company.

Merely Informative
The Gracious, Sensitive Host

The legendary corollary to this principle is that thoughtful hosts and hostesses have sometimes done the opposite—namely do whatever a guest may have done, however stupid, to avoid embarrassing the guest. Stories abound of missteps that guests have made, ranging from drinking a finger bowl of water (see below) to

continued on next page

eating whole artichokes, leaves and all. A skilled host or hostess can sometimes head off potential problems with a helpful comment or a reference to how he or she once was baffled about what to do with, for example, a finger bowl. If you are uncertain, wait and watch. Or simply ask.

Many movies, ranging from *My Fair Lady* to *Pretty Woman,* have included memorable scenes on etiquette, in particular the challenges of dining.

c. *Serving and Clearing.* Plates are served from your left and cleared from your right. If you need help remembering this, think L-L and R-R—LAY from the left, REMOVE from the right.

Why there is such a rule may be a harder question. One answer may be consistency and predictability, so that if you move to give the waiter more room, you don't end up colliding with him. It would help, of course, if all waiters learned the rule as well.

Waiters in some restaurants, including some expensive ones, completely disregard this convention. When this happens, you may smugly, but silently, note the error of their ways. That may help if you're feeling defensive because you weren't able to read the French menu.

4. **Etiquette Books.**

There are many books on etiquette. A number are well-recognized, and a number have been updated. Here are three that are both:

Emily Post's Etiquette, New York: HarperCollins Publishers, 1992, published in its 15th edition, is a traditional standby, now written by Emily Post's granddaughter-in-law, Elizabeth Post. It is traditional, but has been updated.

The New Manners for the '90s, Scribner, 1990, by Letitia Baldrige is also traditional, but adventuresome in addressing new topics not commonly covered in books on manners.

Miss Manners' Guide to Excruciatingly Correct Behavior, Budget Book Service, 1997, by Judith Martin is delightful, entertaining, practical, and opinionated. Although it does not answer every traditional etiquette question, its outspoken, commonsense advice is likely to cause you to keep reading past the question you had in mind.

If you named an etiquette book that can be found in a bookstore, count your answer as correct and give yourself two points.

5. **Introductions.**   In the matter of introductions, one person typically introduces two individuals who don't know each other. The person making the introduction introduces one person to the other and tells each the name of the other.

Traditionally, a younger person is introduced to an older person; a less important person is introduced to a more important person; a friend is introduced to a parent. The idea is that it is respectful to an individual to present or introduce another person to him or her. Thus, "Ambassador Kampelman, I would like to introduce Allison Lutz, my roommate." Or, "Uncle Peter, this is Eric Edelson, who just got back from working out west this summer. "

An easy (but not foolproof) way to get it right is to turn to the more "important" person and mention her or his name first. "Dr. Pichard, this is my friend, Joey Frank." "Mrs. Carlson, I would like for you to meet my sister, Kaia Joye."

6. **Proposing a Toast.**   Two excellent rules of thumb for a toast are (1) keep it brief, and (2) conclude on a sincere, upbeat note, even if most of your toast is devoted to a story, or is humorous.

Other useful rules of thumb include:

- At a dinner party, let the host propose the first toast.
- For the key parts of the toast, speak directly to the person you're toasting.
- If you anticipate giving a toast, decide on the theme and practice before a mirror in advance.
- Stand, unless everyone is at one small table.
- Don't drink in response to a toast if you are the one being toasted.

7. **Etiquette Conventions**

a. The right arm—A man traditionally offers a woman his right arm and walks on the left. There are debates on what appropriate exceptions are. If you just learn the basic rule, you'll be ahead of the game.

b. Knife and fork together—The signal that you have finished eating, which most waiters will recognize, is to place your knife and fork closely parallel to one another diagonally across the center of your plate. If they are crossed or placed randomly on your plate, your waiter may not know whether you are finished.

c. Right shoulder or right lapel—Although this is probably not a matter of etiquette, it is best to wear a name tag or badge on your right shoulder. The reason is practical: it is easier for other people to read than if it is on your left or on your left coat pocket. People shake hands with their right hands. In doing so, each person's right shoulder is usually closer to the other person's line of vision than the left shoulder, so it's easier to see.

d. When you receive a formal or engraved invitation that calls for a response (see question 10), there is an established, if pretentious, convention you should be aware of: write in ink on white or off-white paper the following, with each line centered on the page:

Mr. and Mrs. Robert Huffman
accept with pleasure
the kind invitation of
the King of Siam
for Friday, the thirteenth of June.

or:

Ms. Patsy Palmer
very much regrets
that she is unable to accept
the kind invitation of
the King of Siam
for Friday, the thirteenth of June.

An alternative to such a formal response is a gracious note that says essentially the same thing. However, a gracious written invitation is also an option for the person who chooses instead to send a printed or engraved invitation. It's safest to respond with comparable formality. An e-mail response is not likely to be viewed as appropriate by anyone who has decided that engraved invitations were appropriate to the occasion.

Merely Informative Kissing

A bit of etiquette trivia: When kissing someone whom you are greeting socially, which cheek should you kiss, or kiss first? (This question is more important in Europe, perhaps, than in the United States.)

The "correct" answer is that the right cheek is kissed first. Like many conventions, this has some logic. When shaking hands with your right hand, the other person, if not directly in front of you, is likely to be slightly to your right. If greeting that person is to include cheek-kissing, you will find that the person's right cheek is closer and more convenient than the left. Reaching across to kiss the left cheek is slightly more suggestive of an embrace than a social kiss. While it's not a serious mistake to go for the left cheek, it can cause some uncertain head bobbing if the other person is not quite sure where you're headed with your kiss.

---

8. **Etiquette Anachronisms.**   The only thing more reckless than asking this question is trying to answer it. There is no consensus on the right answers to some of these questions, and disagreement over the answers can become heated. (If you get into an argument over it, feel free to leave the author out of it.) Thus, if you have given thoughtful answers to this question, count them as correct, whether or not they agree with the answers below. (Once again, this is a much friendlier test than the SAT.)

Controversial or not, these situations do happen in real life, and you make a choice when you react, even if you do it without thinking. If you do think about them, some basic principles may provide helpful guidance, and a few recent etiquette books offer advice on these subjects.

One helpful principle to remember is that the essence of good etiquette is consideration for others, so it's relevant to assess whether the gesture you are contemplating will be appreciated by the recipient. If you think it will be unwelcome or resented, good etiquette suggests that you not persevere.

The principle of consideration for others also suggests that the anachronistic part of the five situations described in this question is the phrase, "with a female." Although that has been the traditional pattern, the answers today may be applicable without regard to gender.

Having offered these general observations, here goes:

a. *Elevators.* In a crowded elevator or crowded elevator lobby, the people closest to the elevator doors should enter or exit them first. Waiting for people behind you to leave or enter first can cause a traffic jam and annoy everyone involved.

If you are the first to enter an elevator, a courteous gesture is to step in, step to the side, and hold the door open as others enter. If there are only two or three people present, offer the others the opportunity to leave before you, regardless of their gender.

Merely Informative
Hats and Elevators

If you are fond of anachronisms, you may wish to ponder the relative merits of men removing their hats in elevators, the dilemma being the traditional courtesy of a man's removing his hat indoors versus the practical reality that an elevator with men holding their hats in their hands will accommodate fewer passengers than one in which the men leave their hats on their heads.

Should you find yourself in an elevator wondering whether you should remove your hat, bicycle helmet, backwards baseball cap, or headphones, it's probably a safe bet to leave them on.

---

b. *Standing for a woman.* Whether to stand when another person enters the room (or approaches your conversation group or comes to your table at a restaurant) probably should depend on what is likely to happen next. If, for example, you're going to welcome the other person with a handshake, or introduce her or him to others, standing is a good idea and a welcoming gesture. (It is the same principle as bending over to meet a young child—so that you can meet eye-to-eye.) Likewise, if the approaching person is an older person or a special guest to whom you wish to offer your seat, standing is a logical first step.

If the setting is casual, if you're simply going to wave a greeting, or if there is a lot of coming and going, standing likely makes less sense.

The rationale underlying the tradition of standing for women but not for men is far less accepted than it once was, although the traditional view still has its passionate adherents. If, as now seems likely, the tradition of standing for women does fade away, the convention that men should stand to shake hands, but that women may remain seated while shaking hands, probably will disappear at the same time.

c. *Opening a door for a female.* The correct answer probably should be gender-neutral. Holding a door for another is a thoughtful courtesy, particularly if the other person is carrying things, is elderly, is in a hurry, or is someone to whom you wish to show respect. The fact that women, on average, may be able to bench press slightly less than men is irrelevant when it comes to most doors, as well as a dangerous generalization.

An appropriate alternative in the case of a door that opens away from you is to go through the doorway first and hold the door open for those following you. To be avoided: dealing with a hard-to-open door that opens away from you by pushing the door itself so that you are struggling with one arm to hold the door open and partially blocking the doorway with the rest of your body.

The same principle generally applies to car doors. If a car is locked and you have the keys, it is courteous to unlock your passenger's door first. However, the days of a demure date sitting passively in the passenger seat until her escort comes around to open the door and help her out have disappeared, along with passive women. Absent some special circumstances, such a ritual is likely to be viewed as contrived. More to the point, the woman may be driving.

Remember to factor in the other person's expectations. Your grandmother might be proud of your going around the car to open her car door, and she might be grateful for a helping hand in getting out of the seat.

d. *Walking on the curb side.* The original rationale of protecting the woman from passing carriages that might splash mud is no longer applicable, and, in any event, doesn't apply to sunny days.

Today, this is probably a matter of etiquette only when accompanying someone who is unsteady or a young child who might dart toward the traffic, or when there are in fact puddles by the curb and buses and taxis that always seem to seek them out. It should be noted nonetheless that some otherwise fiercely independent women still welcome this tradition as a thoughtful gesture. In the end, it's best to know your audience.

e. *Pulling out a chair.* Although there is probably no rational distinction between formal and informal meals, this question most often presents itself at formal meals. In that setting, this is a tradition that dies hard.

If you decide that your dinner partner would appreciate assistance with her chair, then use the trick known to the best *maitre d*'s: slide the chair not only with your hands and arms, but also by placing the tip of the sole of your shoe at the bottom of a back leg of the chair. With the use of your foot, you can easily and helpfully slide the chair in as your dinner partner sits down.

Other tips:

- In a professional setting, such as a business lunch, this bit of traditional etiquette is likely to be unwelcome, or worse. Leave the problem to the *maitre d'* but don't be the first one to sit down.
- Don't ignore elderly men who may appreciate a little help with a heavy chair.

9. **Hi-Tech Etiquette.**   What new forms of rudeness or impoliteness have arrived with new technologies in your lifetime? Here are three—you may come up with others that are equally correct.

   a. *Call waiting*—Think of a telephone conversation with someone who has call waiting as though it were a live conversation. You have stopped someone and engaged her in conversation or that person has stopped you to have a conversation. In the middle of your conversation, someone comes up behind the person who is talking to you and taps her on the shoulder. Mid-sentence, she says to you, "Don't go anywhere." Then she turns around and talks to the person who interrupted you both. While she talks with the intruder—for just a minute or two, possibly longer—you look at the back of her head and wait for her to finish. She returns. Then it happens again.

   Rude? You bet it is. Is call waiting inherently rude? Probably yes. You, after all, reached the other party. You got there first. You are in the midst of a conversation. Then, you are preempted by a beep, buzz, or silent vibration. You, not the intruder, then have to wait.

   Is there a polite and considerate way to deal with call waiting? Apart from the most obvious answer—don't get call waiting on your phone—there are other ways, albeit imperfect, to minimize the rudeness. One is to ignore a call waiting signal and to tell the person with whom you are talking (if that person can hear the tone) to ignore it as well. Although the tone may still be annoying, your response is flattering, in a back-handed sort of way. If you have call waiting and choose to answer it, excuse yourself from the conversation, be very quick about it, and apologize for the interruption. If you have a helpful explanation—"Sorry, I'm on call for my boss. I apologize"—then give it.

b. *"Flaming" on the Internet*—The practice of "flaming"—sending an anonymous, nasty message back to someone who has said something you disagreed with or found stupid—is a verbal terrorist tactic. Anonymous criticism, like anonymous violence, is cowardly. Nasty anonymous criticism is even worse. The risks of cyberspace, some might say, another snag, however, in our fabric of civility.

c. *Cellular phones*—Unlike call waiting, cellular phones arguably are not inherently impolite. Quite the contrary, they are marvels of telecommunications for which we seem to have a ravenous appetite. They do present new opportunities, however, for displaying a wide range of human behaviors.

For example, using them can be ostentatious (in a meeting); in bad taste (at a funeral); dangerous (while driving a stick-shift car); or risky (when discussing confidential information).

Inconsiderate use of a cell phone can also be impolite or unwelcome, as, for example, when a woman seated in front of me at a theater stood during intermission, turned away from her friends (presumably out of consideration for them), and broadcast directly to me a lengthy conversation with someone about whether and how "the rash" had worsened. One can hope the conversation was with her babysitter, but I can't be certain.

Moral: Etiquette is not just about forks and fussy rules.

10. **Invitation Terms.**

a. Informal. This term, which is a frequent source of confusion, does not mean casual. Rather, it means business dress or coat and tie when it appears on a formal (printed or engraved) invitation.

In the context of a formal invitation, the terms "formal" or "black tie" signify that the intended dress is a tuxedo or evening dress. "White tie," which tends to be used only for diplomatic or exceedingly formal events, is the most formal category. Men wear fly collars, white bow ties, and tails; women wear long gowns.

The term "casual" on a written or printed invitation typically means that coats and ties and cocktail dresses are not expected. An invitation to a cookout, for example, might say "casual" so that guests may wear relaxed clothing suitable to the event planned. A slightly dressier variant is "business casual," a term that usually suggests attire dressier than shorts or jeans, but not so dressy as to include high heels or coats and ties.

b. RSVP. This term, which also appears as "R.S.V.P." or "Rsvp," is an abbreviation for the French phrase, *repondez s'il vous plait,* which means please reply.

An invitation containing an R.S.V.P. indicates that the planning that is going into the event to which you are being invited (and the event's cost) requires that the host know in advance approximately how many guests will attend. For this reason, failing to respond to an RSVP is thoughtless unless the invitation is a mass mailing or is for a fund-raising event.

Merely Informative
Other Perils of Fancy Meals

If you happen to get lots of formal invitations, there are a couple of other items with which you may want to be familiar, because both offer wonderful opportunities to embarrass yourself.

One is the finger bowl. The finger bowl is something you may encounter at highly formal dinners. As the name suggests, finger bowls are bowls in which you are expected to dip your fingers to remove food particles or grease. Although not common, finger bowls are most likely to be used after you've eaten lobster or shrimp served in their shells, or some other messy food for which you are likely to have needed to use your hands. As you might guess, finger bowls are intended for genteel use, not for an exuberant sponge bath. The appropriate response is to dip your fingertips into the water, which may be slightly warm, and dry them inconspicuously on your napkin. Then act like you've done this all your life.

Finger bowls occasionally come with a slice of lemon floating in them. This can be a misleading clue and should not be taken as a hint that you have been served an unusual, clear soup. It is a mistake to eat the lemon or drink the water in your finger bowl, thinking that it must be a flavorless soup, although both have been done.

A second formal dinner phenomenon is the *demitasse. Demitasse,* sometimes offered on a luncheon or dinner menu, is a small cup of coffee. (*Demi* means half, *tasse* means cup, both in French.) Unlike espresso, which is about the same size, a *demitasse* doesn't necessarily mean richer or thicker coffee. Just less.

More Where This Came From

For more wisdom from Miss Manners, refer to *Miss Manners Rescues Civilization,* New York: Crown Publisher, 1996, by Judith Martin. In the first chapter ("The Case Against Etiquette") she addresses the charges that etiquette is no fun, elitist, trivial, insincere, hypocritical, weak, pretentious, stuffy, artificial, lethal, mean, and rude.

For the other end of your bookshelf, you might try *Tiffany's Table Manners for Teenagers,* New York: Randow House, 1989, by Walter Hoving, a short, lighthearted treatise on etiquette that filled with illustrations, although quite authoritative on a variety of small subjects and unmistakably Tiffany.

Round out your references with one of the standards referred to in the answer to question 4 and with *Multicultural Manners,* New York: John Wiley & Sons, 1996 by Norine Dresser, mentioned in the section, Multicultural Basics.

The RAT's Mouse

If you want to find out even more on the subject of etiquette, use your computer mouse to check the following:

- **www.albion.com/netiquette/index.html** The site for Virginia Shea's book, *Netiquette*; see especially the chapters on core rules and the netiquette quiz
- **www.bartleby.com/95** Emily Post's book on etiquette (the first version of which was published in 1922)
- **www.adolescentadulthood.com** A bit lighter; links to "dating" and "dining etiquette"
- **www.thetearoom.8m.com** Includes etiquette guidance on dress, gifts, invitations, the Internet, tipping, table manners, table settings

22. MULTICULTURAL BASICS—ANSWERS

1. **Cultural Rituals.** The identified rituals:

   a. *Bar mitzvah*—This ritual, the female equivalent of which is a bat mitzvah, is a rite of passage that marks a Jewish boy's reaching age 13—the age of religious responsibility. Bar mitzvahs generally are marked by a lengthy service that includes readings from the *Torah* (the first five books of the Bible), gifts, and a celebration.

   b. *The Hajj*—Each year more than 2 million Muslims participate in this pilgrimage to the Holy City of Mecca, a ritual in which all practicing Muslims are expected to participate at least once during their lifetime.

   c. *Baptism*—Baptism, a ritual performed with or in water and recounted in various books of the Old Testament, is regarded as the formal ceremony by which believers formally become Christians or members of a particular Christian church.

2. **Ethnic Groups.** The answer is Polish-American. Nationwide, Polish Americans constitute one of many ethnic groups in the United States.

Merely Informative
Foreign-born Residents of the U.S.

According to the 1990 census, the largest groups of foreign-born residents of the United States were residents born in Mexico (21.7 percent), the Philippines (4.6 percent), Canada (3.8 percent), and Cuba (3.7 percent).

Source: *The 1994 Information Please Almanac*, Boston: Houghton Mifflin, 1994 p. 836.

---

3. **Holidays.**

   a. *Mardi Gras*—A day of festive celebration marking the end of the carnival period that precedes Lent (the 40 weekdays preceding Easter). Mardi Gras falls on Shrove Tuesday, the day before Ash Wednesday, which begins the 40-day period of Lent that ends on Easter Sunday. As popularized in the city of New Orleans, Mardi Gras is an extravagant festival characterized

MULTICULTURAL BASICS

by public celebration, including grand balls, elaborate costumes, and street parades.

The corresponding celebration in Rio de Janeiro is Carnival, an equally celebratory occasion that immediately precedes Lent. If your answer was Carnival, give yourself two points.

Merely Informative
Mardi Gras in Australia

In Australia, Mardi Gras is the occasion for the annual gay and lesbian festival held in Sydney, reputed to be the biggest such event in the world.

---

    b. *Ramadan*—During Ramadan, the ninth month of the Muslim year, Muslims fast from sunrise to sunset. During this period, commercial activity tends to proceed at a reduced pace, with shorter business hours and modified daily schedules.

    c. *Kwanzaa*—This African-American cultural festival is observed from December 26 to January 1. Based on the Swahili term for first fruits of the harvest, Kwanzaa celebrates the seven principles of unity, self-determination, collective work, cooperative economics, purpose, creativity, and faith. Kwanzaa is observed with music, dance, and the ritual lighting of seven candles.

4. **Judaism.**

    a. *Rosh Hashana*—The Jewish New Year is celebrated on the first two days of Tishri, the first month of the Jewish year. It is an occasion during which observant Jews are expected to attend synagogue services.

    b. *Yarmulke*—A yarmulke is a skullcap worn by Orthodox and Conservative Jewish men and boys during religious services, study, or meals. As a sign of respect, non-Jewish male visitors to synagogues typically wear yarmulkes, which are usually available at the entrance of the synagogue.

    c. *Kosher*—The strict observance of Jewish dietary laws in the preparation of foods allows them to be designated as "kosher." Kitchens in which such laws are followed are sometimes referred to as "kosher" kitchens, and those that observe them strictly "keep kosher."

d. *Hasidic Jews*—This sect of strict Orthodox Judaism originated in Poland. Practitioners of Hasidism generally wear plain black and white clothes, and the men usually leave their hair and beards untrimmed.

5. **National Cultural Habits.**

   a. *False.* Tea, or *chai,* is the ubiquitous beverage in China and a sacrosanct national tradition in England; however, in Brazil, the national hot beverage is decidedly coffee.

   b. *False.* On the contrary, the evening meal in most Latin countries tends to come late in the evening. In Spain and Mexico, for example, the dinner hour may begin as late as 10 P.M. To help compensate for this schedule, the tradition of an afternoon siesta still continues in some rural areas.

   c. *False.* In Arabic countries, some African countries, Indonesia, and China, it is not uncommon for men to hold hands as a gesture of friendship. This practice, which has no sexual implications, is common both in public and in private gatherings.

   d. *False.* The opposite is the case. Although smoking patterns are changing in many countries, it is nonetheless correct to observe that smoking is considerably more common in Canada and Asia, than in the United States.

6. **Famous Authors.**   Toni Morrison, Maya Angelou, Alex Haley, and Langston Hughes are all African-Americans. Each is a celebrated author whose publications have garnered national and international acclaim.

   Toni Morrison, a professor of humanities at Princeton University, was awarded the Nobel Prize for Literature in 1993, the Pulitzer Prize for fiction for *Beloved,* and the 1978 National Book Critics Circle Award for *Song of Solomon.* Maya Angelou, a poet who has won the Langston Hughes award, the Women in Film award, and the Springam Award, has received nominations for both the National Book Award (*I Know Why the Caged Bird Sings*) and the Pulitzer Prize (*Just Give Me A Cool Drink of Water 'fore I Die*). Alex Haley, the author of *Roots,* was awarded a Pulitzer Prize Special Citation in 1977. Langston Hughes, an author of fiction, poetry, drama, history, biography, and children's books, wrote in Paris and Harlem and was elected to the National Institute of Arts and Letters in 1961.

7. **Music and Dance.** Each of the following types of music or dance is associated primarily with one particular culture.

    a. The tango—Argentina. Buenos Aires is the spiritual capital of the tango, a romantic, sometimes sensual dance that is popular around the world.

    b. "'Tis a Gift to Be Simple" is a hymn of the American religious group known as the "Shakers." It has become widely known, in part through being featured in Aaron Copeland's renowned symphonic piece, "Appalachian Spring." (*Correct answers include America, Appalachia, Kentucky, and the Shakers.*)

    c. Yodeling—Switzerland. (Austria or Germany are also correct answers.) This form of singing, with its interspersed high, falsetto notes, has popularly been associated with with herding sheep in the Alps.

    d. The hora—Judaism (or Israel, Jewish groups in various countries, or Romania). A festive, energetic dance, the hora is often performed at weddings and typically includes lifting the bride and groom, seated in chairs, above the heads of the dancers.

    e. Mariachi bands—Mexico. The distinctive sound of mariachi bands combines stringed instruments and prominent trumpets to produce a recognizable sound that is native to Mexico.

8. **Expressions.**

    a. *Australia—G'day mate* is the classic, friendly greeting common to Australia, and to Australians wherever they may be found.

    b. *Germany—Gesundheit* is the German equivalent of "God bless you" and has become an international response to a sneeze.

    c. *China—Gambei,* the Chinese expression used in proposing a toast, is the Chinese version of the English term *cheers,* the Spanish *salud,* and the Norwegian and Danish *skoal.* A ritual part of formal Chinese occasions, toasts of "gambei," when combined with the potent Chinese liquor, mao tai, can be a fearsome form of hospitality.

    d. *Israel, or Jewish tradition anywhere—Chutzpah* is a Yiddish term used to refer to brash or nervy behavior, sometimes as a compliment, sometimes in a derogatory sense.

    e. *France—C'est la vie,* a French idiom that has come to connote a carefree approach to whatever life may bring, literally means "It is life." Its rough Italian equivalent is *Que sera, sera.*

f. *Saudi Arabia, or any other Arabic country*—This qualifying expression, meaning "God willing," is typically combined with comments or phrases referring to expected future events as, for example, in "I will see you again on my next trip, *Enshallah.*"

9. **Islamic Culture.**   The correct terms are these:

a. *Mecca*—Wherever practicing Muslims are in the world, at prayer time, their practice is to say their prayers facing Mecca, the birthplace of Mohammed and thus the holy city of Islam.

b. *Mosques*—Mosques are the Islamic equivalent of churches and synagogues. Minarets, slender towers that are often attached to mosques, are not places of worship, but are traditionally the places from which calls to prayer are chanted or broadcast.

c. *Friday*—The Muslim weekend is Thursday and Friday, and Friday is the holy day.

d. *Worry beads*—Muslims frequently carry smooth wooden worry beads and handle them absently during conversation or prayer.

10. **Rude Gestures.**   One of the unsung perils of international travel is the risk that some gesture that may be common, unexceptional, or even humorous in your own culture is offensive in another. The examples are many. Among some of the better known are these:

- Blowing your nose in public is considered impolite in Japan and Korea. If you do turn away and blow your nose, a disposable tissue is considered more appropriate than a handkerchief.
- Talking to someone while your hands are in your pockets is considered impolite in England, Switzerland, and a number of other European countries.
- Crossing your legs so as to show the soles of your shoes is considered rude throughout the Arab world and in certain other Muslim countries.
- Pointing with a finger rather than an open hand is considered rude in England, India, Japan, Indonesia, and many other countries.
- The "ok" sign—forming a circle with your thumb and index finger—which is a common sign of approval in the United States, means zero in France and money in Japan. In Scandinavia, however, it is often considered insulting; in Spain, it is considered rude; and in Russia and Brazil, it is considered vulgar.

- The V-sign, when made with the palm facing in, is insulting in Canada and England, and obscene in New Zealand and Australia.
- The thumb's up sign of approval in the United States and Canada is considered offensive in such countries as Russia and Nigeria and in the Middle East.
- Whistling is regarded as impolite in India.
- Chewing gum in public is considered impolite in France and other northern European countries, particularly when you're talking with another person.
- A man's winking at a woman is generally considered inappropriate in Australia and Taiwan.
- Waving and shouting a public greeting to a friend in Germany or The Netherlands is considered ill-mannered.
- Touching or standing too close to someone with whom you are talking but don't know well may be seen as rude in China, Japan, Canada, or Sweden.
- On the other hand, backing away from someone who is standing close to you or touching you when talking with you may be considered unfriendly or impolite in Mexico, Brazil, or other Latin countries.
- Public displays of affection between members of the opposite sex are inappropriate in China, Indonesia, Turkey, Germany, Thailand, and most Islamic countries. Kissing in public is regarded as disgraceful in Japan.
- Being late for an appointment is rude in Germany, where punctuality is perhaps more commonly expected than in any other country.

More Where This Came From

There is a wealth of cultural contradictions to be found in body language, gift giving, dietary behavior, superstitions, punctuality, forms of address, negotiating styles, health practices, religious worship, values, and more.

An informative discussion of cross cultural practices that can be the source of miscommunication, embarrassment, or amusement can be found in *Kiss, Bow, or Shake Hands,* Holbrook, Massachusetts: Bob Adams, Inc., 1994, by Morrison, Conaway, and Borden.

Multicultural Manners, New York: John Wiley & Sons, 1996, by Norine Dresser, also reviews a host of taboos and potential cultural disconnects.

The RAT's Mouse

- **www.export.seda-cog.org/cultural_tips.htm** Cultural tips for different countries, hand gestures included
- **www.library.thinkquest.org/10007/** Celebrations around the world; pick a country to see how Christmas, Easter, birthdays, etc., are celebrated there
- **www.worldbook.com/fun/holidays/html/holidays.htm** Information on world religions

23. AMERICANA—ANSWERS

1. **The National Anthem.**

The Star Spangled Banner

Oh! say, can you see, by the dawn's early light,
What so proudly we hailed at the twilight's last gleaming?
Whose broad stripes and bright stars, thro' the perilous fight,
O'er the ramparts we watched were so gallantly streaming?
And the rockets' red glare, the bombs bursting in air,
Gave proof thro' the night that our flag was still there.
Oh! say does that star-spangled banner yet wave
O'er the land of the free and the home of the brave?

Francis Scott Key, 1814

AMERICANA

Merely Informative
More on the National Anthem

Moderately-well known facts: *The Star-Spangled Banner* was written by Francis Scott Key during the naval bombardment of Fort McHenry by British warships in Baltimore Harbor during the War of 1812. It was inspired by the fact that at dawn the American flag was still flying over the walls of the fort.

Less-well-known facts: Key watched the battle from a British ship to which he and another Washingtonian had gone to attempt to negotiate the release of an American the British had taken prisoner. Francis Scott Key was a lawyer. The tune

continued on next page

---

came from an old English drinking song that had become known as both a military march and a political song in America. The flag Key saw was big (over 50 feet long) and now hangs in the Smithsonian.

The Star-Spangled Banner actually has four verses, not one. The fourth verse contains two lines you may recognize: "Then conquer we must, when our cause it is just, And this be our motto—'in God is our trust.'"

2. **Demographics.**   The answer is *b*; women outnumber men in the United States.

As of the 1990 census, there were approximately 6 million more women than men in the United States, with women accounting for just over 51 percent of the total population.

According to *The World Almanac* (2000), as of 1999, approximately 273 million people lived in the United States, 13 percent of whom were black or African American, and the median age in 1998 was 35.2, the highest ever.

3. **U.S. Currency.**   The fronts and backs depict the following:

Bill	Front	Back
$1 bill	George Washington	The great seal of the U.S.
$2 bill	Thomas Jefferson	Monticello (earlier versions), or "The Signing of the Declaration of Independence" (1976 version)
$5 bill	Abraham Lincoln	The Lincoln Memorial
$10 bill	Alexander Hamilton	U.S. Treasury building
$20 bill	Andrew Jackson	The White House
$50 bill	Ulysses Grant	The U.S. Capitol building
$100 bill	Benjamin Franklin	Independence Hall in Philadelphia

Merely Informative
More about Folding Money

There is a certain logic to what is portrayed on the front and back of many of these bills. The $5 bill is obvious. Monticello is the Charlottesville, Virginia, home

continued on next page

that Jefferson designed and where he lived. Alexander Hamilton was the first secretary of the Treasury. Andrew Jackson, the seventh president, was the first president to open the White House to the people of the United States. The dome and the Senate and House wings of the Capitol were added while Ulysses Grant was president. Benjamin Franklin was a leading figure in the Constitutional Convention in Philadelphia, where Independence Hall is located.

Each bill is a "Federal Reserve Note" and "legal tender for all debts." Each bears the motto, "In God We Trust" and bears the signatures of the Treasurer of the United States and the secretary of the Treasury at the time the bill was printed.

There once were denominations of $500 (William McKinley), $1,000 (Grover Cleveland), $5,000 (James Madison), $10,000 (Salmon P. Chase), and $100,000 (Woodrow Wilson), but they were all discontinued after 1969.

4. **The National Debt.** The answer is *c*, $20,000.

As of late October 2000, the national debt of the United States was approximately $5.6 trillion. On a per capita basis, the debt for every child, woman, and man in the United States was just over $20,000.

Merely Informative
The Dynamics of National Debt

Our national debt has grown dramatically since 1960, when it was just over $290 billion. In late 1979, the national debt was just under $1 trillion ($908 billion). From 1980 to 1992, it increased more than fourfold. By the year 2000, the public debt had grown to approximately $5.6 trillion dollars.

The national debt grows whenever the federal government spends more money than it collects in revenues (primarily through taxes). Thus, when the federal government has a budget deficit, the national debt rises. The largest budget deficits were incurred in 1991 ($269 billion), 1992 ($290 billion), and 1993 ($255 billion).

The federal government funds budget deficits by borrowing money, primarily from the public. It does so by selling Treasury bonds and notes, on which it pays interest. Interest on that debt is paid out of taxes the federal government collects. Thus, the cost of borrowing money for this year is spread over future years when interest on federal bonds and notes is due.

continued on next page

As the debt has grown, the cost of interest paid on the outstanding federal debt has itself become an increasingly significant budget item. In 1995, nearly 15 percent of federal government outlays were to pay interest on money the government had borrowed. In dollar terms, that interest cost was approximately $226 billion. The government spends 15 percent for interest payments, compared to 19 percent for national defense and 17 percent for all domestic programs other than the "entitlement" programs (Social Security, Medicare, Medicaid, other retirement programs).

In 1998, the federal government had its first surplus since 1969. In 1999, the budget surplus was $124 billion. In the year 2000, the government budget again showed a surplus, the first time in about a half-century that we enjoyed three consecutive years of such surpluses.

5. **State Capitals.**

State	Capital
The Northeast and Mid-Atlantic:	
Maine	Augusta
Vermont	Montpelier
New Hampshire	Concord
Massachusetts	Boston
Connecticut	Hartford
Rhode Island	Providence
New York	Albany
New Jersey	Trenton
Pennsylvania	Harrisburg
Delaware	Dover
Maryland	Annapolis
The Southeast and Appalachians:	
Virginia	Richmond
West Virginia	Charleston
Kentucky	Frankfort
Tennessee	Nashville
Arkansas	Little Rock
North Carolina	Raleigh
South Carolina	Columbia

Georgia	Atlanta
Florida	Tallahassee
Alabama	Montgomery
Mississippi	Jackson
Louisiana	Baton Rouge

The Midwest:

Ohio	Columbus
Indiana	Indianapolis
Illinois	Springfield
Michigan	Lansing
Wisconsin	Madison
Minneapolis	St. Paul
Iowa	Des Moines
Missouri	Jefferson City

The West:

North Dakota	Bismarck
South Dakota	Pierre
Nebraska	Lincoln
Kansas	Topeka
Oklahoma	Oklahoma City
Texas	Austin
New Mexico	Santa Fe
Arizona	Phoenix
Colorado	Denver
Utah	Salt Lake City
Wyoming	Cheyenne
Montana	Helena
Idaho	Boise
Nevada	Carson City
Washington	Olympia
Oregon	Salem
California	Sacramento

Noncontiguous States:

Alaska	Juneau
Hawaii	Honolulu

6. **U.S. Presidents**

1. George Washington
2. John Adams
3. Thomas Jefferson
4. James Madison
5. James Monroe
6. John Quincy Adams
7. Andrew Jackson
8. Martin van Buren
9. William Henry Harrison
10. John Tyler
11. James Polk
12. Zachary Taylor
13. Millard Fillmore
14. Franklin Pierce
15. James Buchanan
16. Abraham Lincoln
17. Andrew Johnson
18. Ulysses S. Grant
19. Rutherford B. Hayes
20. James Garfield
21. Chester Arthur
22. Grover Cleveland
23. Benjamin Harrison
24. Grover Cleveland
25. William McKinley
26. Theodore Roosevelt
27. William Howard Taft
28. Woodrow Wilson
29. Warren Harding
30. Calvin Coolidge
31. Herbert Hoover
32. Franklin Delano Roosevelt
33. Harry Truman
34. Dwight Eisenhower
35. John F. Kennedy
36. Lyndon Baines Johnson
37. Richard M. Nixon
38. Gerald Ford
39. Jimmy Carter
40. Ronald Reagan
41. George Bush
42. William Clinton
43. George W. Bush

Merely Informative About the Presidents

Four sets of presidents were related: John Quincy Adams (6) was the son of John Adams (2); Benjamin Harrison (23) was the grandson of William Henry Harrison (9); Franklin Delano Roosevelt (32) was a cousin of Teddy Roosevelt (26); and George W. Bush (43) is the son of George Bush (41).

One-third of the presidents (14 of 42) served as vice-president before becoming president. Eight were born in Virginia. Seven were military leaders before becoming president.

The president who served the longest was Franklin Delano Roosevelt; he was elected president four times and died three months into his fourth term. The

continued on next page

presidents who served the shortest terms were William Henry Harrison (one month) and James Garfield (eight months). On a cold winter day, William Henry Harrison delivered the longest inaugural address ever, caught pneumonia, and died one month later. James Garfield was shot by a disappointed office seeker in July following his inauguration and died in September.

The youngest presidents inaugurated were Teddy Roosevelt (42), John F. Kennedy (43), and Bill Clinton (46). The oldest inaugurated were Ronald Reagan (69), William Henry Harrison (68), and George Bush and Zachary Taylor (both 64).

One president was a bachelor (James Buchanan). Six were twice married. William Henry Harrison had 10 children; by two wives, John Tyler had 14.

The first Catholic to become president was John F. Kennedy. As of 2000, no Jew, African-American, or woman has yet held the office.

7. **Mission to the Moon.**

   a. The first astronaut who walked on the moon was Neil Armstrong.

   b. The NASA space program that succeeded in reaching the moon was the Apollo program, and the spaceship was *Apollo 11*.

   c. The first manned lunar landing was July 20, 1969, at 10:56 P.M., EDT.

Merely Informative
Man on the Moon

The two other astronauts on the *Apollo 11* mission were Lt. Col. Michael Collins and Col. Edwin "Buzz" Aldrin, Jr. When he took his first step on the surface of the moon, Neil Armstrong meant to say "One small step for a man; one giant step for mankind." In fact, he said "One small step for man; one giant step for mankind."

8. **The Supreme Court.**

   Sandra Day O'Connor was the first woman appointed to be a justice of the U.S. Supreme Court. Justice O'Connor of Arizona was nominated by President Ronald Reagan on July 7, 1981.

   Thurgood Marshall was the first African-American justice of the U.S. Supreme Court. He was nominated in October 1967, by President Lyndon B. Johnson.

9. **The Constitution.**   Here are a few of the better-known amendments to the Constitution:

1st Amendment (1791)	Prohibits Congress from passing any law denying freedom of speech or freedom of the press.
	Prohibits Congress from passing any law that would establish a religion or prohibit freedom of religion.
	Prohibits Congress from passing any law denying the right of the people to assemble or to petition the government.
4th Amendment (1791)	Established the right of the people to be protected from unreasonable searches and seizures.
13th Amendment (1865)	Abolished slavery.
14th Amendment (1868)	Conferred citizenship on former slaves and all others born or naturalized in the United States. Guaranteed due process of law and equal protection of the laws by the states.
15th Amendment (1870)	Gave former slaves the right to vote.
18th Amendment (1919)	Prohibited the manufacture, sale, or transportation of "intoxicating liquors."
19th Amendment (1920)	Gave women the right to vote.
21st Amendment (1933)	Repealed the 18th Amendment.
26th Amendment (1971)	Lowered the voting age in the United States to 18 years of age.

10. **Ancestral Groups.**   The answer is *d*, Poland.

Although several areas in the United States have strong Polish-American communities, Poland ranks 9th on the list of ancestral groups. According to 1990 statistics, the four leading ancestral groups of Americans are German (57,948,000, or 23.3 percent of all ancestral groups), Irish (38,735,000, or 15.6 percent), English (32,651,000, or 13.1 percent), and African (23,777,000, or 9.6 percent).

Source: *The 1994 Information Please Almanac*, p. 836.

The RAT's Mouse

More Americana can be found on the following web sites. Use a computer and mouse.

- **www.unitedstates-on-line.com** Presidents, map, flags, quizzes
- **www.americanafunz.com** American jokes, humorous sayings, quotations, cartoons, etc.
- **www.azstarnet.com/~rgrogan/flag3.htm** Photo of manuscript of national anthem; the anthem's history; Frances Scott Key
- **www.treas.gov/opc/opc0034.html** A site about U.S. paper currency with frequently asked questions
- **www.supremecourtus.gov** Official site of the U.S. Supreme Court

E. IMPROVING YOUR QUALITY OF LIFE

24. DANCING—ANSWERS

1. **Famous Tap Dancers.**   Among some of the most well-known tap dancers are Fred Astaire, Ginger Rodgers, Gregory Hines, Dan Dailey, Savion Glover, Gene Kelly, Bill (Bojangles) Robinson, and Donald O'Connor.

2. **Movie Dance Scenes.**   There are lots. Some of the classics include:
   - *Scent of a Woman* (Al Pacino's tango)
   - *Strictly Ballroom* (Australian ballroom dance competitions)
   - *Shall We Dance?* (a Fred Astaire-Ginger Rogers classic)
   - *Flashdance* (disco in Pittsburgh)
   - *Saturday Night Fever* (John Travolta in his best duds)
   - *Witness* (the unforgettable dance in the barn loft)
   - *Singing in the Rain* (Gene Kelly's number in the rain; Donald O'Connor's dance in the studio)
   - *Dirty Dancing* (official and unofficial dance lessons in the Catskills)
   - *The King and I* (East meets Western dance)
   - The Fred Astaire-Ginger Rodgers films are considered classics; each one has one or more great dance scenes. Some of their best films include *Top Hat, Swing Time,* and *Shall We Dance?*

DANCING

3. **Dancers and Dance Groups.**   Correct answers are these:

   a. Riverdance

   b. The Rockettes

   c. Michael Jackson

4. **Ballet.**   For ballets, correct answers include:

   The Nutcracker
   Swan Lake
   Giselle
   Sleeping Beauty
   Don Quixote

   (See the answer to question 4(b) in the section on The Fine Arts for summaries of the stories of several classic ballets.)

   Great male ballet dancers have included *Mikhail Baryshnikov* and *Rudolf Nureyev* (both Russian; both studied in Leningrad (St. Petersburg), danced with the Kirov Ballet, and moved to the West); early in the twentieth century, *Vaslav Nijinsky* (born in Russia of Polish extraction; also trained in St. Petersburg).

   There have been many famous ballerinas. Among the greats have been *Natalia Makarova* (born in Leningrad [St. Petersburg], danced with the Kirov); *Margot Fonteyn* (*prima ballerina assoluta* of the Royal Ballet, regular partner of Rudolf Nureyev, president of the Royal Academy of Dancing); *Anna Pavlova* (also Russian, early twentieth century); *Martha Graham* (American dancer and choreographer); *Suzanne Farrell* (New York City Ballet).

Merely Informative
Isadora Duncan

Isadora Duncan, a pioneer of modern dance and interpretive dance, greatly influenced twentieth-century ballet. A creative free spirit who established dance schools in Berlin, Paris, and Moscow, she is quoted as having said, "I am an enemy of the ballet, which I consider a false and preposterous art." A dramatic, creative innovator who usually danced barefoot, Isadora Duncan died on the French Riviera when, riding in an open car, the long scarf she was wearing got tangled in the rear wheel of the car and broke her neck.

5. **Dance Directors.** *Choreographer.* Although some choreographers, such as George Balanchine, have also directed dancers, typically a dance master or director performs that responsibility.

Merely Informative Choreographers

Among the most illustrious choreographers are *George Balanchine, Merce Cunningham, Sergei Diaghilev, Michel Fokine, Bob Fosse, Martha Graham, Paul Taylor,* and *Twyla Tharp.*

---

6. **Dance Rhythm.** You may think this is really silly, but these are the first steps in dancing. If you can do each of these three simple rhythm exercises and learn to do them naturally, without thinking, learning to dance will not be difficult. If you can do the third exercise—shifting your weight—in time to a rumba, it is relatively easy to learn the basic steps for that dance.

7. **Dance Position.** In fact, there are a number of variations of ballroom dance position. For certain Latin dances, for example, dancers hold their arms differently from the way they would for a waltz. In a tango, the dancers' bodies are more parallel than facing directly.

For the basic closed ballroom dance position, however, the man and woman directly face each other, standing 6–8 inches apart, feet together, toes facing forward, shoulders squarely facing their partners.

The man places his right hand in the center of the woman's back (below her shoulder blades, above her bottom). The woman places her left hand comfortably on the man's right shoulder, holding it firmly, but lightly, not pressing down.

The woman places her right hand in the man's left hand, comfortably extended to the side (a slight bend in both elbows). The grip should be neither limp nor a squeeze; rather, it should be comfortably firm.

The reason for dance position is that it helps couples dance smoothly together. Once in dance position, the position of the arms of the man, who traditionally leads, should not change relative to his body. Thus, his dance position provides a frame that, as he moves, cues his partner on steps and direction. A slight movement by the man is not an attempt to change the dance position the two have assumed. Rather, it is a cue for the direction of the next steps, a turn, or a reversal of direction. Slight pressure by the man's hand on the woman's back is also a common way for a man to initiate leads. Throughout a dance, dancers typically maintain, or return to, ballroom dance position.

Learning ballroom dance position is—this should not be a surprise—the first step in learning any ballroom dance.

Merely Informative
Waltzes and Foxtrots

Two of the most common ballroom dances are the waltz and the fox-trot. Both are done in dance position. The principal difference between the two is the music to which they are danced.

A waltz has three steps that are repeated and recurring rhythm patterns of three beats ("three beats to the measure"). The fox-trot has four steps. As a result, it is danced to music that has—you guessed it—patterns of four beats.

All things being equal, it is much easier to dance a waltz when a waltz is playing and a fox-trot when a fox-trot is playing, because the simple secret of dancing is that it should be done in time to the music—that is, your steps should follow the beat of the music.

There are times, however, when dance floors are occupied by dancers who are apparently determined to dance somewhat independently of the music. An alternative pastime to dancing is to watch for (this is better than dancing with) someone whose dancing is inspired by something other than the beat of the music.

More Where This Same From

Victor Silvester, *Modern Ballroom Dancing,* Trafalgar Square Publishing, 1993. (From page 44: before you begin dancing, "count at least one bar of music or more than one, to yourself.")

8. **Ballroom Dancing.**

   i. The answer is *b*, the man leads and the woman follows.

Merely Informative Alternatives

If this tradition is gender-offensive to you, one solution is simply to reverse the roles. Let the woman lead and the man follow. To do this effectively, however, you should also reverse ballroom dance positions, with the woman assuming the man's traditional position. The same accommodation can be made by two dancers of the same sex, if that is preferred.

In addition, there are a number of dances, or movements to music, that don't involve ballroom dance position at all. These often can be done without having either person lead, without touching, without any apparent interpersonal interaction, and with a random number of people.

What is not a workable solution is for a couple to decide that neither should lead, or that both should. For reasons wholly unrelated to gender dominance, this doesn't work. It particularly doesn't work if the dance is a jitterbug or, worse yet, a polka.

ii. The answer is *a*, he begins with his left, she with her right.

In virtually all dances that are danced in ballroom dance position, the woman begins with her right foot, the man, with his left. This is a useful rule to master because it helps avoid the common beginner's trauma of stepping on your partner's feet. That something that does happen, however and you should not let it be traumatic. Rather than stopping in your tracks and trading lengthy apologies, you should smile, keep dancing, and say something to help the moment pass—"Sorry, my fault entirely," "Oops," or "Gotcha," or "Your turn next."

9. **Dances.** The correct answers are these:

    a. *The Electric Slide*—A popular, anyone-can-participate dance that can be learned or picked up quickly and enjoyed by everyone watching to see if the participants, in fact, turn together and end up facing the same direction.

    b. *The Zydeco Two-Step*—Popular in the West and Southwest, and spreading eastward.

c. *The Macarena*—Generously referred to as a dance even though no foot movement is involved. After being a craze, the Macarena found an apparently permanent home at professional football and baseball games.

d. *The Charleston*—A durable vestige of the Roaring '20s, the Charleston requires coordination, energy, and a free spirit.

For descriptions of these and others, see *Social Dance* by Jane Harris, Anne Pittman, and Marlys Waller.

10. **Latin Dances.**   Correct answers are these:

a. Tango

b. Samba, Rumba, Cha Cha, Conga, Meringue, Mambo, Salsa

More Where This Came From

An excellent, well-illustrated book describing how to dance a wide variety of dances is *Let's Dance*, Black Dog and Leventhal Publishing, 1998, by Paul Bottomer.

Another instructional book, which ranges from ballroom to line dances to Latin to Country Western, is *Social Dance*, Needham Heights, Massachusetts: Allyn & Bacon, 1998, by Jane Harris, Anne Pittman, and Marlys Waller.

Dancing—The Pleasure, Power and Art of Movements, Harry N. Abrams, 1998, by Gerald Jonas, is rich history of dance, including classical dance theater, social dance, modernizing dance, and others.

Ballet 101, A Complete Guide to Learning and Loving the Ballet, New York: Hyperion, 1998, by Robert Greskovic, is a comprehensive resource on ballet.

The RAT's Mouse

Web sites having to do with dancing, accessible by using a computer mouse, include the following:

- **www.dancetv.com/** Learn dances online—waltz, fox-trot, swing; order instructional videos
- **www.eecs.umich.edu/~zaher/ballroom/team.html** University of Michigan's ballroom dance team's homepage, with pictures, ballroom dance links, and an "online studio"
- **www.geocities.com/Hollywood/9766/fred.html** Classic movies and oldies, complete with dancing
- **www.themave.com/Astaire/** A Fred Astaire page—biography, audio files, images, etc.
- **www.bestanimations.com/Music/Dancers/FamousBaby/FamousBaby/FamousBaby.htm** Famous on-line dancing baby

25. FRIENDS AND ACQUAINTANCES—ANSWERS

1. **Handshakes.**

    Keys of a good handshake include the following:
    - Shake hands with a firm, but not crushing grip.
    - Slightly shake the other person's hand; don't pump it up and down.
    - Look the person with whom you are shaking hands directly in the eyes.
    - Make sure that the notch between your thumb and your index finger makes contact with the other person's hand. Avoid—or correct—handshakes in which you don't have a good grip and are just shaking the other person's fingers with your fingers.
    - Say your name as you shake hands. It's not a bad idea to do so even with people you may know casually and who probably remember your name in any event.

2. **Talking to People You Don't Know.**

If you encounter a stranger with whom you would like to have a conversation—in an elevator, at a subway stop, in line—several things can make initiating a conversation easier:

- Make eye contact if possible
- Smile
- Say hello
- Say something else, immediately; if you don't, and you allow a silence to set in, it can become more awkward to try to break the ice again.

3. **Remembering Names.**   A few accepted techniques:

- Repeat the person's name when you are introduced, as in, "Hello, Nina. Nice to meet you."
- Within the next 10 seconds, recall and say that person's name to yourself ("Annemarie; Annemarie; Annemarie").
- Use the person's name in the conversation that follows, as in, "Max, where did you buy that great tie?"
- Make some mental association—an image—to help you remember the person's name. The image can be a silly one; in fact, it will be easier to remember if it is. For George, for example, you might want to picture him wearing George Washington's hat. For Sandra you might picture sanding your wooden desk or surfing on a large piece of sand paper. (You may laugh, but people pay money to get tips like this!)
- Write the name down later (Eli—met at homecoming dance).
- Keep a list or file of names and look at them every now and then.

4. **The Art of Good Conversation.**   Some simple tips:

- Ask the other person about himself or herself. Most people are willing to talk about themselves.
- Fish for common ground. If you're at Charlie's house, you might ask, "How do you know Charlie?" If the other person simply says, "I don't," you may want to try one more time.
- Follow your nose. If a response from the other person contains a clue to a new topic, follow it up: "I don't really know Charlie; I'm here with his brother, Jeff." You: "Jeff. Point him out to me." Or, "Jeff. Was he a big brother who picked on Charlie when they were kids?" Or, if you want to

take a small risk: "Oh, Jeff. He's the one whose taste I've always admired . . . . Actually, I don't really know Jeff."

- Avoid questions that can be answered with a yes or a no. Ask questions that require the other person to talk, such as, "Kansas. What's it like to grow up in Kansas?" "What do you think they mean when they say, 'reboot your computer'?" "What was the worst thing that happened to you today?" (Most lawyers who try to learn this—they call it not asking "leading questions"—spend years trying to get it right. In fact, you can probably master it in two or three attempts.)

- Don't respond with one-word answers. Keep the effort moving. Should you have the good fortune to be asked a question or offered a friendly lead-in, don't let your entire response be "yes" or "no" or "I'm not sure." Even if your most honest answer to the question, "What do you think of this place?" is "Not much," don't leave it at that. Try "Not much. They should paint that far wall pink." Or "Not much. My burrito was made with burrito meat."

- Don't give up and take the first un-huh as a terminal answer. Be prepared to carry the conversation for a few cycles. If your first exchange dies a quick, quiet death, try again quickly. If it consistently goes nowhere, you don't have to make the effort a long-term project.

More Where This Came From

How to Start a Conversation and Make Friends, New York: Simon and Schuster, 2001, by Don Gabor and Mary Power (short and helpful);

Common American Phrases in Everyday Contexts: A Detailed Guide to Real-Life Conversation and Small Talk, Unknown, by Richard A. Spears (1991);

Conversationally Speaking: Tested New Ways to Increase Your Personal and Social Effectiveness, Lowell House, 1997, by Alan Garner.

5. **Making Yourself Likable.**

Here are some easy rules of thumb. There are others, and if third parties agree that yours are thoughtful, count them as correct answers.

- Smile.
- Remember people's names. (According to Dale Carnegie, "A person's name is to that person the sweetest and most important sound in any language.")
- Encourage others to talk about themselves. Ask your friend questions about herself. What she's doing? How are things going? How does she feel about something?
- Become genuinely interested in other people. (Dale Carnegie again: "You can make more friends in two months by becoming genuinely interested in other people than you can in two years by trying to get other people interested in you.")
- Be a good listener. (Good and patient listeners usually develop a reputation as excellent conversationalists!)
- Learn to find appropriate occasions to compliment others—about projects they've done, successes they've had, their clothes, their ideas.
- Identify and talk about things you have in common with others.
- Laugh. Look for the humor in things and share it.

Merely Informative
How to Win Friends

Among many excellent books on friendships, a few of which are listed below, Dale Carnegie's *How to Win Friends and Influence People,* New York: Pocket Books, 1964, remains a classic, even though it is was first written more than a half-century ago. Carnegie's list of "six ways to make people like you" include most of those listed above plus his last: "Make the other person feel important—and do it sincerely."

---

6. **Friendships.**   *True.*

Although some of the most enriching friendships can be between people who are quite different, most experts believe that friendships thrive on similarity. This is not a recent observation; it has been attributed to, among others, Aristotle. Of various possible similarities, similarity in values appear to be the most important, easily outweighing similarities in background, work, age, race, class, or sex.

Friendships are universally available. Great friendships can be developed regardless of a person's age, economic condition, intelligence level, or attractiveness.

7. **Characteristics Valued by Friends.**   Count either *a* or *c* as a correct answer.

Different surveys produce different answers to the question, what characteristic is considered to be the most important to a close friendship?

One study that suggests that a sense of humor is the correct answer can be found in R. Robinson, *The Friendship Book,* North Hollywood, California: Newcastle Publishing Co., (1992), pp. 25–26. Perhaps more common is the answer of loyalty. According to Latty Cotton Pogrebin, "More commonly, people completed the sentence [A friend is someone who . . .] with 'a friend is someone who is loyal.'"

8. **The Sociology of Friendships.**   The answer is *a*, their 20s.

"Research shows that people in their twenties spend more time with friends than does any other age group except the over-seventies," says Pogrebin. The 30s, 40s, and 50s tend to be crowded with the demands of work, child rearing, professional and community activities, and the like.

9. **Undermining Relationships.**

Relationships or friendships can be damaged by a variety of types of behavior:

- Failing to maintain a confidence
- Gossiping about a friend, especially talking critically about a friend behind his or her back
- Failing to repay a debt
- Getting interested in a friend's girlfriend or boyfriend (either wait for their relationship to end on its own, or be prepared to lose the friendship)
- Being jealous
- Being dishonest, even if giving an honest opinion would be unwelcome or unsettling

- Bluntly or continually criticizing a friend
- Attempting to make the relationship grow at a pace with which a friend is not comfortable
- Suffocating a friend; not leaving space or allowing freedom in the relationship
- Neglecting the friendship

10. **Building Friendships.**

There are lots of right answers to this question, ranging from practical and specific to quite abstract. For a start, each of the following 15 techniques is a correct response:

- Return a friend's phone calls promptly.
- Remember a friend's birthday or other special occasion. Call or send a card.
- See each other or communicate regularly. Stay in touch, even if you're apart.
- Express your friendship. Saying, "You are a good friend," or "Alvin, I appreciate your hearing me out," reinforces a friendship. So do positive comments about a friend that get back to that friend through a third person.
- Evidence friendship by gestures of friendship. They need not be verbal; actions can be expressions of friendship. Doing a favor, helping change a flat tire, buying a friend an ice cream cone, picking up a jacket left behind—all are little acts of friendship.
- Expand your relationship beyond its original context. If you got to know one another at work, do things together outside of work. If you met through a sport or activity, transplant the relationship to another context.
- Resolve disagreements amicably. Dealing honestly with disagreement or conflict is another way of expressing and sustaining true friendship. Doing so may entail apologizing, admitting you were wrong, or trying hard to see something from a friend's point of view, rather than just your own.
- Find things to laugh about together. Seeing the humor in life is bonding and invigorating. Being able to make others laugh is a gift.
- Be supportive and encouraging. We all can use that from time to time.
- Be empathetic—make the effort to try to stand in a friend's shoes and see something the same way he or she does.

- Share personal history. To develop a strong friendship, it's almost always necessary to know about a friend's past and for the friend to know about yours. Sharing that history provides context for who and what that person is today. Since we are all shaped by our past, that information is an essential part of a serious friendship. Ask a friend about his or her personal history.
- Have fun together. The fun factor can be an important ingredient in a friendship. According to Jan Yager, "One of the most sought-after qualities in a friend is the ability to 'have fun together.'"
- Be loyal, which means being there through thick and thin. This concept, found in most marriage vows, captures the notion that strong friendships are for more than just good times. They can be valuable in times of need, distress, and grief and in moments of joy and triumph. Stick up for your friends.
- Come through when you're needed. If a friend asks you for something that is important to him or her, you should come through. This often includes attending an event that, although of only marginal interest to you, is important to her.
- Dream together. Our hopes and dreams animate us, but few people know our deepest dreams. Sharing them with a friend can be an intimate and trusting act. If I share my dreams with you, I reveal a part of myself and articulate a personal vision; when you learn what my dreams are, you move them to a different level. It is not just for our generation that a special connection is created when one person confides, "I have a dream."
- Invest time. Friendships bond with time: time together produces common experiences, adventures, memories. Sharing highs and lows, peaks and pains, tragedies and passages—all are the stuff of enduring friendships. Spend time together.

Merely Informative
Giving the Special Gift of a Friend

Each of us has our own set of friends, and some of our friendships are special ones. Introducing one friend to another can be thought of as giving a gift. Stated differently, certain friendships are treasures. When we share a treasured friend, we give someone a great gift.

More Where This Came From

Dale Carnegie, *How to Win Friends and Influence People.* New York: Pocket Books, 1934, (a timeless classic).

Larry King, *How to Talk to Anyone, Anytime, Anywhere.* New York: Crown Trade Paperbacks, 1994.

William J. Bennett, *The Book of Virtues.* New York: Simon and Schuster, 1993, Chapter 4, pp. 267–343.

L.T. Pogrebin, *Among Friends.* McGraw-Hill, 1987.

J. Yager, *Friendshifts.* Hannacroix Creek Books, Inc., 1999.

Psychology Today's "The Friendship Bond."

Dick and Ruth Foth, *When the Giant Lies Down.* Wheaton, Illinois: Victor Books, 1995 (relationships discussed from a biblical perspective).

The RAT's Mouse

If you want to use your computer to learn more, use your mouse to check the following web sites:

- **www.oxygen.com** This is Oprah Winfrey's site, which contains articles on many subjects; search for friendships, social situations, relationships
- **www.ncbi.org** National Coalition Building Institute, an organization that works to reduce prejudice and conducts workshops at schools and colleges around the country
- **www.bluemountain.com** Send greeting cards online
- **www.queendom.com/communic.html** An Impersonal Communication Skills Test
- **www.memoryimprovement.co.uk** Tips for remembering names, numbers, lists, etc.

26.   NUTRITION—ANSWERS

1. **Snack Foods.**   There are actually quite a few. Any of the following are correct answers.

    • Unbuttered popcorn
    • Pretzels
    • Carrot or celery sticks
    • Apples
    • Chocolate skim milk
    • Cheerios and other cereals to which no sugar has been added (with skim milk or dry)
    • Raisins (or other dried fruits, such as dried apricots)
    • Yogurt (low fat or nonfat), frozen or regular
    • Trail mix without chocolate

2. **Fat.**   The answer is *a*, 65 fat grams.

    According to the Surgeon General's Report on Nutrition and Health, fat grams should account for no more than 30 percent of an individual's daily total caloric intake. (Twenty percent is better). For a diet of 2,000 calories per day, 30 percent is a maximum of 65 grams of fat a day. (Twenty percent is 44 grams of fat.)

3. **Sources of Fiber.**   Good sources of fiber include:

    • whole grain breads
    • bran cereals
    • fruits
    • vegetables
    • cooked peas and beans

4. **High Blood Pressure.**   Sodium.

    High blood pressure, or hypertension, is often associated with diets high in sodium, a common source of which is table salt. Salt—sodium chloride—contains about 40 percent sodium. Since diets commonly contain far more sodium than the body requires, individuals with high blood pressure are often encouraged to reduce their sodium intake.

NUTRITION

Garlic salt or onion salt are not helpful substitutes. Since both are salts, both are high in sodium. So are soy sauce, green olives, dill pickles, bouillon, and most fast foods.

Because high blood pressure also correlates with obesity, high-fat diets also may be associated with high blood pressure. Among the dietary steps commonly suggested to moderate high blood pressure are reducing or eliminating salt from the diet, losing weight, stopping smoking, and drinking alcohol in moderation only.

5. **Food Groups.**   The answer is *b*, breads, cereals, rice, and pasta.

The Dietary Guidelines for Americans, published by Human Nutrition Information Service of the U.S. Department of Agriculture, suggest eating from 6 to 11 servings a day of breads, cereals, rice, and pasta, particularly whole grain products. Examples of this food group are ready-to-eat cereals, bread or toast, rice, tortillas, popcorn, noodles, crackers, bagels, muffins, hamburger and hot dog rolls, pretzels, grits, and oatmeal. Whole grain varieties include brown rice; corn tortillas; granola; whole wheat, rye, and pumpernickel bread; graham crackers; and popcorn.

Recommended daily servings of the other groups are 2–4 servings of fruits; 3–5 servings of vegetables; 2–3 servings of meats, poultry, fish, beans and peas, eggs, and nuts; and 2 servings of milk, yogurt, and cheese.

6. **Nutrients.**   The other four types of nutrients are vitamins, minerals, fats, and water.

Vitamins and minerals are needed, although not in large quantities, for the regulation of metabolism and normal growth and functioning of the body. Even though a high-fat diet presents a variety of health risks, fat is a nutrient and the most concentrated source of food energy or calories. Water, sometimes called the "forgotten nutrient," is essential in many ways to the human body, which is itself about 70 percent water.

7. **Meats.**
   a. Three Low-Fat Meats
      White meat generally has lower fat content than dark meat. Three good choices are turkey (white meat), chicken (white meat), and fish.

b. Three High-Fat Meats

Unless it is especially lean, red meat generally has higher fat content, particularly "prime" and "choice" cuts. Among the most common are the:

- steaks,
- hamburger,
- prime rib and other roast beef,
- pork ribs (also called spare ribs, ribs, short ribs),
- hot dogs,
- luncheon meats such as bologna, and salami,
- bacon, and
- sausage (bacon and sausage are among the highest in fat content).

Merely Informative
Fat Meat; Lean Meat

Cuts of beef that contain "marbling" are often more tender than leaner cuts without marbling. "Marbling" simply refers to fat. If a cut is marbled, it has bits of fat throughout the meat.

Flank steak (London broil) is a red meat with lower fat content. Hamburgers made with ground sirloin generally have less fat than hamburgers made from ground chuck. Lean steaks often can be made more tender by marinating them before cooking.

---

8. **Variations on a Theme.**   The answer is *sugars*.

Each is a sugar that is found naturally in foods. Sucrose, which becomes white table sugar, is taken from sugar cane and sugar beets. Lactose is a sugar found in milk and milk products. Most fruits contain glucose, sucrose, and fructose.

Merely Informative
Honey and Brown Sugar

Are honey and brown sugar more nutritious than white table sugar? Not according to the Human Nutrition Information Service of the U.S. Department of Agriculture: "Though honey and brown sugar contain traces of some vitamins and minerals, the amounts of these nutrients are insignificant."

9. **Colas.**   The answer is *d*, 9.

A typical cola contains 9 teaspoons of sugar, or roughly the same as 3 half-cup servings of ice cream or 4½ doughnuts. Diet colas contain artificial sweeteners, not sugar.

Merely Informative
Sugar

Although sugar does not cause obesity directly, it is a rich source of calories, and too many calories can cause obesity. Science has not shown any direct link between sugars and development of diabetes or heart disease; however, obesity is associated with increased risk for both. And most of the conscious world knows that high consumption of sugar promotes tooth decay.

---

10. **Nutritious Foods.**   Different foods have different nutritional benefits. The Center for Science in the Public Interest publishes the "Nutrition Scoreboard," a rating system by which foods are given points for their content of "dietary fiber, naturally occurring sugars and complex carbohydrates, protein, vitamins A and C, iron, and calcium." Points are deducted for "fat content (especially saturated fat), sodium, cholesterol, added refined sugars, and caffeine."

Based on the Center's ranking system, the following are among the most nutritious foods (shown with their point scores). Each one listed below that you named counts toward a correct answer.

Vegetables		*Beans*	
Baked sweet potato	184	Kidney beans	91
Baked potato	83	Navy beans	82
Spinach	76	Black-eyed peas, lima beans	78
Broccoli, kale	52–55		
Fruits		*Dairy*	
Half a cantaloupe	134	Nonfat yogurt	58
Strawberries	65	Skim milk	40
Orange	62	Low-fat yogurt	36
Uncooked prunes	51	Low-fat milk (1% milkfat)	28
Meat and Poultry		*Beverages*	
Steamed clams	19	Orange juice	55
Turkey breast	10	Grapefruit juice	42
Tuna (in water)	6	Prune juice	40

Merely Informative
Least Nutritious Foods

Because points are deducted from and added to the Nutrition Scorecard, some foods had negative scores. Ranked among the least nutritious in the terms discussed above:

Burger King Double Whopper with Cheese	−194
Ben & Jerry's Heath Bar Crunch Ice Cream	−183
Cheesecake	−161
McDonald's Sausage and Egg Biscuit	−144
KFC Extra Tasty Crispy Thigh	−121
2 sausage links	−112
Regular hamburger	−92
Sirloin steak	−86
Salami or luncheon meat	−81
2 Reese's Peanut Butter Cups	−77
Oscar Mayer Beef Frank	−76
Vanilla ice cream	−73
One tablespoon of butter	−66

More Where This Came From

College Students on the Go: Introduction to Healthy Living, Needham Heights, Massachusetts: Simon & Schuster, 1996, by Drs. Maher Abbas, Daniel Adame, and Unnur Gylfadottir (1996) (covers nutritional basics, late-night snack attacks, eating in the dorm, eating disorders, places to eat out, healthy recipes by students; its authors describe it as "perhaps one of the most practical and useful books you will acquire as a college student.")

 *The RAT's Mouse*

Your computer mouse can lead you to any of the following:

- **www.discoveryhealth.com/DH/ihtlH/WSDSC000/325/325.html** Discovery page, including basic facts, lots of information, articles; good site

- **www.ificinfo.health.org/** International Food Information Council; extensive site covering food labeling, sweeteners, caffeine, fats and replacements, etc.
- **www.ganesa.com/food/index.html** A site on the food pyramid
- **www.health.yahoo.com/** Yahoo health site; includes section on nutrition and other information

27. MUSIC—ANSWERS

1. **Music Personalities.**

    a. The Beatles: George Harrison, John Lennon, Paul McCartney, and Ringo Starr.

    b. Violinists who are known internationally include Itzhak Perlman, Jascha Heifetz, Isaac Stern, and Yehudi Menuhin. Your grandparents might identify Fritz Kreisler as one of the world's greats.

2. **American Music.**   Types of music that originated in the United States include:

    - *Jazz*—a form of distinctly American music, often improvised, that grew out of black musical traditions in the early twentieth century; jazz evolved into jazz bands and then "big bands," including the bands of Count Basie, Louis Armstrong, Glenn Miller, and Duke Ellington.
    - *Gospel*—joyful, often rhythmic religious music common in Southern, particularly Southern black and evangelical, Protestant churches; gospel grew out of Negro spirituals and was later popularized by such singers as Mahalia Jackson.
    - *Blues*—a particular type of soulful jazz, often in the form of work songs or spirituals that reflected worry or despondency.
    - *Country and western*—music of the southeastern and southwestern United States, often with themes of love, tragedy, and the trials and disappointments of everyday life; popular in rural areas, centered in the Grand Old Opry in Nashville, Tennessee, and characterized by stringed instruments, including "fiddles"; also called country music.
    - *Rock and roll*—an enormously popular type of fast tempo music that combined elements of country, blues, and gospel music; this upbeat music was pioneered by such singers as Chuck Berry and Elvis Presley

and adopted by numerous British groups, including the Beatles and the Rolling Stones; also called rock or rock music.

- *Bluegrass*—a type of folk music featuring such instruments as guitar, banjo, and violin and a rapid tempo; found in the mountains of Appalachia, particularly including West Virginia and Kentucky.
- *Rap*—another popular music genre of the late twentieth century characterized by chanted rhymes accompanied by music with a strong beat from synthesizers or drums and other percussion instruments.

See *The Dictionary of Cultural Literacy,* Boston: Houghton Mifflin Company, 1988, by Hirsch, Kett, and Trefil for descriptions of certain of these and other types of music.

3. **Musicals.**   Here are some possibilities:

    a. Show: *Phantom of the Opera*
       Music/lyrics: Andrew Lloyd Webber; Tim Rice
       Songs: "The Music of the Night," "All I Ask of You," and others (other Andrew Lloyd Webber classics include *Jesus Christ, Superstar; Evita; Cats; Joseph and the Amazing Technicolor Dreamcoat; Starlight Express*)

    b. Show: *Grease*
       Music/lyrics: Warren Casey and Jim Jacobs
       Songs: "Summer Nights," "We Go Together" (3,388 Broadway performances, and a film classic)

    c. Show: *Cabaret*
       Music/lyrics: John Kander and Fred Ebb
       Songs: "Wilkommen," "Mein Herr," "Money, Money" (also by Kander and Ebb: *Chicago,* which includes the song, "And All That Jazz")

    d. Show: *The Lion King*
       Music/lyrics: Elton John and Tim Rice
       Songs: "Can You Feel the Love Tonight?," "Circle of Life," "Hakuna Matata"

    e. Show: *Fiddler on the Roof*
       Music/lyrics: Sheldon Harnick and Jerry Bock
       Songs: "If I Were a Rich Man," "Sunrise, Sunset," "Tradition," "Matchmaker," "To Life," and others

MUSIC

 f. Show: *The Sound of Music*
  Music/lyrics: Richard Rogers and Oscar Hammerstein
  Songs: "Edelweiss," "Do-Re-Mi," "Maria," "Climb Every Mountain," "My Favorite Things," and others. (other Rogers and Hammerstein musicals include *Oklahoma, South Pacific, Carousel, The King and I*)

 g. Show: *Beauty and the Beast* (Walt Disney)
  Music/lyrics: Alan Menken, Howard Ashman, and Tim Rice
  Songs: "Beauty and the Beast," "Be Our Guest," "Belle," "Something There," and others

 h. Show: *My Fair Lady*
  Music/lyrics: Alan Jay, Lerner and Frederick Loewe
  Songs: "Get Me to the Church on Time," "Rain in Spain," "I Could Have Danced All Night," "Wouldn't It Be Loverly," "On the Street Where You Live," and others (also *Camelot, Paint Your Wagon*)

 i. Show: *Annie*
  Music/lyrics: Martin Charnin and Charles Strouse
  Songs: "It's the Hard Knock Life," "Tomorrow," "You're Never Fully Dressed without a Smile," and others (one of the all-time family favorites; 2,377 Broadway performances)

 j. Show: *The Fantasticks*
  Music/lyrics: Harvey Schmidt and Tom Jones
  Songs: "Try to Remember," "Soon It's Gonna Rain" (over 15,000 performances)

 k. Show: *Guys and Dolls*
  Music/lyrics: Frank Loesser
  Songs: "Luck Be a Lady," "Fugue for Tinhorns," "A Bushel and a Peck," "Sit Down You're Rockin' the Boat," "Take Back Your Mink"

4. Instruments.

 a. *percussion instruments:* bass drum, kettle drum, timpani, cymbals, gong

 b. *brass instruments:* trumpet, trombone, coronet, French horn, English horn, tuba, sousaphone

   c. *woodwind instruments:* clarinet, oboe, bassoon, flute, piccolo

   d. *strings:* violin, viola, cello, bass

5. **Jazz Musicians.**   The answer is *c*, Jerry Garcia.

Louis Armstrong, also known as "Satchmo," was a legendary trumpet player. Dizzy Gillespie, also a trumpet player, led a popular jazz band. Dave Brubeck was a creative jazz musician whose quartets and quintets developed a distinctive style.

Jerry Garcia was the lead guitarist and vocalist for The Grateful Dead, which gained a large cult following. Garcia, later became well known for his necktie designs.

6. **Singing Parts.**

For male singing groups, the four traditional parts are first tenor, second tenor, baritone, and bass.

For female singing groups, the usual parts are first soprano, second soprano, alto, and contralto (or soprano 1, soprano 2, alto 1, alto 2).

In mixed choruses, the four are generally soprano, alto, tenor, and bass.

7. **Composers.**

You have many choices in choosing among pre-twentieth-century composers. Among the more well known are

- *Johann Sebastian Bach.* Richard Wagner called Bach "the most stupendous miracle in all music." This prodigious German composer (1685–1750) produced volumes of musical compositions for orchestra, piano, chamber groups, organ, and choruses. In addition, with two wives, Bach fathered twenty children. Seven generations of Bachs were musical professionals.
- *Ludwig van Beethoven.* Also German, this musical genius composed nine symphonies during his life (1770–1827), much of which he spent in Vienna. At age 30, Beethooven began going deaf. He continued composing, and in 1824, when he was completely deaf, he conducted the premiere of his Ninth Symphony.
- *Frederic Chopin.* Chopin (1810–1849) was born in Poland, and his music was a source of nationalist inspiration during Poland's domination by Czarist Russia, and again during World War II. Most of his

compositions—169 in all—were for the piano, and a substantial number of them are considered masterpieces.

- *Joseph Haydn.* Born in Austria (1732–1809), Haydn, a teacher of Mozart, came to be known as the father of the symphony, sonata, and string quartet. Haydn began under a patronage system in which composers were, not unlike other household workers, simply servants, composing on request and at the direction of their patrons.
- *Wolfgang Amadeus Mozart.* A musical prodigy who became the standard by which to measure musical genius, Mozart (1756–1791) began playing the harpsichord at age 3, went on tour at age 6, and variously identified chords while blindfolded, reproduced pieces from memory after hearing them once, and played keyboards covered with cloth. During his brief 35 years, Mozart was reviled by Antonio Salieri, a powerful, rival Vienna musician. He died poor and was buried in a pauper's grave, after having produced an extraordinary series of new works in the year he died.
- *Peter Ilich Tchaikovsky.* The greatest Russian composer (1840–1893) was a troubled and sensitive artist who was supported and subsidized for thirteen years by an affluent widow with whom he communicated intensively, but whom he never met face-to-face. Tchaikovsky composed such classics as the *Romeo and Juliet* fantasy-overture, the *1812 Overture,* the *Nutcracker Suite,* and music for the ballets, *Swan Lake* and *Sleeping Beauty.*

8. **Music Terms.**

   a. Singing just below proper pitch is singing "flat." By contrast, singing just slightly higher than the proper note is singing "sharp," a much less common phenomenon.

   b. Middle C. Middle C is used as a reference point: "Start on C above middle C."

   c. *A cappella,* a term taken from the Italian word for chapel; thus, singing in the style of a chapel.

   d. Syncopation. Calypso music, for example, is often syncopated. The song, *Kiss the Girl* in the musical animated film, *The Little Mermaid,* uses syncopation.

9. **Music Miscellany.**

   a. *American Pie* was written about Buddy Holly, Richie Valens, and "The Big Bopper."

   b. Johann Strauss. Among his famous Viennese waltzes are *The Blue Danube, Tales of the Vienna Woods, The Skaters' Waltz,* and *The Emperor's Waltz.*

   c. Hip hop.

10. **Lyrics.**   Obviously, the choice is yours. Knowing one verse and the chorus counts as a correct answer. If you're having trouble, here are a few popular candidates: *Tomorrow, Margaritaville, My Girl, Don't Cry for Me, Argentina, You've Lost That Loving Feeling, Amazing Grace.*

More Where This Came From

Classical Composers, An Illustrated History, New York: CLB, 1999, by Peter Gammond is a readable, elegant reference book on composers.

Stanley Sadie (ed.), Vladimir Ashkenazy, *The Billboard Illustrated Encyclopedia of Classical Music,* London: Watson-Guptill Publications, 2000, is also a comprehensive reference book.

If you're cramming for an introductory music course, you might like *Introduction to Music,* New York: McGraw-Hill, 1992, by Ronald Pen.

Jazz 101, New York: Hyperion, 2000, by John E. Szwed, is a helpful introduction to jazz, and *Opera for Beginners, Writers and Readers,* 1996, by Ron David, is an irreverent introduction to the world of opera.

The New Rolling Stone Encyclopedia of Rock & Roll, New York: Fireside, 1995, is a comprehensive reference source of rock & roll facts and personalities.

The RAT's Mouse

For more information using your computer mouse . . .

- **www.music.yahoo.com/** A general and dependable music site
- **www.musicals.net/** A site about musicals with links to lots of musicals; musical news

- **www.aliasrecords.com/Americanmusicclub.htm** American music, including new bands (popular, rock), tour dates, merchandise, etc.
- **www.wnur.org/jazz/** An in-depth jazz site that explains styles of jazz, profiles artists, describes instruments

28. FAMILY FACTS—ANSWERS

Obviously, the correct answers to many of the questions in this section are specific to your own family, so you need to answer them and then confirm your answers with another member of your family—probably an older one. If family members living near you don't know all of the answers, you may need to do a little research or call or write other members of the family.

If you're adopted, or if you have one or more stepparents, you may wish to provide answers for your natural parents, your adoptive or stepparents, some combination of the two, or both.

1. **Names.**

Family names may derive from your ancestors' occupations—for example, the last name, Taylor, which may reflect an ancestor's occupation. Other family names may have no literal meaning in English but may have some meaning in another language or another country. Other names may have been shortened (as in the case of some immigrants to the United States who adopted shortened versions of their original family names), or the spelling may have changed over time.

See *American Surnames*, Genealogical Publishing Company, 1997, by Elsdon C. Smith.

2. **Key Dates for Your Parents.**

In addition to the birthdays of your father and mother, and their anniversary date (the date that they were married), other interesting tidbits are their ages when they got their first jobs; their ages when you were born; their ages when their first and last children were born; the ages they will be when their last child finishes school.

3. **Your Mother's Names.**

   Your mother's last name may or may not be the same last name she had when she was born. Many women take the last name of their husbands when they marry. If they do, they are likely to use their last name as a middle name, sometimes called a "maiden name."

   Some women simply elect to keep their maiden names after marriage. Some keep their family name for professional reasons or as a *nom de plume* if they happen to be writers.

   Other women, when married, choose to adopt a hyphenated last name that combines both the husband's and the wife's last name.

Merely Informative Latin Names

The conventions for names in most Latin countries are even more complicated. Most Latins carry both their father's and their mother's family names. Thus, the son of a father whose family name is Reyes and a mother whose family name is Lopez might be named José Reyes Lopez. The father's family name comes before the mother's family name, and in casual conversation, Jose would likely be known simply as José Reyes.

If José Reyes Lopez marries Nina Rodriguez Velez, Nina becomes Nina Rodriguez de Reyes. For professional purposes, she likely will remain Nina Rodriguez Velez.

If José and Nina have a daughter, she might be named Isabel Reyes Rodriguez. More informally, she would simply be Isabel Reyes.

When she gets married . . .

The key thing to remember is that if you run into José Reyes Lopez, the "last" name you want to use in introducing him, if you use only one, is the name that appears in the middle—Reyes—not the one at the end—Lopez.

FAMILY FACTS

4. **First Cousins.**   First cousins are the children of your aunts and uncles. If your mother was an only child and had no brothers or sisters, then you would have no first cousins on your mother's side of the family. Conversely, if one or both of your parents had a number of brothers and sisters, and if they married and had children, all of those children would be your first cousins.

5. **Second Cousins.**   The most correct answer is *d*.

   Second cousins are, in fact, the children of your parents' first cousins.
   The children of your first cousins are generally regarded as "first cousins
   once removed." Your cousin's cousins may be no relation to you at all.
   However, it is also true that the term, "cousin," is loosely used to refer to a
   wide variety of relatives. In fact, in some parts of the country, the word is
   used almost as a term of endearment for anyone with whom you believe you
   have a common ancestor.

6. **The Old Country.**   Except for Native Americans, all citizens of the United
   States have family roots that go back to another country. Although some families may have to go back several generations to find their immigrant ancestors,
   those roots are there, whether or not you can find them.

7. and 8. **Grandparents and Your Grandparents' Home Towns.**   Your grandparents on your mother's side of the family are your maternal grandparents;
   your grandparents on your father's side are your paternal grandparents.

   If your grandparents are alive, you can ask them about their family histories,
   including their own parents and grandparents. The best information about your
   family history comes from living family members, and what they pass on can
   become part of your family's oral history and tradition.

9. **Family Health History.**   The answer is *b*, which is *not* correct.

   Although your blood type may not be the same as that of your parents (or
   of your siblings), your blood type—whether it's O, A, B, or AB—is, determined genetically.

   Certain diseases, or susceptibility to disease, can be transmitted genetically; hemophilia and cystic fibrosis are two such illnesses.

   For other kinds of health risks, genetics can make you more susceptible to
   certain types of diseases. Being aware of those genetic patterns or traits in
   your parents or grandparents can be helpful to you in avoiding health risks or
   an early death. Cancer and heart disease are examples of diseases for which a
   genetic susceptibility may exist in families. Thus, if one or more of your
   parents or grandparents died early of a heart attack or stroke, that might alert
   you that you could be genetically susceptible to heart disease yourself.

   Other health problems may have been caused, or worsened, by lifestyle
   choices that you may wish to avoid. For example, if you had a parent or

grandparent who smoked heavily or was obese and died of heart disease, that might influence your lifestyle choices.

It is for reasons such as these that a doctor is likely to ask about your family health history during the course of a physical examination.

10. **Your Family Tree.** Once you have developed your family tree, save it and pass it on. It will be fun for other members of your family.

More Where This Came From

Sources on learning about your family tree and family facts include the following:

The Sleuth Book for Genealogists, Betterway Publications, 2000, by Emily Anne Croom;

The Everything Family Tree Book, Holbrook, Massachusetts: Adams Media Corporation, 1997, by William G. Hartley;

Ancestors (A Beginner's Guide to Family History and Genealogy), by Jim and Terry Willard;

Genealogy via the Internet, Alexander Books, 1997, by Ralph Roberts.

The RAT's Mouse

Additional information accessible through the touch of a computer's mouse include the following:

- **www.familytreemagazine.com/** A link to the *Family Tree Magazine*, a good start for beginners in tracing their roots
- **www.usaafter.com/** Offers free family tree builders software, genealogy information, links to other sites
- **www.kuntakinte.org/** Celebration of the heritage, culture, and history of Africans, African Americans, and African Caribbeans
- **www.familyheritageshop.com/** For those of European descent

29.   THE FINE ARTS—ANSWERS

1.   Classical Music

You may surprise yourself. Here are a few classical melodies that you may know:

- *Peter and the Wolf,* by Peter Ilich Tchaikovsky
- *Bolero,* by Maurice Ravel
- *Pomp and Circumstance,* by Edward Elgar (the march played at graduations)
- *Lullaby,* by Johannes Brahms
- *The William Tell Overture,* by Antonio Rossini
- *The Wedding March,* by Felix Mendelssohn

Again, any classical pieces that you can identify by ear count as correct answers. Here are a few more of the most recognizable classical pieces:

- *Toreador Song* by Georges Bizet
- "The Hallelujah Chorus," from George Frideric Handel's *Messiah*
- *Humoresque* by Antonin Dvořák
- *The Blue Danube* by Johann Strauss
- "Dance of the Sugar Plum Fairy" from Tchaikovsky's *Nutcracker Suite*
- *The 1812 Overture* by Tchaikovsky

More Where This Came From

For example, take a look at *The NPR Guide to Building a Classical CD Collection,* New York: Workman Publishing, 1999, by Ted Libbey, which includes a Classical Checklist for Teenage Listeners and a Top Ten list.

2.   Plays.

Some of Shakespeare's most well known plays: *Hamlet, Macbeth, Romeo and Juliet, A Midsummer Night's Dream, Merchant of Venice, As You Like It, Julius Caesar, Othello.*

Plays by twentieth-century playwrights include: *Glass Menagerie* and *A Streetcar Named Desire* by Tennessee Williams; *Death of a Salesman* and *The Crucible* by Arthur Miller; *Who's Afraid of Virginia Woolf* by Edward Albee; *A Raisin in the Sun* by Lorraine Hansberry; *The Circle* by

W. Somerset Maugham; *Ah, Wilderness!, The Iceman Cometh, Long Day's Journey into Night, The Hairy Ape* by Eugene O'Neill; *Twelve Angry Men* by Reginald Rose.

For each category, there are additional correct answers. If your answers are correct, give yourself two points.

3. **Film Classics.**
   a. There are numerous correct answers. Some of the great black-and-white classics include:
      - *All Quiet on the Western Front* starring Lew Ayres (1930)
      - *Mutiny on the Bounty* with Charles Laughton and Clark Gable (1935)
      - *Gone with the Wind* starring Vivien Leigh and Clark Gable (1939)
      - *Stagecoach* starring John Wayne (1939)
      - *The Grapes of Wrath* starring Henry Fonda (1940)
      - *Citizen Kane* starring Orson Wells (1941)
      - *Casablanca* starring Humphrey Bogart and Ingrid Bergman (1943)
      - *Going My Way* starring Bing Crosby (1944)
      - *A Streetcar Named Desire* starring Vivien Leigh and Marlon Brando (1951)
      - *From Here to Eternity* starring Burt Lancaster and Deborah Kerr (1953)
      - *On the Waterfront* starring Marlon Brando, Eva Marie Saint, and Rod Steiger (1954)
      - *Some Like It Hot* starring Tony Curtis, Jack Lemon, Marilyn Monroe (1959)
      - *Psycho* starring Anthony Perkins, Janet Leigh (1960)

   b. In order, they were *Star Wars* (1977), *The Empire Strikes Back* (1980), and *Return of the Jedi* (1983).

   Other defining characters of the Star Wars Trilogy included Luke Skywalker, Han Solo, Darth Vader, Princess Leia, Chewbacca, and Obi-Wan Kenobi.

4. **Art Museums.**   Famous art galleries and museums are scattered around the world. Here are the locations of those listed:

THE FINE ARTS

Uffizi	Florence, Italy
Metropolitan Museum of Art	New York
Louvre	Paris
Tate	London
Hermitage	St. Petersburg, Russia
Musée d'Orsay	Paris

Both Washington, D.C., and London have National Galleries. London's is the National Gallery, on Trafalgar Square; Washington's is The National Gallery of Art, which is on the Mall. Count either as a correct answer.

Merely Informative
Other Terrific Museums

There are many other great museums, among them are the Prado in Madrid, The Municipal Museum in Amsterdam, The Chicago Art Institute, the National Gallery in London, and The Museum of Modern Art ("MOMA") in New York.

Art museums renowned for their architecture include the Guggenheim museums in New York City and Bilbao, Spain; The Getty Center in Los Angeles; and the East Wing of the National Gallery in Washington.

In addition, many regional cities have distinguished local museums that display excellent art and save you the hassle of traveling to a major city. The Clark Art Institute in Williamstown, Massachusetts; the Museum of Fine Arts in St. Petersburg, Florida; The Nelson-Atkins Museum of Art in Kansas City, Missouri; the Columbus Museum of Art in Columbus, Ohio; and the Modern Art Museum of Fort Worth, Texas, are but a few examples of dozens of such museums. See *The New York Times Traveler's Guide to Art Museum Exhibitions 2000,* Harry N. Abrams, 2000, (ed. Fletcher Roberts).

---

5. **Sculptors.**   The correct matches are the following:

Alexander Calder	c. mobiles
Auguste Rodin	d. *The Thinker*
Henry Moore	b. *Reclining Figure*
Michaelangelo	a. *David*

6. **Impressionist Painters.**   The answer is *c*, Rembrandt van Rijn.

Rembrandt, one of the Olympian figures of art, was Dutch. Although he, too, was innovative in his use of light, he lived in the 1600s, predating the Impressionists by more than 200 years.

Auguste Renoir, unparalled in his ability to capture "shimmering color and flickering light," produced happy, colorful scenes, including famous paintings of parties, parks, and gardens. Mid-career, Renoir shifted his artistic attention to large paintings of female nudes. Ultimately crippled by rheumatoid arthritis, in his later years, Renoir painted with brushes tied to his crippled fingers and became a sculptor when confined to his wheelchair.

Widely regarded as the greatest of the Impressionists, Claude Monet was a master of light and color. Some of his famous works—*Water Lilies, Cathedral at Rouen*—are multiple paintings of the same scene under varying light conditions. A pioneer with light and color harmony, Monet ultimately became blind.

A participant in the 1874 exhibition that prompted the term, "Impressionists," Edgar Degas is best known for his paintings of ballerinas and female bathers. A regular at rehearsals at the Paris opera, Degas used pastels (chalk) and oils, and ultimately became a sculptor as his eyesight began to fail.

7. **Symphony Orchestras.**

Many American cities have symphony orchestras. Among those with the richest histories:

Boston Symphony
Cleveland Symphony
Philadelphia Orchestra
Los Angeles Philharmonic
New York Philharmonic
Chicago Symphony
National Symphony (Washington, D.C.)

Merely Informative 🐿
Personalities of Orchestras

The Boston Symphony—One of the country's grand symphonies, with one of the most important summer music festivals at Tanglewood (in western Massachusetts), plus a sister orchestra, the Boston Pops, that has set the standard for light classics. Among its famous conductors: Seiji Ozawa, Serge Koussevitzky, Charles Munch, and Eric Leinsdorf.

The Cleveland Symphony—One of the most recorded orchestras in America, with a summer festival at Blossom Center (outside of Cleveland), this symphony is noted for adventuresome programming.

The Philadelphia Orchestra—Noted for its woodwinds, it was the first American orchestra to visit China (1973). Among its famous conductors: Eugene Ormandy.

The Los Angeles Philharmonic—Soon to move to its new home in the Walt Disney Concert Hall, this symphony has a strong commitment to contemporary music. It performs during the summer at the Hollywood Bowl. Past conductors: Otto Klemperer, Zubin Mehta, Andre Previn.

The New York Philharmonic—The oldest orchestra in America (since 1842). In 1986, its free concert in Central Park attracted more than 800,000 people, the largest recorded attendance ever for a classical concert. Famous conductors: Gustav Mahler, Arturo Toscanini, Leonard Bernstein, and Zubin Mehta.

The National Symphony is now conducted by Leonard Slatkin, whose predecessors included Mstislav Rostropovich, Antal Dorati, and Howard Mitchell.

Other excellent American symphony orchestras include Chicago Symphony, Dallas Symphony, Pittsburgh Symphony, San Diego Symphony, and Atlanta Symphony.

Many other American cities also have symphony orchestras. Some of the world's greatest orchestras are located outside the United States. Among numerous exceptional symphonies are the Berlin Philharmonic, the Academy of St. Martin-in-the-Fields, the Vienna Philharmonic, and the London Symphony.

---

8. **Personalities in the Arts.** The answer is *c*.

Although it is true that Picasso's sculpture "Bull's Head" was done with a bicycle seat and handlebar, Picasso neither died young nor led a monastic life. To the contrary, he lived beyond 90 and was a prolific artist and womanizer well into his 80s, during which he again married, punctuating a long life reportedly filled with romances.

Each of the other statements is true. Leonardo da Vinci, a quintessential Renaissance man, was a painter, sculptor, architect, scientist, and engineer. He would have done well on *The RAT* of his day.

Vincent van Gogh's tumultuous and intense life ended while he was in his 30s, living in the south of France in an asylum. Two years before his death, in 1888, following an altercation with fellow artist Paul Gaugin, van Gogh did cut off his own earlobe and presented it to a prostitute.

Andy Warhol's pop art includes not only famous paintings of Campbell's soup cans, but also portraits of Marilyn Monroe, Elvis Presley, Mao Tse-tung, and a box of Brillo pads.

More Where This Came From

For an "exhilarating joyride" through the history of art, try *Instant Art History,* New York: Fawcett Columbine, 1995, by Walter Robinson (1995).

9. **Architecture.**

   a. *Classic columns.* The three classic styles of columns are Doric, Ionic, and Corinthian. To help remember, you may want to recall that the circular features on either side of the top of an Ionic column resemble two *eyes*.

   The church of Saint-Suplice in Paris shows all three styles of columns. Construction on Saint-Suplice began in 1646, took 134 years to complete, and produced, as one Paris guidebook put it, "very mixed styles."

   b. *Twentieth-century Architects.* Some of the more famous, together with one of each of their famous buildings:

   - Frank Lloyd Wright (The Guggenheim Museum in New York)
   - Walter Gropius (Harvard Graduate Center)
   - Mies van der Rohe (The Seagram Building in New York)
   - Eero Saarinen (Dulles Airport in Washington, D.C.)
   - I.M. Pei (the East Wing of the National Gallery of Art in Washington, D.C.)
   - Philip Johnson (Pennzoil Place in Houston)
   - Louis I. Kahn (the Salk Institute in La Jolla, California)
   - Buckminster Fuller (creator of the geodesic dome)

More Where This Game From 🍳

Twentieth-Century American Architecture—The Buildings and Their Makers, New York: W.W. Norton, 2000, by Carter Wiseman (2000). This book was described by one reviewer as "About as good a summary of American architecture of this century as anyone is likely to write."

10. **Ballet and Opera.**   You are entitled to two points if you can provide the three pieces of information called for about any classic ballet or opera that is performed publicly.

a. *Opera*

Many operas have endured as classics. The following are among them:

1. *Madam Butterfly*
   Composer: Giacomo Puccini

   An American military officer, Lieutenant Pinkerton, arranges a temporary contract marriage with a Japanese girl, "Butterfly," while he is stationed in Japan. She falls in love with him and treats the marriage as continuing, even after Pinkerton returns to America. Three years later, Pinkerton writes that he is returning to Japan with his new American wife, but the news of his marriage does not reach Butterfly, who, with her son by Pinkerton, expectantly awaits his return. Butterfly is ultimately confronted with the truth, and the new Mrs. Pinkerton asks if they may adopt Pinkerton's son. Butterfly consents, blindfolds her son, and before Pinkerton returns for his son, she kills herself with her father's sword to preserve her honor.

2. *Don Quixote*
   Composer: Jules Massenet

   At a feast in the town square at which many knights seek to impress the beautiful Dulcinea, the comical knight, Don Quixote, and his companion, Sancho Panza, appear. Amused by Don Quixote's serenade, Dulcinea promises that she will be the knight's loved one if he can recover her necklace, which bandits have stolen. Don Quixote and Sancho, on horse and donkey, go in search of the bandits, even though the knight's only battle experience has been charging hogs and tilting at windmills. Finding the bandits, Don Quixote bravely attacks, but is captured and threatened with death. So impressed with the knight's intense love for Dulcinea, however, the bandits give him the necklace. Triumphantly returning, the knight is embraced by Dulcinea, but told that she is not the woman he thinks and that she will not marry him. Alone with Sancho, the dying Don Quixote thanks him for having given him his dreams.

3. *Hansel and Gretel*
Composer: Engelbert Humperdinck.

Hansel and Gretel, scolded by their mother, are punished by being sent to the woods to pick berries. On returning home, their father is alarmed because the wicked Crunch Witch, who lures children with magic cakes, lives in the woods. In the woods, Hansel and Gretel play, eat all the berries they have picked, and, as night falls, realize they are lost. Afraid, they pray to angels and, with help from the Sandman, fall asleep. On awakening, they see the witch's hut and begin to nibble at the gingerbread wall that surrounds it. The witch captures Hansel, puts him in a cage, and asks Gretel to help fatten Hansel before cooking him into gingerbread. Warned by her brother, Gretel asks the witch to show her how to check the hot oven. When she does, Gretel and Hansel, who has escaped, push her into the oven, and all the children who have been turned into gingerbread are turned back into children.

Other classics: *Aida* and *La Traviata,* by Giuseppe Verdi; *The Barber of Seville* and *William Tell* by Giacchino Antonio Rossini; *Carmen* by Georges Bizet; *La Boheme* by Giacomo Puccini; *The Ring* by Richard Wagner; *Faust* and *The Magic Flute* by Wolfgang Amadeus Mozart; *Romeo and Juliet* by Charles François Gounod.

More Where This Came From

The stories of these and other operas may be found in *The Story of a Hundred Operas,* Doubleday, 1989; Edith Dodway, *56 of the Best Operas,* New York: A.L. Burt Company, 1915; and similar books. Summaries with a lighter touch may be found in *When the Fat Lady Sings,* Sound and Vision Limited, 1990, by David W. Barber.

b. *Ballet*

Here are a few of the more famous ballets:

1. *The Nutcracker*
   Composer: Peter Ilich Tchaikovsky

   A popular Christmas ballet, *The Nutcracker* begins at a Christmas party where a little girl, Clara, is given a gift of a nutcracker by her godfather, Counsellor Drosselmeyer. Clara falls asleep and dreams that mice are attacking her toys. Clara saves her toys and, in gratitude, the Nutcracker takes her on a journey to the Kingdom of Sweets, where dance numbers center around the Sugar Plum Fairy, the Snow Queen, Chinese dancers, and others.

2. *The Sleeping Beauty*
   Composer: Tchaikovsky

   This classic, fairy tale ballet is based on the tale of a young infant, Aurora, who is placed under a spell by a wicked fairy to sleep for 100 years when she pricks her finger. Courted by several princes, she pricks her finger on a spindle given to her by an old woman and falls asleep. One hundred years later, a young prince out hunting is presented with a vision of Aurora, for whom he searches. He finds her, awakens her with a kiss, and, in the third act, they marry.

3. *Swan Lake*
   Composer: Tchaikovsky

   The most popular of all ballets, *Swan Lake* is the story of a prince who, on his 21st birthday, is urged by his mother to marry. Escaping with his friends to go hunting, the prince comes upon a flight of swans. Demanding the right to shoot the first one, the prince discovers that the swans are maidens under a magician's spell that requires them to live as swans by day and become humans only at night. The prince, in love with the lead swan, Odette, is tricked at a palace reception into proposing to someone who appears to be Odette, but who is, in fact, the magician's daughter. Now unable to be released from her spell, the grieving Odette is met by the prince by the lake with the other swans. The prince and Odette plunge into the lake. The magician dies, the other swans are returned to human form, and the prince and Odette are united in death.

Other famous classical ballets involving stories of love, the supernatural, tragedy, and death include *La Sylphide, Giselle,* and *Coppelia.* Other ballets set to familiar stories include *Romeo and Juliet, Cinderella,* and *Don Quixote. Fancy Free* is a story of three sailors on shore leave in New York; *Revelations* has Negro spirituals as its theme; *Apollo* has the god Apollo choosing the muse of dance over the muses of poetry and mime, as all ascend Mount Olympus.

More Where That Came From

For a pictorial, illustrated book on ballet, see *The Colorful World of Ballet,* by C. Crisp and E. Thorpe, London: Octopus Books Ltd., 1977.

The RAT's Mouse

There are many excellent web sites relating to the fine arts. Here are a few, accessible with a computer and a mouse:

- **www.classicalusa.com** Many links to music sites, classical and jazz, art, video theater, film
- **www.musicweb.uk.net** Composer profiles, CD reviews, music societies
- **www.rollingstone.com** Site for *Rolling Stone* magazine; includes reviews, top hit lists, local music, etc.
- **www.netpopular.com/art.htm** Links to museums worldwide
- **www.artchive.com/74nadar.htm** About first Impressionist exhibit in 1874, it features Renoir, Monet, Pissaro, Boudin, Cezanne, Moristo, Degas, and Sisley
- **www.operabase.com** Crammed with information—world-premier performances, weekly highlights, performance and artist searches; its world map covers 600 opera houses and festivals
- **www.abt.org/home.html** Site of the American Ballet Theater; see its "dictionary" of ballet terms, photos, performance dates
- **www.aha.ru~vladmo** Russian classical ballet site—key figures, companies, photos, etc.

30. PRINCIPLES AND PRIORITIES—ANSWERS

1. **Making Important Decisions.**   Among the many good questions you might ask yourself (or things you might do) before making an important decision:

    - Do I have all of the relevant information I need to make this decision?
    - Have I considered (and written down) all the pros and cons?
    - Have I considered all options or alternatives?
    - Have I asked another person whose judgment I trust for his or her opinion?
    - What are the likely long-term effects of any decision I make?
    - What might be the unintended consequences of my decision?
    - What would someone with more experience, greater wisdom, or stronger values do?
    - How will I feel about one choice versus another one year from now?
    - What are the worst-case scenarios and best-case scenarios of my possible decisions?
    - Have I, time permitting, thought about the question after a night's sleep or after living with the idea for a couple of days?

2. **Traits of Successful People.**   Good habits that may increase your effectiveness and serve you well include:

    - persistence,
    - goal-setting,
    - diligence and hard work,
    - careful preparation or planning,
    - follow-through,
    - inquisitiveness,
    - cheerfulness,
    - a positive attitude,
    - a can-do attitude,
    - a deep sense of personal responsibility,
    - a sense of humor, and
    - a solid sense of right and wrong.

Merely Informative
Habits of Effective People

A long-time best seller, *The 7 Habits of Highly Effective People,* identifies seven principles as keys to success and excellence. They are

1. Be proactive (exercise initiative and take responsibility).
2. Begin with the end in mind (visualize at the outset how you want things to turn out).
3. Put first things first (manage yourself so that you do what is, in fact, most important).
4. Think Win/Win (think cooperatively to achieve mutual benefit).
5. Seek first to understand, then to be understood (communicate better by first listening, diagnosing, and understanding).
6. Synergize (cooperate creatively so that two together can produce more than two acting alone).
7. "Sharpen the saw" (take time regularly to renew yourself physically, mentally, emotionally, and spiritually).

PRINCIPLES AND PRIORITIES

3. **Fabulous Books.** The choice is, of course, yours. Among the possibilities:

   - The Complete Works of Shakespeare
   - An anthology of poetry
   - The Bible
   - A songbook
   - *The Odyssey* by Homer
   - *Lessons of History* by Will and Ariel Durant
   - *Gone with the Wind* by Margaret Mitchell
   - *Winnie the Pooh* by A. A. Milne
   - *War and Peace* by Leo Tolstoy
   - *Ulysses* by James Joyce
   - A dictionary
   - Any of your own favorites that you like to read and reread, whether it's a biography of Lincoln, poems by Maya Angelou, or a book by Dr. Seuss.

Merely Informative
Reading Good Books

"The man who does not read good books has no advantage over the man who can't read them." Mark Twain.

4. **Personal Goals.**   You set them; they are your goals. The accumulated wisdom about goals is that they should be aspirational or ambitious; require some sustained effort on your part; and improve your abilities, experience level, discipline, character, or solvency.

5. **A Poem.**   *You have broad latitude on this question, except that very short rhymes and limericks are discouraged. You get credit for a correct answer if you can recite from memory a complete poem of any length; one or more verses of a longer poem; or ten or more lines from an important play. What is most important is that you have committed to memory lines of some poem that is important to you.*
    Among the many possibilities are:
    a. "Dreams" by Langston Hughes
        Hold fast to dreams
        For if dreams die
        Life is a broken-winged bird
        That cannot fly.
        Hold fast to dreams
        For when dreams go
        Life is a barren field
        Frozen with snow.
    b. Sonnet No. 18 by William Shakespeare
        Shall I compare thee to a summer's day?
        Thou art more lovely and more temperate;
        Rough winds do shake the darling buds of May,
        And summer's lease hath all too short a date:
        Sometimes too hot the eye of heaven shines,
        And often is his gold complexion dimmed;
        And every fair from fair sometimes declines,
        By chance or nature's changing course untrimmed;
        But thy eternal summer shall not fade,

Nor lose possession of that fair thou ow'st;
Nor shall death brag thou wander'st in his shade,
When in eternal lines to time thou grow'st:
So long as men can breathe, or eyes can see,
So long lives this, and this gives life to thee.

c. The Twenty-third Psalm, Book of Psalms, The Bible
The Lord is my shepherd, I shall not want;
He makes me lie down in green pastures.
He leads me beside still waters;
He restores my soul.
He leads me in paths of righteousness for his name's sake.
Even though I walk through the valley of the shadow of death,
I fear no evil; for thou art with me;
thy rod and thy staff, they comfort me.
Thou preparest a table before me in the presence of my enemies;
thou anointest my head with oil, my cup overflows.
Surely goodness and mercy shall follow me all the days of my life;
and I shall dwell in the house of the Lord forever.

Excerpts from a few classics . . .

d. "The Night Before Christmas" by Clement C. Moore
'Twas the night before Christmas, when all through the house
Not a creature was stirring, not even a mouse.
The stockings were hung by the chimney with care
In hopes that Saint Nicholas soon would be there.
The children were nestled all snug in their beds,
While visions of sugar plums danced in their heads.
And Mama in her kerchief and I in my cap,
Had just settled down for a long winter's nap.
. . .
He was dressed all in fur from his head to his foot,
And his clothes were all tarnished with ashes and soot.
A bundle of toys he had flung on his back,
And he looked like a peddler just opening his pack.
His eyes—how they twinkled! His dimples—how merry!
His cheeks were like roses, his nose like a cherry!
His droll little mouth was drawn up like a bow,
And the beard on his chin was as white as the snow.

The stump of a pipe he held tight in his teeth,
And the smoke it encircled his head like a wreath.
He had a broad face and a little round belly
That shook when he laughed like a bowl full of jelly.
He was chubby and plump, a right jolly old elf,
And I laughed when I saw him in spite of myself.
A wink of his eye and a twist of his head
Soon gave me to know I had nothing to dread.
He spoke not a word but went straight to his work,
And filled all the stockings; then turned with a jerk,
And laying his finger aside of his nose,
And giving a nod, up the chimney he rose.
He sprang to his sleigh, to his team gave a whistle,
And away they all flew like the down of a thistle.
But I heard him exclaim ere he drove out of sight,
"Happy Christmas to all and to all a good night!"

e. "Casey at the Bat" by Ernest Lawrence Thayer

It looked extremely rocky for the Mudville nine that day;
The score stood two to four, with but an inning left to play.
So, when Cooney died at second, and Burrows did the same,
A pallor wreathed the features of the patrons of the game.
A straggling few got up to go, leaving there the rest,
With that hope which springs eternal within the human breast.
For they thought: "If only Casey could get a whack at that,"
They'd put even money now, with Casey at the bat.
. . .
The sneer is gone from Casey's lips, his teeth are clenched in hate,
He pounds with cruel vengeance his bat upon the plate;
And now the pitcher holds the ball, and now he lets it go,
And now the air is shattered by the force of Casey's blow.
Oh, somewhere in this favored land the sun is shining bright,
The band is playing somewhere, and somewhere hearts are light;
And somewhere men are laughing, and somewhere children shout,
But there is no joy in Mudville; Mighty Casey has struck out.

f. "The Cremation of Sam McGee," by Robert Service

There are strange things done in the midnight sun
By the men who moil for gold;

The Arctic trails have their secret tales
That would make your blood run cold;
The Northern Lights have seen queer sights,
But the queerest they ever did see
Was that night on the marge of Lake Lebarge
I cremated Sam McGee.
Now Sam McGee was from Tennessee, where the cotton blooms
and blows.
Why he left his home in the South to roam 'round the Pole,
God only knows.
He was always cold, but the land of gold seemed to hold him
like a spell;
Though he'd often say in his homely way that "he'd sooner live in hell."
. . .
Some planks I tore from the cabin floor, and I lit the boiler fire;
Some coal I found that was lying around, and I heaped the fuel higher;
The flames just soared, and the furnace roared—
such a blaze you seldom see;
And I burrowed a hole in the glowing coal, and I stuffed in
Sam McGee.
. . .
I do not know how long in the snow I wrestled with grisly fear;
But the stars came out and they danced about ere again I
ventured near;
I was sick with dread, but I bravely said: "I'll just take a peep inside.
I guess he's cooked, and it's time I looked"; . . .
then the door I opened wide.
And there sat Sam, looking cool and calm, in the heart of the
furnace roar;
And he wore a smile you could see a mile, and he said:
"Please close that door.
It's fine in here, but I greatly fear you'll let in the cold and storm—
Since I left Plumtree, down in Tennessee, it's the first time
I've been warm."

g. "The Road Not Taken" by Robert Frost
Two roads diverged in a yellow wood,
And sorry I could not travel both

And be one traveler, long I stood
And looked down one as far as I could
To where it bent in the undergrowth;
Then took the other, as just as fair,
And having perhaps the better claim,
Because it was grassy and wanted wear;
Though as for that the passing there
Had worn them really about the same,
And both that morning equally lay
In leaves no step had trodden black.
Oh, I kept the first for another day!
Yet knowing how way leads on to way,
I doubted if I should ever come back.
I shall be telling this with a sigh
Somewhere ages and ages hence:
Two roads diverged in a wood, and I—
I took the one less traveled by,
And that has made all the difference.

Merely Informative
Things You've Memorized

Individuals who have been isolated—climbing a mountaintop, alone on an Outward Bound program, in a prisoner-of-war cell—sometimes report that knowing poetry by heart helped them to pass the time, stay connected with the world, and keep mentally alert.

---

6. **An Older Friend.**   Through a friendship with someone two to three times your age, you are likely to find someone who has:
   - a different perspective on life from yours;
   - opinions different from your own;
   - a perspective shaped by considerably more experience than you have had;
   - a reliable confidant or advisor;
   - a perspective that will help you appreciate being young;
   - settled values and interesting reasons for them;

- actually has witnessed things that you think of only as history;
- an interest in what you and your friends think about certain things, and why; and
- other attributes that will help you appreciate older people and why they are, as they should be, treasured in many societies.

7. **Learning from Mistakes.** Selecting the wrong color socks should not be on this list. Neither should wrong answers on tests, even a test as important as *The RAT*. Try, instead, for something like an occasion on which you were rude, insensitive, or thoughtless. Or situations in which you failed to plan ahead, prepare sufficiently, or meet a commitment you made.

   If you're still stuck, consider acts of unkindness, selfishness, or spitefulness toward a brother, sister, or parent. That almost always works. Virtually any situation that you are able to recall in which your integrity or your sense of personal responsibility failed provides a correct answer to this question.

8. **Listening.** You are probably doing a good job of listening well when you:
   - listen more than you talk (If you want to be a good listener, a listening-talking ratio of 70–30 is not bad.);
   - actually pay attention to *what* is being said (The opposite, which you may recognize, is looking earnestly at someone who is talking but having your mind a thousand miles away.);
   - maintain eye contact;
   - periodically react, even if minimally. Relevant comments or questions are one sign that you're listening. So are periodic expletives, or a timely, "I don't believe that." Even occasional guttural responses show that your vital signs are working;
   - use affirming body language—leaning forward, sitting up in your chair, taking occasional notes, and responsive facial expressions are all signs of good listening; slouching, arms folded across the chest, or a baseball hat pulled down low over your eyes don't suggest a high level of attentiveness.

Merely Informative Listening in Japan

In Japan, people often close their eyes when they are listening carefully. If you're not in Japan, however, people with their eyes closed may be asleep. Hence, in most countries, closed eyes are not regarded as positive feedback to a speaker.

---

9. **Role Models.**   Role models can serve an important function in your own growth and development. Although in sports training it is sometimes called "imaging," observing people you admire and emulating their traits or abilities can work in all fields of endeavor, from academic curiosity to music, from public speaking to posture.

    For this question, shoot a little higher and identify:

    a. two nonrelatives who have greatly influenced your life;

    b. someone you believe to be one of the three greatest figures of the 20th century, and why you think so; or

    c. an individual you would like to be like—a true role model.

10. **A Principle for Life.**   *What is required for a correct answer to this question is simply that you consider various possibilities and identify at least one principle that you think is a worthy goal for a lifetime.*

    Many principles are worthy and durable candidates for an entire lifetime. Examples of principles that have been embraced or articulated by others include:

    - "You commit a sin of omission if you do not utilize all the power that is within you." Oliver Wendell Holmes
    - "I expect to pass through this world but once. Any good therefore that I can do, or any kindness that I can show to my fellow-creature, let me do it now. Let me not defer or neglect it, for I shall not pass this way again." Attributed to Stephen Grellet
    - "Don't compromise yourself. You are all you've got." Janis Joplin
    - "Do what you can, with what you have, where you are." Theodore Roosevelt
    - "'Why not?'" Mason Cooley
    - "Life has two rules: number 1, Never quit! Number 2, Always remember rule number 1." Duke Ellington

- "Pinpoint Your Passion." Maria Shriver, *Ten Things I Wish I'd Known— Before I Went Out into the Real World,* New York: Warner Books, 2000.
- "If you do not live your life completely, realizing goals you hold to be worthwhile, making your unique contribution to the world, nobody ever will. Your song will die with you." Richard Edler, *If I Knew Then What I Know Now,* Berkely Publishing Group, 1997.
- "Do unto others as you would have them do unto you." Matthew 7:12
- "Grant me the courage to change the things that I can change, the serenity to accept the things I cannot, and the wisdom to know the difference." Attributed to Rheinhold Neibuhr, and often referred to as "The Serenity Prayer"
- "Keep your feet on the ground and your eyes on the stars." Millie Moyer, and perhaps others

Merely Informative Principles from Kindergarten

In his best-selling book, *All I Really Need to Know I Learned in Kindergarten,* Robert Fulghum cites fifteen things he learned in kindergarten that he maintains are "all I really need to know about how to live and what to do and how to be." The things he learned are the following:

- Share everything.
- Play fair.
- Don't hit people.
- Put things back where you found them.
- Clean up your own mess.
- Don't take things that aren't yours.
- Say you're sorry when you hurt somebody.
- Wash your hands before you eat.
- Flush.
- Warm cookies and cold milk are good for you.
- Live a balanced life—learn some and think some and draw and paint and sing and dance and play and work every day some.
- Take a nap every afternoon.
- When you go out into the world, watch out for traffic, hold hands, and stick together.

continued on next page

- Be aware of wonder. Remember the little seed in the Styrofoam cup: The roots go down and the plant goes up and nobody really knows how or why, but we are all like that.
- Goldfish and hamsters and white mice and even the little seed in the Styrofoam cup—they all die. So do we.
- And then remember the Dick-and-Jane books and the first word you learned—the biggest word of all—LOOK.

From *All I Really Need to Know I Learned in Kindergarten* by Robert L. Fulghum, copyright © 1986, 1988, by Robert L. Fulghum. Used by permission of Villard Books, a division of Random House, Inc.

More Where This Came From

A couple of multipurpose reference works that deal with some of life's larger themes:

The Book of Virtues, New York: Simon & Schnster, 1993, by William J. Bennett (self-described as a "'how-to' book for moral literacy" that collects poems, stories, and excerpts of classic works under headings of ten character traits).

Chicken Soup for the Teenage Soul, Volumes I and II, Deerfield Beach, Florida: Health Communications, Inc., 1998, by Jack Canfield, Mark Victor Hansen, and Kimberly Kirberger (stories on such topics as friendship, family, making a difference, and growing up).

An Incomplete Education, New York: Ballantine Books, 1995, by Judy Jones and William Wilson. A bird's eye view of such sweeping topics as science, religion, music, economics, and others; described as "cheerfully, subversively anti-academic."

The RAT's Mouse

Principles and priorities through a computer mouse:

- **www.2.bc.edu/~caser/7habits.html** Excerpts from *Seven Habits of Highly Successful People*
- **www.rolemodel.net/** Features a role model of the week
- **www.listen.org/pages/quotes.html** The importance of being a good listener; quotes about listening
- **www.classiclit.about.com/arts/classiclit** Large site exploring pre-World War II literature, with articles, links to other sites
- **www.Oxygen.com** A good site for searches on mentors, role models, decision making, books, and other topics
- Also see **www.thriveonline.oxygen.com/season/new_year/resolutions/** For information on how to keep New Year's resolutions

More Where This Came From
The RAT's Bookshelf

The Rat is filled with helpful guideposts to point curious readers to "More Where This Came From"—more details, more stories, and more little-known facts on subjects important in real life. As fascinating as these other books are, however, there are more listed than will fit in a backpack or on a short shelf.

Thus as a parting favor, *The RAT* takes an entirely arbitrary stab at identifying a few good books that might be worth keeping close at hand. To make this list, a book must cover not just one subject addressed by *The RAT*, but several. A few are a bit hefty for carrying around in a backpack (although we do know that backpacks can hold extraordinary amounts of materials). But they probably would fit on a short shelf, and most of us find ourselves with an empty short shelf in the real world.

With that thought in mind, here are few possibilities in the spirit of *The RAT*:

- A dictionary. Dictionaries seem to have improved to the point that many of the best now have small photographs and illustrations, a little information on famous people, and even a few foreign phrases, as well as correct spellings.
- *The Little Know-How Book* by Bob Scher. One of my favorites, this little book is practical, entertaining, and full of real-world advice.
- *An Incomplete Education* by Judy Jones and William Wilson. Weighing in at more than 650 pages, this ambitious book is designed to fill educational gaps in areas ranging from economics to religion, philosophy to film. Enormous amounts of information in bite-sized servings.
- *Where's Mom Now That I Need Her?* and its companion, *Where's Dad Now That I Need Him?*—books on "Surviving Away from Home" by Betty Rae Frandsen, Katheryn J. Frandsen, and Kent P. Frandsen. A little heavy on the recipes, but advice ranging from laundry and clothing to avoiding becoming a victim of crime.
- *Ten Things I Wish I'd Known—Before I Went Out into the Real World* by Maria Shriver. An expanded version of a successful commencement address that discusses work, behavior, failure, laughter, marriage, and more.
- *The Dictionary of Cultural Literacy: What Every American Needs to Know* by E. D. Hirsch, Jr. Joseph F. Kett, and James Trefil. Cultural knowledge defined in dictionary format across 23 broad categories, including Mythology and

Folklore, Earth Sciences, Technology, World Politics, Idioms, Business and Economics, Conventions of Written English, as well as a few of the real-world subjects addressed in *The RAT*. Too big for your coat pocket.

- *Welcome to the Real World* by Stacy Kravetz. With an emphasis on getting a job and getting the upper hand on your finances, this book contains post education advice from an author who quickly made her way to a job with the *Wall Street Journal*.
- A current almanac with a decent index. Mountains of information and statistics and facts enough to settle countless disagreements. Keep it next to the dictionary.
- *The Big Book of Life's Instructions: Simple Solutions for Complicated Lives* by Sheree Bykofsky and Paul Fargis. With an eclectic spirit that the *The RAT* applauds, this book, available in paperback, tackles scores of useful topics on twenty different subject areas. Tips on bargaining, tea parties, carving a pumpkin, finding a good lawyer, etc.
- *The Bible.* Not only does the Bible contain material considered sacred by three of the world's greatest religions, but as the most widely known book in the English language, the Bible's history, literature, stories, and personalities permeate the cultures of English-speaking peoples. A little intimidating perhaps, but it's on the most bookshelves of all.

INDEX